The Complete Instant Pot Cookbook for Beginners

1500 Days Recipes for Fast, Easy, and Delicious Meals - From Comfort Food Classics to Global Cuisine, Explore the Endless Possibilities of Your Multi-Cooker

Ronald K. Aranda

Copyright© 2023 By Ronald K. Aranda

All rights reserved worldwide.

No part of this book may be reproduced or transmitted in any form or by any means, electronic or mechanical, including photo- copying, recording or by any information storage and retrieval system, without written permission from the publisher, except for the inclusion of brief quotations in a review.

Warning-Disclaimer

The purpose of this book is to educate and entertain. The author or publisher does not guarantee that anyone following the techniques, suggestions, tips, ideas, or strategies will become successful. The author and publisher shall have neither liability or responsibility to anyone with respect to any loss or damage caused, or alleged to be caused, directly or indirectly by the information contained in this book.

Table of Contents

Chapter 7 Stews and Soups 68

Chapter 8 Vegetables and Sides 83

INTRODUCTION

Are you finding it time-consuming and overwhelming to cook at home? The bad news is that you may be missing some essential kitchen supplies, leading to standing over the stove for prolonged periods. Luckily, the Instant Pot is a smart and advanced cooker that doesn't require constant monitoring or stirring. Using an Instant Pot can save you time and effort in preparing dinner entirely.

The Instant Pot can cook food up to 70% faster than conventional cookware, and it's convenient to use since it's hands-free. By simply making your favorite ketogenic meal in the Instant Pot, you can relax and enjoy, spending quality time away from the kitchen.

For those who don't want to spend the entire day cooking over a hot stove, the Instant Pot is the ideal appliance as it cooks meals much faster than regular pots and cookers, making it an excellent choice for busy households. Despite being a cliché, your health is your most valuable asset. Properly preparing your food is crucial for your well-being and values.

The Instant Pot aims to enhance the palatability and succulence of your meals. High-temperature cooking improves the flavor of your food while using less oil and other additives, thus preserving most of the meal's natural flavors and nutrients. The Instant Pot also ensures a perfect balance of flavors, as it's almost impossible to overcook the food, resulting in dull and bland dishes.

Chapter 1 Know Your Instant Pot

Before you start cooking with your Instant Pot, it's essential to take some time to get to know your appliance. Familiarizing yourself with its features, limits, and functions will make your cooking experience much smoother and efficient. Knowing your Instant Pot well will allow you to cook a wide variety of dishes, from soups and stews to rice, pasta, and even desserts, with confidence and ease.

What is an Instant Pot?

An Instant Pot is a multi-functional electric pressure cooker that has become a staple appliance in many kitchens around the world. The Instant Pot allows for quick and easy cooking of a wide variety of meals, making it perfect for busy families or individuals who want to save time and effort in the kitchen. The Instant Pot works by trapping steam inside a sealed pot, which increases the pressure and temperature inside the pot, allowing food to cook faster. The pot has a pressure valve that regulates the pressure inside the pot and a sealing ring that keeps the steam from escaping. With its high pressure and temperature cooking capabilities, the Instant Pot can reduce cooking time by up to 70% compared to traditional cooking methods.

In addition to its pressure cooking capabilities, the Instant Pot can also function as a slow cooker, rice cooker, steamer, sauté pan, yogurt maker, and more. Its versatile cooking functions and easy-to-use settings make it a popular choice among home cooks, food bloggers, and professional chefs alike. With the Instant Pot, you can cook a wide variety of dishes, from soups and stews to rice, pasta, and even desserts.

The Instant Pot has also gained popularity due to its ability to enhance the flavor and texture of food. The high pressure and temperature cooking process help to retain the nutrients and natural flavors of the food, resulting in healthy and delicious meals. Additionally, the Instant Pot allows for hands-free cooking, which means you can spend less time in the kitchen and more time with your loved ones.

Instant Pot Mania: The Factors Driving its Popularity

The Instant Pot is a popular cooking appliance because it offers a variety of benefits to home cooks. From convenience and speed to healthier cooking and versatility, the Instant Pot is a must-have for anyone who wants to make home cooking easier, faster, and more enjoyable.

Convenience: The Instant Pot has taken the cooking world by storm with its versatility and convenience. This multi-functional kitchen appliance offers a wide range of cooking options, including pressure cooking, slow cooking, rice cooking, steaming, and more. With the Instant Pot, you no longer need to clutter your kitchen with multiple appliances for different cooking methods. This one-stop-shop kitchen gadget can help you prepare a variety of dishes, from stews and soups to rice and even cheesecake. The pressure cooking function of the Instant Pot cooks food faster than conventional cooking methods by using high-pressure steam to cook the food evenly and thoroughly. The slow cooking function is ideal for those who like to prepare meals in advance, and the rice cooking function ensures perfectly cooked rice every time. The steaming function is great for cooking vegetables and seafood while retaining their nutrients. The Instant Pot's convenience lies in its ability to cook a complete meal in one appliance. You can start with a sauté function to brown your meat or vegetables, followed by pressure cooking or slow cooking to finish off the meal. With the Instant Pot, you can even prepare multiple dishes simultaneously, saving you time and effort.

Speed: The Instant Pot has revolutionized the way we cook our meals, and one of the main reasons for its popularity is its ability to cook food much faster than traditional methods. With its advanced technology, the Instant Pot is capable of cooking food up to 70% faster than conventional cooking methods. This is because the Instant Pot uses pressure cooking to cook food at high temperatures, which significantly reduces the cooking time. Gone are the days when you had to spend hours in the kitchen to prepare a healthy, home-cooked meal. With the Instant Pot, you can have a delicious meal on the table in a fraction of the time it would take to cook it on the stove or in the oven. This is especially convenient for busy individuals and families who don't have a lot of time to spend in the kitchen. Whether you're a working parent, a college student, or anyone who values their time, the Instant Pot is a lifesaver. Moreover, the Instant Pot's ability to cook food quickly doesn't sacrifice the quality of the food. In fact, the pressure cooking method used in the Instant Pot ensures that the food is cooked evenly and retains its nutrients and flavor. This means that you can still enjoy a healthy, delicious meal without compromising on taste or quality.

Healthier Cooking: Pressure cooking has gained a reputation as one of the healthiest cooking methods available. One of the primary reasons for this is because pressure cooking helps to retain more nutrients and vitamins in the food compared to other methods like boiling or frying. The Instant Pot, with its ability to cook food quickly and under high pressure, is an

excellent example of a pressure cooker that can preserve the nutritional value of your food. Moreover, the Instant Pot offers a significant advantage over traditional cooking methods when it comes to reducing the amount of added fat and calories in your meals. Because the Instant Pot requires less oil and fat than traditional cooking methods, it can help you prepare healthier meals that are less greasy and more nutritious. This is especially important for individuals who are trying to follow a healthier diet or lose weight. Additionally, using an Instant Pot can save you money in the long run by reducing the amount of food waste you produce. By cooking food faster and more efficiently, the Instant Pot ensures that your ingredients are cooked evenly and thoroughly, resulting in less food waste. With all these benefits, it's no wonder that the Instant Pot has become a popular appliance in many households worldwide, providing an easy and convenient way to cook healthy meals while saving time and money.

Ease of Use: The Instant Pot is renowned for its user-friendliness, making it an excellent choice for people who have little or no experience with pressure cooking. Its straightforward settings and safety features make it easy to use, even for beginners. The appliance comes with several safety features, including a safety lid lock, which prevents the lid from being opened when the pot is under pressure. The Instant Pot also includes multiple cooking modes that are simple to navigate, including pressure cook, sauté, and slow cook, among others. You can also easily adjust the temperature and pressure settings to suit your needs. The appliance also has an automatic keep-warm feature that will keep your food warm for up to 10 hours after cooking, which is a convenient feature if you are not ready to eat immediately. The appliance is also incredibly versatile and can cook a variety of foods, from soups and stews to rice, pasta, and even yogurt. Many Instant Pot models also have pre-programmed settings for specific types of food, making it even easier to cook your favorite dishes.

Potential Issues with an Instant Pot

While the Instant Pot is a versatile and popular cooking appliance, it does have some potential limitations to consider. One limitation is its size. Depending on the model, the Instant Pot may have a smaller capacity than some traditional cooking pots, which could limit the amount of food you can prepare at one time. Additionally, while the Instant Pot can be used for a variety of cooking methods, it may not be the best option for every recipe. For example, some dishes may require a specific type of cookware or cooking method to achieve the desired texture or flavor.

Another limitation to consider is the learning curve. While the Instant Pot is designed to be user-friendly, it can still take some time to learn how to use it properly. The appliance has several settings and functions that may be unfamiliar to those who are new to pressure cooking, and it can take some trial and error to figure out the best cooking times and settings for different recipes.

Lastly, the Instant Pot may not be the best option for those who prefer a hands-on approach to cooking. Since the appliance is designed to be hands-free, some people may feel like they have less control over the cooking process. Additionally, the pressure cooking method can result in a slightly different texture than other cooking methods, which may not be preferable for some dishes.

Useful Tips for Using an Instant Pot

Using an Instant Pot can be a bit intimidating for first-time users, but with a few tips and tricks, it can become an easy and convenient cooking tool.

Read the Manual First: Using an Instant Pot can be an incredibly convenient and time-saving way to prepare meals, but it's important to understand how to use it properly before getting started. The first step is to read the manual that comes with your Instant Pot thoroughly. The manual will provide you with important information on how to use the appliance safely and effectively. It will also provide you with an overview of the different features of your Instant Pot, such as the pressure cooking function, sautéing function, and more.

Use the right cooking time: While the Instant Pot is known for its ability to cook meals quickly, it's important to remember that different recipes require different cooking times. One of the most important things to do when using your Instant Pot is to carefully follow the recipe instructions. This means using the recommended amount of ingredients and adjusting the cooking time as necessary. Additionally, it's important to consider factors such as the type and size of the food being cooked. For example, a whole chicken will require more cooking time than chicken pieces or strips. Vegetables also cook at different rates, with some taking longer than others.

Use enough liquid. When using an Instant Pot, the pressure cooking function is one of the most popular features. However, it's essential to ensure that enough liquid is used in the pot to create steam. Steam is what creates pressure in the Instant Pot, which in turn cooks the food. As a general rule, you should use at least one cup of liquid for every recipe. However, keep in mind that certain foods, such as grains and beans, may require more liquid. It's always best to consult the recipe instructions and adjust the liquid amount accordingly.

Don't overfill the pot: Overfilling your Instant Pot can lead to uneven cooking, burnt food, or even damage to the appliance. It's important to follow the manufacturer's recommendations and not exceed the maximum fill line. When you overfill the pot, there may not be enough room for the steam to build up, which can cause the pressure valve to malfunction or the food to cook unevenly. It's also important to note that the size of your Instant Pot matters. If you have a small Instant Pot, filling it up too much can lead to the same problems mentioned above. Similarly, if you have a larger Instant Pot, it may be tempting to fill it up to the brim to save time, but this can also cause issues.

Release pressure carefully: After the cooking cycle is complete, it's important to release the pressure from the Instant Pot before opening the lid. The reason for this is that pressure builds up inside the pot during the cooking process, which can be dangerous if released suddenly. To release the pressure, there are two methods: natural release and quick release. With natural release, you simply let the Instant Pot sit for a specified amount of time (usually 10-15 minutes) until the pressure releases on its own. With quick release, you use the valve on the top of the lid to manually release the pressure. It's important to follow the instructions for your specific model of Instant Pot, as the process may vary depending on the model. When releasing the pressure, it's crucial to do so carefully to avoid steam burns. Always keep your face and hands away from the steam, and use oven mitts or a towel to turn the valve. It's also important to note that some recipes may require a natural release, while others may call for a quick release. Be sure to follow the recipe instructions for the correct method.

Use the sauté function: Using the sauté function on your Instant Pot can add depth and complexity to your recipes by allowing you to brown meat and sauté vegetables before pressure cooking. This step not only enhances the flavor of your dishes but also helps develop a richer color and texture. To use the sauté function, simply press the "Sauté" button on your Instant Pot and allow it to heat up. Once the display reads "Hot," you can add your ingredients and start sautéing. When sautéing, it's important to use a high heat setting and to stir your ingredients regularly to prevent burning. You can also deglaze the pot by adding a small amount of liquid, such as broth or wine, to the bottom of the pot and scraping up any browned bits with a wooden spoon. This not only helps prevent burning but also adds more flavor to your dish. Using the sauté function is particularly useful for recipes that call for browning meat before pressure cooking, such as stews and chili. It's also a great way to add flavor and texture to vegetarian dishes, such as sautéed mushrooms or onions. By taking advantage of the sauté function on your Instant Pot, you can create dishes that are not only quick and easy to make but also packed with flavor.

Instant Pot Cleaning and Maintenance

Keeping your Instant Pot clean and maintained is essential for ensuring that it continues to function properly and lasts for a long time. Here are some tips for cleaning and maintaining your Instant Pot:

1.Clean the pot and lid after every use: After each use, the pot and lid should be cleaned thoroughly to remove any residue or food particles that may be stuck on them. To do this, start by unplugging the Instant Pot and letting it cool down completely. Once it is cool, remove the inner pot and the lid.

Next, wash the inner pot and lid with warm, soapy water. You can use a sponge or a soft cloth to scrub the surface gently. Make sure to pay special attention to any crevices or hard-to-reach areas to ensure that they are thoroughly cleaned. Rinse the pot and lid with clean water and dry them with a clean towel or allow them to air dry.

If there is any stubborn food residue on the pot or lid, you can use a non-abrasive cleaner or a mixture of baking soda and water to help remove it. It's important to avoid using abrasive cleaning pads or harsh chemicals, as they can damage the surface of the Instant Pot.

2.Remove and clean the sealing ring: The sealing ring is the rubber gasket that sits inside the lid. It's important to remove and clean it after each use to prevent any buildup of food or debris. Simply wash it with warm, soapy water and allow it to dry completely before reinserting it.

In addition to cleaning the sealing ring after each use, it's also important to inspect it regularly for any signs of wear or damage. Over time, the sealing ring may become stretched or cracked, which can compromise its ability to create an airtight seal. If you notice any damage or wear, it's important to replace the sealing ring with a new one. Replacement sealing rings can be purchased from the manufacturer or from various retailers online. It's a good idea to keep a spare on hand, just in case you need to replace the ring during a cooking session. Proper maintenance and care of the sealing ring can help ensure the longevity and effectiveness of your Instant Pot.

3.Clean the exterior: Wipe down the exterior of the Instant Pot with a damp cloth to remove any food splatters or spills. Avoid using harsh chemicals or abrasive cleaners that could damage the finish.

4.Check and clean the vent and float valve: The vent and float valve are crucial components of the Instant Pot's pressure cooking function. The vent is responsible for releasing excess steam during the cooking process, while the float valve helps regulate the pressure inside the pot. It's important to check these components regularly to ensure they are working properly. If the vent or float valve becomes clogged or dirty, it can impact the pressure release and cause the Instant Pot to malfunction. To clean them, remove the lid and inspect the vent and float valve for any debris or buildup. Use a small brush or toothpick to gently remove any dirt or debris. Rinse with warm water and dry thoroughly before reassembling the lid. Regularly cleaning the vent and float valve will help keep your Instant Pot functioning properly and ensure that your meals come out perfectly every time.

5.Maintain the electrical components: Avoid immersing the base of the Instant Pot in water or other liquids. Instead, wipe it down with a damp cloth and dry it thoroughly.

6.Replace parts as needed: Over time, some parts of your Instant Pot may wear out or become damaged. Check the manual for your specific model to see which parts can be replaced and how to order them.

By following these tips, you can keep your Instant Pot clean and well-maintained, ensuring that it continues to function properly for years to come.

A Perfect Guide for Instant Pot Cooking Beginners

The purpose of this cookbook is to introduce the Instant Pot and provide a variety of recipes for people to explore the benefits of pressure cooking. This cookbook is designed for anyone who is interested in healthy cooking with less time and effort, convenience, and delicious meals.

Our cookbook aims to achieve several goals. Firstly, we aim to provide a comprehensive guide on how to use the Instant Pot, from basic features to advanced settings. This includes information on how to adjust cooking times for different types of food and how to use the different cooking functions. Secondly, we aim to introduce a range of recipes that showcase the versatility of the Instant Pot, from classic dishes to innovative new creations. We have included recipes for all meals of the day, including breakfast, lunch, and dinner. Lastly, we aim to encourage people to embrace the benefits of pressure cooking, such as healthier cooking and easy cleanup.

The cookbook is perfect for anyone who wants to cook meals that are not only healthy but also delicious. It is ideal for those who have busy lifestyles and are looking for quick and easy meal options that don't require a lot of preparation or cleanup time. Additionally, the cookbook is a great resource for those who are health-conscious and want to reduce their cooking time without sacrificing flavor.

With the Instant Pot, you can enjoy the benefits of pressure cooking, such as healthier meals and easy cleanup. Pressure cooking can help you achieve your health and fitness goals by reducing your cooking time and retaining more nutrients in your food. Additionally, pressure cooking is a convenient way to cook meals that are tender and delicious without the need for excessive oil or fat.

We encourage you to try out the recipes in this cookbook and explore the benefits of pressure cooking for yourself. From tender beef stew to perfectly cooked rice, there is something for everyone in this cookbook. With the Instant Pot, you can cook your favorite meals in a healthier and more convenient way. Say goodbye to lengthy cooking times and hello to the deliciousness of pressure cooking!

In conclusion, we hope this cookbook inspires you to embrace the benefits of pressure cooking and try out new recipes that are not only healthy but also delicious. With the Instant Pot, you can cook a variety of meals with ease and without the need for unhealthy oils. We invite you to join us on this culinary journey and discover the wonders of pressure cooking!

Chapter 2 Snacks and Appetizers

Brussels Sprouts with Aioli Sauce

Prep time: 5 minutes | Cook time: 7 minutes | Serves 4

1 tablespoon butter
½ cup chopped scallions
¾ pound (340 g) Brussels sprouts
Aioli Sauce:
¼ cup mayonnaise
1 tablespoon fresh lemon juice
1 garlic clove, minced
½ teaspoon Dijon mustard

1. Set your Instant Pot to Sauté and melt the butter. 2. Add the scallions and sauté for 2 minutes until softened. Add the Brussels sprouts and cook for another 1 minute. 3. Lock the lid. Select the Manual mode and set the cooking time for 4 minutes at High Pressure. 4. Meanwhile, whisk together all the ingredients for the Aioli sauce in a small bowl until well incorporated. 5. When the timer beeps, perform a quick pressure release. Carefully remove the lid. 6. Serve the Brussels sprouts with the Aioli sauce on the side.

Per Serving:
calories: 167 | fat: 13.8g | protein: 3.4g | carbs: 8.6g | net carbs: 5.4g | fiber: 3.2g

Green Goddess White Bean Dip

Prep time: 1 minutes | Cook time: 45 minutes | Makes 3 cups

1 cup dried navy, great Northern, or cannellini beans
4 cups water
2 teaspoons fine sea salt
3 tablespoons fresh lemon juice
¼ cup extra-virgin olive oil, plus 1 tablespoon
¼ cup firmly packed fresh flat-leaf parsley leaves
1 bunch chives, chopped
Leaves from 2 tarragon sprigs
Freshly ground black pepper

1. Combine the beans, water, and 1 teaspoon of the salt in the Instant Pot and stir to dissolve the salt. 2. Secure the lid and set the Pressure Release to Sealing. Select the Bean/Chili, Pressure Cook, or Manual setting and set the cooking time for 30 minutes at high pressure if using navy or Great Northern beans or 40 minutes at high pressure if using cannellini beans. (The pot will take about 15 minutes to come up to pressure before the cooking program begins.) 3. When the cooking program ends, let the pressure release naturally for 15 minutes, then move the Pressure Release to Venting to release any remaining steam. Open the pot and scoop out and reserve ½ cup of the cooking liquid. Wearing heat-resistant mitts, lift out the inner pot and drain the beans in a colander. 4. In a food processor or blender, combine the beans, ½ cup cooking liquid, lemon juice, ¼ cup olive oil, ½ teaspoon parsley, chives, tarragon, remaining 1 teaspoon salt, and ½ teaspoon pepper. Process or blend on medium speed, stopping to scrape down the sides of the container as needed, for about 1 minute, until the mixture is smooth. 5. Transfer the dip to a serving bowl. Drizzle with the remaining 1 tablespoon olive oil and sprinkle with a few grinds of pepper. The dip will keep in an airtight container in the refrigerator for up to 1 week. Serve at room temperature or chilled.

Per Serving:
calorie: 70 | fat: 5g | protein: 3g | carbs: 8g | sugars: 1g | fiber: 4g | sodium: 782mg

Colby Cheese and Pepper Dip

Prep time: 5 minutes | Cook time: 5 minutes | Serves 8

1 tablespoon butter
2 red bell peppers, sliced
2 cups shredded Colby cheese
1 cup cream cheese, room temperature
1 cup chicken broth
2 garlic cloves, minced
1 teaspoon red Aleppo pepper flakes
1 teaspoon sumac
Salt and ground black pepper, to taste

1. Set your Instant Pot to Sauté and melt the butter. 2. Add the bell peppers and sauté for about 2 minutes until just tender. 3. Add the remaining ingredients to the Instant Pot and gently stir to incorporate. 4. Lock the lid. Select the Manual mode and set the cooking time for 3 minutes at High Pressure. 5. When the timer beeps, perform a quick pressure release. Carefully remove the lid. 6. Allow to cool for 5 minutes and serve warm.

Per Serving:
calories: 241 | fat: 20.8g | protein: 10.6g | carbs: 3.0g | net carbs: 2.6g | fiber: 0.4g

Cheese Stuffed Mushrooms

Prep time: 15 minutes | Cook time: 8 minutes | Serves 4

1 cup cremini mushroom caps
1 tablespoon chopped scallions
1 tablespoon chopped chives
1 teaspoon cream cheese
1 teaspoon sour cream
1 ounce (28 g) Monterey Jack cheese, shredded
1 teaspoon butter, softened
½ teaspoon smoked paprika
1 cup water, for cooking

1. Trim the mushroom caps if needed and wash them well. 2. After this, in the mixing bowl, mix up scallions, chives, cream cheese, sour cream, butter, and smoked paprika. 3. Then fill the mushroom caps with the cream cheese mixture and top with shredded Monterey Jack cheese. 4. Pour water and insert the trivet in the instant pot. 5. Arrange the stuffed mushrooms caps on the trivet and close the lid. 6. Cook the meal on Manual (High Pressure) for 8 minutes. 7. Then make a quick pressure release.

Per Serving:
calories: 45 | fat: 4g | protein: 3g | carbs: 1g | net carbs: 1g | fiber: 0g

Herbed Mushrooms

Prep time: 5 minutes | Cook time: 10 minutes | Serves 4

2 tablespoons butter
2 cloves garlic, minced
20 ounces (567 g) button mushrooms
1 tablespoon coconut aminos
1 teaspoon dried rosemary
1 teaspoon dried basil
1 teaspoon dried sage
1 bay leaf
Sea salt, to taste
½ teaspoon freshly ground black pepper
½ cup chicken broth
½ cup water
1 tablespoon roughly chopped fresh parsley leaves, for garnish

1. Set your Instant Pot to Sauté and melt the butter. 2. Add the garlic and mushrooms and sauté for 3 to 4 minutes until the garlic is fragrant. 3. Add the remaining ingredients except the parsley to the Instant Pot and stir well. 4. Lock the lid. Select the Manual mode and set the cooking time for 5 minutes at High Pressure. 5. When the timer beeps, perform a quick pressure release. Carefully open the lid. 6. Remove the mushrooms from the pot to a platter. Serve garnished with the fresh parsley leaves.

Per Serving:
calories: 94 | fat: 6.8g | protein: 5.7g | carbs: 5.3g | net carbs: 3.6g | fiber: 1.7g

Lemon Artichokes

Prep time: 5 minutes | Cook time: 5 to 15 minutes | Serves 4

4 artichokes
1 cup water
2 tablespoons lemon juice
1 teaspoon salt

1. Wash and trim artichokes by cutting off the stems flush with the bottoms of the artichokes and by cutting ¾–1 inch off the tops. Stand upright in the bottom of the inner pot of the Instant Pot. 2. Pour water, lemon juice, and salt over artichokes. 3. Secure the lid and make sure the vent is set to sealing. On Manual, set the Instant Pot for 15 minutes for large artichokes, 10 minutes for medium artichokes, or 5 minutes for small artichokes. 4. When cook time is up, perform a quick release by releasing the pressure manually.

Per Serving:
calories: 60 | fat: 0g | protein: 4g | carbs: 13g | sugars: 1g | fiber: 6g | sodium: 397mg

Southern Boiled Peanuts

Prep time: 5 minutes | Cook time: 1 hour 20 minutes | Makes 8 cups

1 pound raw jumbo peanuts in the shell
3 tablespoons fine sea salt

1. Remove the inner pot from the Instant Pot and add the peanuts to it. Cover the peanuts with water and use your hands to agitate them, loosening any dirt. Drain the peanuts in a colander, rinse out the pot, and return the peanuts to it. Return the inner pot to the Instant Pot housing. 2. Add the salt and 9 cups water to the pot and stir to dissolve the salt. Select a salad plate just small enough to fit inside the pot and set it on top of the peanuts to weight them down, submerging them all in the water. 3. Secure the lid and set the Pressure Release to Sealing. Select the Steam setting and set the cooking time for 1 hour at low pressure. (The pot will take about 20 minutes to come up to pressure before the cooking program begins.) 4. When the cooking program ends, let the pressure release naturally (this will take about 1 hour). Open the pot and, wearing heat-resistant mitts, remove the inner pot from the housing. Let the peanuts cool to room temperature in the brine (this will take about 1½ hours). 5. Serve at room temperature or chilled. Transfer the peanuts with their brine to an airtight container and refrigerate for up to 1 week.

Per Serving:
calories: 306 | fat: 17g | protein: 26g | carbs: 12g | sugars: 2g | fiber: 4g | sodium: 303mg

Porcupine Meatballs

Prep time: 20 minutes | Cook time: 15 minutes | Serves 8

1 pound ground sirloin or turkey
½ cup raw brown rice, parboiled
1 egg
¼ cup finely minced onion
1 or 2 cloves garlic, minced
¼ teaspoon dried basil and/or oregano, optional
10¾-ounce can reduced-fat condensed tomato soup
½ soup can of water

1. Mix all ingredients, except tomato soup and water, in a bowl to combine well. 2. Form into balls about 1½-inch in diameter. 3. Mix tomato soup and water in the inner pot of the Instant Pot, then add the meatballs. 4. Secure the lid and make sure the vent is turned to sealing. 5. Press the Meat button and set for 15 minutes on high pressure. 6. Allow the pressure to release naturally after cook time is up.

Per Serving:
calories: 141 | fat: 2g | protein: 16g | carbs: 14g | sugars: 3g | fiber: 1g | sodium: 176mg

Herbed Shrimp

Prep time: 5 minutes | Cook time: 5 minutes | Serves 4

2 tablespoons olive oil
¾ pound (340 g) shrimp, peeled and deveined
1 teaspoon paprika
1 teaspoon garlic powder
1 teaspoon onion powder
1 teaspoon dried parsley flakes
½ teaspoon dried oregano
½ teaspoon dried thyme
½ teaspoon dried basil
½ teaspoon dried rosemary
¼ teaspoon red pepper flakes
Coarse sea salt and ground black pepper, to taste
1 cup chicken broth

1. Set your Instant Pot to Sauté and heat the olive oil. 2. Add the shrimp and sauté for 2 to 3 minutes. 3. Add the remaining ingredients to the Instant Pot and stir to combine. 4. Secure the lid. Select the Manual mode and set the cooking time for 2 minutes at Low Pressure. 5. When the timer beeps, perform a quick pressure release. Carefully remove the lid. 6. Transfer the shrimp to a plate and serve.

Per Serving:
calories: 146 | fat: 7.7g | protein: 18.5g | carbs: 3.0g | net carbs: 2.3g | fiber: 0.7g

Taco Beef Bites

Prep time: 10 minutes | Cook time: 15 minutes | Serves 6

10 ounces (283 g) ground beef
3 eggs, beaten
⅓ cup shredded Mozzarella cheese
1 teaspoon taco seasoning
1 teaspoon sesame oil

1. In the mixing bowl mix up ground beef, eggs, Mozzarella, and taco seasoning. 2. Then make the small meat bites from the mixture. 3. Heat up sesame oil in the instant pot. 4. Put the meat bites in the hot oil and cook them for 5 minutes from each side on Sauté mode.

Per Serving:

calories: 132 | fat: 6g | protein: 17g | carbs: 1g | net carbs: 1g | fiber: 0g

Broccoli with Garlic-Herb Cheese Sauce

Prep time: 5 minutes | Cook time: 3 minutes | Serves 4

½ cup water
1 pound (454 g) broccoli (frozen or fresh)
½ cup heavy cream
1 tablespoon butter
½ cup shredded Cheddar cheese
3 tablespoons garlic and herb cheese spread
Pinch of salt
Pinch of black pepper

1. Add the water to the pot and place the trivet inside. 2. Put the steamer basket on top of the trivet. Place the broccoli in the basket. 3. Close the lid and seal the vent. Cook on Low Pressure for 1 minute. Quick release the steam. Press Cancel. 4. Carefully remove the steamer basket from the pot and drain the water. If you steamed a full bunch of broccoli, pull the florets off the stem. (Chop the stem into bite-size pieces, it's surprisingly creamy.) 5. Turn the pot to Sauté mode. Add the cream and butter. Stir continuously while the butter melts and the cream warms up. 6. When the cream begins to bubble on the edges, add the Cheddar cheese, cheese spread, salt, and pepper. Whisk continuously until the cheeses are melted and a sauce consistency is reached, 1 to 2 minutes. 7. Top one-fourth of the broccoli with 2 tablespoons cheese sauce.

Per Serving:

calories: 134 | fat: 12g | protein:4 g | carbs: 5g | net carbs: 3g | fiber: 2g

Lemon-Butter Mushrooms

Prep time: 10 minutes | Cook time: 4 minutes | Serves 2

1 cup cremini mushrooms, sliced
½ cup water
1 tablespoon lemon juice
1 teaspoon almond butter
1 teaspoon grated lemon zest
½ teaspoon salt
½ teaspoon dried thyme

1. Combine all the ingredients in the Instant Pot. 2. Secure the lid. Select the Manual mode and set the cooking time for 4 minutes at High Pressure. 3. Once cooking is complete, do a natural pressure release for 5 minutes, then release any remaining pressure. Carefully open the lid. 4. Serve warm.

Per Serving:

calories: 63 | fat: 4.8g | protein: 2.9g | carbs: 3.3g | net carbs: 2.1g | fiber: 1.2g

Sesame Mushrooms

Prep time: 2 minutes | Cook time: 10 minutes | Serves 6

3 tablespoons sesame oil
¾ pound (340 g) small button mushrooms
1 teaspoon minced garlic
½ teaspoon smoked paprika
½ teaspoon cayenne pepper
Salt and ground black pepper, to taste

1. Set your Instant Pot to Sauté and heat the sesame oil. 2. Add the mushrooms and sauté for 4 minutes until just tender, stirring occasionally. 3. Add the remaining ingredients to the Instant Pot and stir to mix well. 4. Lock the lid. Select the Manual mode and set the cooking time for 5 minutes at High Pressure. 5. When the timer beeps, perform a quick pressure release. Carefully remove the lid. 6. Serve warm.

Per Serving:

calories: 77 | fat: 7.6g | protein: 1.9g | carbs: 1.8g | net carbs: 1.0g | fiber: 0.8g

Roasted Garlic Bulbs

Prep time: 2 minutes | Cook time: 25 minutes | Serves 4

4 bulbs garlic
1 tablespoon avocado oil
1 teaspoon salt
Pinch of black pepper
1 cup water

1. Slice the pointy tops off the bulbs of garlic to expose the cloves. 2. Drizzle the avocado oil on top of the garlic and sprinkle with the salt and pepper. 3. Place the bulbs in the steamer basket, cut-side up. Alternatively, you may place them on a piece of aluminum foil with the sides pulled up and resting on top of the trivet. Place the steamer basket in the pot. 4. Close the lid and seal the vent. Cook on High Pressure for 25 minutes. Quick release the steam. 5. Let the garlic cool completely before removing the bulbs from the pot. 6. Hold the stem end (bottom) of the bulb and squeeze out all the garlic. Mash the cloves with a fork to make a paste.

Per Serving:

calories: 44 | fat: 5g | protein: 0g | carbs: 1g | net carbs: 1g | fiber: 0g

Creamy Spinach

Prep time: 5 minutes | Cook time: 4 minutes | Serves 4

2 cups chopped spinach
2 ounces (57 g) Monterey Jack cheese, shredded
1 cup almond milk
1 tablespoon butter
1 teaspoon minced garlic
½ teaspoon salt

1. Combine all the ingredients in the Instant Pot. 2. Secure the lid. Select the Manual mode and set the cooking time for 4 minutes at High Pressure. 3. Once cooking is complete, do a quick pressure release. Carefully open the lid. 4. Give the mixture a good stir and serve warm.

Per Serving:

calories: 101 | fat: 8.1g | protein: 4.2g | carbs: 2.6g | net carbs: 2.3g | fiber: 0.3g

Broccoli Cheese Dip

Prep time: 5 minutes | Cook time: 10 minutes | Serves 6

4 tablespoons butter
½ medium onion, diced
1½ cups chopped broccoli
8 ounces (227 g) cream cheese
½ cup mayonnaise
½ cup chicken broth
1 cup shredded Cheddar cheese

1. Press the Sauté button and then press the Adjust button to set heat to Less. Add butter to Instant Pot. Add onion and sauté until softened, about 5 minutes. Press the Cancel button. 2. Add broccoli, cream cheese, mayo, and broth to pot. Press the Manual button and adjust time for 4 minutes. 3. When timer beeps, quick-release the pressure and stir in Cheddar. Serve warm.

Per Serving:
calories: 411 | fat: 37g | protein: 8g | carbs: 4g | net carbs: 3g | fiber: 1g

7-Layer Dip

Prep time: 10 minutes | Cook time: 35 minutes | Serves 6

Cashew Sour Cream
1 cup raw whole cashews, soaked in water to cover for 1 to 2 hours and then drained
½ cup avocado oil
½ cup water
¼ cup fresh lemon juice
2 tablespoons nutritional yeast
1 teaspoon fine sea salt
Beans
½ cup dried black beans
2 cups water
½ teaspoon fine sea salt
½ teaspoon chili powder
¼ teaspoon garlic powder
½ cup grape or cherry tomatoes, halved
1 avocado, diced
¼ cup chopped yellow onion
1 jalapeño chile, sliced
2 tablespoons chopped cilantro
6 ounces baked corn tortilla chips
1 English cucumber, sliced
2 carrots, sliced
6 celery stalks, cut into sticks

1. To make the cashew sour cream: In a blender, combine the cashews, oil, water, lemon juice, nutritional yeast, and salt. Blend on high speed, stopping to scrape down the sides of the container as needed, for about 2 minutes, until very smooth. (The sour cream can be made in advance and stored in an airtight container in the refrigerator for up to 5 days.) 2. To make the beans: Pour 1 cup water into the Instant Pot. In a 1½-quart stainless-steel bowl, combine the beans, the 2 cups water, and salt and stir to dissolve the salt. Place the bowl on a long-handled silicone steam rack, then, holding the handles of the steam rack, lower it into the Instant Pot. (If you don't have the long-handled rack, use the wire metal steam rack and a homemade sling) 3. Secure the lid and set the Pressure Release to Sealing. Select the Bean/Chili, Pressure Cook, or Manual setting and set the cooking time for 25 minutes at high pressure. (The pot will take about 10 minutes to come up to pressure before the cooking program begins.) 4. When the cooking program ends, let the pressure release naturally for at least 20 minutes, then move the Pressure Release to Venting to release any remaining steam. 5. Place a colander over a bowl. Open the pot and, wearing heat-resistant mitts, lift out the inner pot and drain the beans in the colander. Transfer the liquid captured in the bowl to a measuring cup, and pour the beans into the bowl. Add ¼ cup of the cooking liquid to the beans and, using a potato masher or fork, mash the beans to your desired consistency, adding more cooking liquid as needed. Stir in the chili powder and garlic powder. 6. Using a rubber spatula, spread the black beans in an even layer in a clear-glass serving dish. Spread the cashew sour cream in an even layer on top of the beans. Add layers of the tomatoes, avocado, onion, jalapeño, and cilantro. (At this point, you can cover and refrigerate the assembled dip for up to 1 day.) Serve accompanied with the tortilla chips, cucumber, carrots, and celery on the side.

Per Serving:
calories: 259 | fat: 8g | protein: 8g | carbs: 41g | sugars: 3g | fiber: 8g | sodium: 811mg

Chinese Spare Ribs

Prep time: 3 minutes | Cook time: 24 minutes | Serves 6

1½ pounds (680 g) spare ribs
Salt and ground black pepper, to taste
2 tablespoons sesame oil
½ cup chopped green onions
½ cup chicken stock
2 tomatoes, crushed
2 tablespoons sherry
1 tablespoon coconut aminos
1 teaspoon ginger-garlic paste
½ teaspoon crushed red pepper flakes
½ teaspoon dried parsley
2 tablespoons sesame seeds, for serving

1. Season the spare ribs with salt and black pepper to taste. 2. Set your Instant Pot to Sauté and heat the sesame oil. 3. Add the seasoned spare ribs and sear each side for about 3 minutes. 4. Add the remaining ingredients except the sesame seeds to the Instant Pot and stir well. 5. Secure the lid. Select the Meat/Stew mode and set the cooking time for 18 minutes at High Pressure. 6. When the timer beeps, perform a natural pressure release for 10 minutes, then release any remaining pressure. Carefully remove the lid. 7. Serve topped with the sesame seeds.

Per Serving:
calories: 336 | fat: 16.3g | protein: 42.6g | carbs: 3.0g | net carbs: 2.0g | fiber: 1.0g

Mayo Chicken Celery

Prep time: 15 minutes | Cook time: 15 minutes | Serves 4

14 ounces (397 g) chicken breast, skinless, boneless
1 cup water
4 celery stalks
1 teaspoon salt
½ teaspoon onion powder
1 teaspoon mayonnaise

1. Combine all the ingredients except the mayo in the Instant Pot. 2. Secure the lid. Select the Manual mode and set the cooking time for 15 minutes at High Pressure. 3. Once cooking is complete, do a natural pressure release for 6 minutes, then release any remaining pressure. Carefully open the lid. 4. Remove the chicken and shred with two forks, then return to the Instant Pot. 5. Add the mayo and stir well. Serve immediately.

Per Serving:
calories: 119 | fat: 2.9g | protein: 21.4g | carbs: 0.7g | net carbs: 0.6g | fiber: 0.3g

Curried Broccoli Skewers

Prep time: 15 minutes | Cook time: 1 minute | Serves 2

1 cup broccoli florets
½ teaspoon curry paste
2 tablespoons coconut cream
1 cup water, for cooking

1. In the shallow bowl mix up curry paste and coconut cream. 2. Then sprinkle the broccoli florets with curry paste mixture and string on the skewers. 3. Pour water and insert the steamer rack in the instant pot. 4. Place the broccoli skewers on the rack. Close and seal the lid. 5. Cook the meal on Manual mode (High Pressure) for 1 minute. 6. Make a quick pressure release.

Per Serving:
calories: 58 | fat: 4g | protein: 2g | carbs: 4g | net carbs: 2g | fiber: 2g

Fast Spring Kale Appetizer

Prep time: 5 minutes | Cook time: 2 minutes | Serves 6

3 teaspoons butter
1 cup chopped spring onions
1 pound (454 g) kale, torn into pieces
1 cup water
½ teaspoon cayenne pepper
Himalayan salt and ground black pepper, to taste
½ cup shredded Colby cheese, for serving

1. Set your Instant Pot to Sauté and melt the butter. 2. Add the spring onions and sauté for 1 minute until wilted. 3. Add the remaining ingredients except the cheese to the Instant Pot and mix well. 4. Lock the lid. Select the Manual mode and set the cooking time for 1 minute at High Pressure. 5. When the timer beeps, perform a quick pressure release. Carefully remove the lid. 6. Transfer the kale mixture to a bowl and serve topped with the cheese.

Per Serving:
calories: 106 | fat: 6.4g | protein: 6.7g | carbs: 8.0g | net carbs: 4.7g | fiber: 3.3g

Lemon-Cheese Cauliflower Bites

Prep time: 5 minutes | Cook time: 8 minutes | Serves 6

1 cup water
1 pound (454 g) cauliflower, broken into florets
Sea salt and ground black pepper, to taste
2 tablespoons extra-virgin olive oil
2 tablespoons lemon juice
1 cup grated Cheddar cheese

1. Pour the water into the Instant Pot and insert a steamer basket. Place the cauliflower florets in the basket. 2. Lock the lid. Select the Manual mode and set the cooking time for 3 minutes at Low Pressure. 3. When the timer beeps, perform a quick pressure release. Carefully remove the lid. 4. Season the cauliflower with salt and pepper. Drizzle with olive oil and lemon juice. Sprinkle the grated cheese all over the cauliflower. 5. Press the Sauté button to heat the Instant Pot. Allow to cook for about 5 minutes, or until the cheese melts. Serve warm.

Per Serving:
calories: 136 | fat: 9.8g | protein: 7.2g | carbs: 5.0g | net carbs: 3.4g | fiber: 1.6g

Creole Pancetta and Cheese Balls

Prep time: 5 minutes | Cook time: 5 minutes | Serves 6

1 cup water
6 eggs
4 slices pancetta, chopped
⅓ cup grated Cheddar cheese
¼ cup cream cheese
¼ cup mayonnaise
1 teaspoon Creole seasonings
Sea salt and ground black pepper, to taste

1. Pour the water into the Instant Pot and insert a steamer basket. Place the eggs in the basket. 2. Lock the lid. Select the Manual mode and set the cooking time for 5 minutes at Low Pressure. 3. When the timer beeps, perform a quick pressure release. Carefully remove the lid. 4. Allow the eggs to cool for 10 to 15 minutes. Peel the eggs and chop them, then transfer to a bowl. Add the remaining ingredients and stir to combine well. 5. Shape the mixture into balls with your hands. Serve chilled.

Per Serving:
calories: 239 | fat: 19g | protein: 14g | carbs: 3g | net carbs: 3g | fiber: 0g

Parmesan Artichoke

Prep time: 1 minute | Cook time: 30 minutes | Serves 2

1 large artichoke
1 cup water
¼ cup grated Parmesan cheese
¼ teaspoon salt
¼ teaspoon red pepper flakes

1. Trim artichoke. Remove stem, outer leaves and top. Gently spread leaves. 2. Add water to Instant Pot and place steam rack on bottom. Place artichoke on steam rack and sprinkle with Parmesan, salt, and red pepper flakes. Click lid closed. Press the Steam button and adjust time for 30 minutes. 3. When timer beeps, allow a 15-minute natural release and then quick-release the remaining pressure. Enjoy warm topped with additional Parmesan.

Per Serving:
calories: 90 | fat: 3g | protein: 6g | carbs: 10g | net carbs: 6g | fiber: 4g

Creamy Scallion Dip

Prep time: 10 minutes | Cook time: 11 minutes | Serves 4

5 ounces (142 g) scallions, diced
4 tablespoons cream cheese
1 tablespoon chopped fresh parsley
1 teaspoon garlic powder
2 tablespoons coconut cream
½ teaspoon salt
1 teaspoon coconut oil

1. Heat up the instant pot on Sauté mode. 2. Then add coconut oil and melt it. 3. Add diced scallions and sauté it for 6 to 7 minutes or until it is light brown. 4. Add cream cheese, parsley, garlic powder, salt, and coconut cream. 5. Close the instant pot lid and cook the scallions dip for 5 minutes on Manual mode (High Pressure). 6. Make a quick pressure release. Blend the dip will it is smooth if desired.

Per Serving:
calories: 76 | fat: 6g | protein: 2g | carbs: 4g | net carbs: 3g | fiber: 1g

Creamy Spinach Dip

Prep time: 13 minutes | Cook time: 5 minutes | Serves 11

8 ounces low-fat cream cheese
1 cup low-fat sour cream
½ cup finely chopped onion
½ cup no-sodium vegetable broth
5 cloves garlic, minced
½ teaspoon salt
¼ teaspoon black pepper
10 ounces frozen spinach
12 ounces reduced-fat shredded Monterey Jack cheese
12 ounces reduced-fat shredded Parmesan cheese

1. Add cream cheese, sour cream, onion, vegetable broth, garlic, salt, pepper, and spinach to the inner pot of the Instant Pot. 2. Secure lid, make sure vent is set to sealing, and set to the Bean/Chili setting on high pressure for 5 minutes. 3. When done, do a manual release. 4. Add the cheeses and mix well until creamy and well combined.

Per Serving:
calorie: 274 | fat: 18g | protein: 19g | carbs: 10g | sugars: 3g | fiber: 1g | sodium: 948mg

Cheddar Chips

Prep time: 10 minutes | Cook time: 5 minutes | Serves 4

1 cup shredded Cheddar cheese
1 tablespoon almond flour

1. Mix up Cheddar cheese and almond flour. 2. Then preheat the instant pot on Sauté mode. 3. Line the instant pot bowl with baking paper. 4. After this, make the small rounds from the cheese in the instant pot (on the baking paper) and close the lid. 5. Cook them for 5 minutes on Sauté mode or until the cheese is melted. 6. Then switch off the instant pot and remove the baking paper with cheese rounds from it. 7. Cool the chips well and remove them from the baking paper.

Per Serving:
calories: 154 | fat: 13g | protein: 9g | carbs: 2g | net carbs: 1g | fiber: 1g

Hummus with Chickpeas and Tahini Sauce

Prep time: 10 minutes | Cook time: 55 minutes | Makes 4 cups

4 cups water
1 cup dried chickpeas
2½ teaspoons fine sea salt
½ cup tahini
3 tablespoons fresh lemon juice
1 garlic clove
¼ teaspoon ground cumin

1. Combine the water, chickpeas, and 1 teaspoon of the salt in the Instant Pot and stir to dissolve the salt. 2. Secure the lid and set the Pressure Release to Sealing. Select the Bean/Chili, Pressure Cook, or Manual setting and set the cooking time for 40 minutes at high pressure. (The pot will take about 15 minutes to come up to pressure before the cooking program begins.) 3. When the cooking program ends, let the pressure release naturally for 15 minutes, then move the Pressure Release to Venting to release any remaining steam. 4. Place a colander over a bowl. Open the pot and, wearing heat-resistant mitts, lift out the inner pot and drain the beans in the colander. Return the chickpeas to the inner pot and place it back in the Instant Pot housing on the Keep Warm setting. Reserve the cooking liquid. 5. In a blender or food processor, combine 1 cup of the cooking liquid, the tahini, lemon juice, garlic, cumin, and 1 teaspoon salt. Blend or process on high speed, stopping to scrape down the sides of the container as needed, for about 30 seconds, until smooth and a little fluffy. Scoop out and set aside ½ cup of this sauce for the topping. 6. Set aside ½ cup of the chickpeas for the topping. Add the remaining chickpeas to the tahini sauce in the blender or food processor along with ½ cup of the cooking liquid and the remaining ½ teaspoon salt. Blend or process on high speed, stopping to scrape down the sides of the container as needed, for about 1 minute, until very smooth. 7. Transfer the hummus to a shallow serving bowl. Spoon the reserved tahini mixture over the top, then sprinkle on the reserved chickpeas. The hummus will keep in an airtight container in the refrigerator for up to 3 days. Serve at room temperature or chilled.

Per Serving:
calories: 107 | fat: 5g | protein: 4g | carbs: 10g | sugars: 3g | fiber: 4g | sodium: 753mg

Oregano Sausage Balls

Prep time: 10 minutes | Cook time: 16 minutes | Serves 10

15 ounces (425 g) ground pork sausage
1 teaspoon dried oregano
4 ounces (113 g) Mozzarella, shredded
1 cup coconut flour
1 garlic clove, grated
1 teaspoon coconut oil, melted

1. In the bowl mix up ground pork sausages, dried oregano, shredded Mozzarella, coconut flour, and garlic clove. 2. When the mixture is homogenous, make the balls. 3. After this, pour coconut oil in the instant pot. 4. Arrange the balls in the instant pot and cook them on Sauté mode for 8 minutes from each side.

Per Serving:
calories: 310 | fat: 23g | protein: 17g | carbs: 10g | net carbs: 5g | fiber: 5g

Rosemary Chicken Wings

Prep time: 10 minutes | Cook time: 16 minutes | Serves 4

4 boneless chicken wings
1 tablespoon olive oil
1 teaspoon dried rosemary
½ teaspoon garlic powder
¼ teaspoon salt

1. In the mixing bowl, mix up olive oil, dried rosemary, garlic powder, and salt. 2. Then rub the chicken wings with the rosemary mixture and leave for 10 minutes to marinate. 3. After this, put the chicken wings in the instant pot, add the remaining rosemary marinade and cook them on Sauté mode for 8 minutes from each side.

Per Serving:
calories: 222 | fat: 11g | protein: 27g | carbs: 2g | net carbs: 2g | fiber: 0g

Cheese Stuffed Bell Peppers

Prep time: 10 minutes | Cook time: 5 minutes | Serves 5

1 cup water
10 baby bell peppers, seeded and sliced lengthwise
4 ounces (113 g) Monterey Jack cheese, shredded
4 ounces (113 g) cream cheese
2 tablespoons chopped scallions
1 tablespoon olive oil
1 teaspoon minced garlic
½ teaspoon cayenne pepper
¼ teaspoon ground black pepper, or more to taste

1. Pour the water into the Instant Pot and insert a steamer basket. 2. Stir together the remaining ingredients except the bell peppers in a mixing bowl until combined. Stuff the peppers evenly with the mixture. Arrange the stuffed peppers in the basket. 3. Lock the lid. Select the Manual mode and set the cooking time for 5 minutes at High Pressure. 4. When the timer beeps, perform a quick pressure release. Carefully remove the lid. 5. Cool for 5 minutes and serve.

Per Serving:
calories: 226 | fat: 17.8g | protein: 8.9g | carbs: 8.7g | net carbs: 7.4g | fiber: 1.3g

Ground Turkey Lettuce Cups

Prep time: 5 minutes | Cook time: 30 minutes | Serves 8

3 tablespoons water
2 tablespoons soy sauce, tamari, or coconut aminos
3 tablespoons fresh lime juice
2 teaspoons Sriracha, plus more for serving
2 tablespoons cold-pressed avocado oil
2 teaspoons toasted sesame oil
4 garlic cloves, minced
1-inch piece fresh ginger, peeled and minced
2 carrots, diced
2 celery stalks, diced
1 yellow onion, diced
2 pounds 93 percent lean ground turkey
½ teaspoon fine sea salt
Two 8-ounce cans sliced water chestnuts, drained and chopped
1 tablespoon cornstarch
2 hearts romaine lettuce or 2 heads butter lettuce, leaves separated
½ cup roasted cashews (whole or halves and pieces), chopped
1 cup loosely packed fresh cilantro leaves

1. In a small bowl, combine the water, soy sauce, 2 tablespoons of the lime juice, and the Sriracha and mix well. Set aside. 2. Select the Sauté setting on the Instant Pot and heat the avocado oil, sesame oil, garlic, and ginger for 2 minutes, until the garlic is bubbling but not browned. Add the carrots, celery, and onion and sauté for about 3 minutes, until the onion begins to soften. 3. Add the turkey and salt and sauté, using a wooden spoon or spatula to break up the meat as it cooks, for about 5 minutes, until cooked through and no streaks of pink remain. Add the water chestnuts and soy sauce mixture and stir to combine, working quickly so not too much steam escapes. 4. Secure the lid and set the Pressure Release to Sealing. Press the Cancel button to reset the cooking program, then select the Pressure Cook or Manual setting and set the cooking time for 5 minutes at high pressure. (The pot will take about 10 minutes to come up to pressure before the cooking program begins.) 5. When the cooking program ends, perform a quick pressure release by moving the Pressure Release to Venting, or let the pressure release naturally. Open the pot. 6. In a small bowl, stir together the remaining 1 tablespoon lime juice and the cornstarch, add the mixture to the pot, and stir to combine. Press the Cancel button to reset the cooking program, then select the Sauté setting. Let the mixture come to a boil and thicken, stirring often, for about 2 minutes, then press the Cancel button to turn off the pot. 7. Spoon the turkey mixture onto the lettuce leaves and sprinkle the cashews and cilantro on top. Serve right away, with additional Sriracha at the table.

Per Serving:
calories: 127 | fat: 7g | protein: 6g | carbs: 10g | sugars: 2g | fiber: 3g | sodium: 392mg

Bok Choy Salad Boats with Shrimp

Prep time: 8 minutes | Cook time: 2 minutes | Serves 8

26 shrimp, cleaned and deveined
2 tablespoons fresh lemon juice
1 cup water
Sea salt and ground black pepper, to taste
4 ounces (113 g) feta cheese, crumbled
2 tomatoes, diced
⅓ cup olives, pitted and sliced
4 tablespoons olive oil
2 tablespoons apple cider vinegar
8 Bok choy leaves
2 tablespoons fresh basil leaves, snipped
2 tablespoons chopped fresh mint leaves

1. Toss the shrimp and lemon juice in the Instant Pot until well coated. Pour in the water. 2. Lock the lid. Select the Manual mode and set the cooking time for 2 minutes at Low Pressure. 3. When the timer beeps, perform a quick pressure release. Carefully remove the lid. 4. Season the shrimp with salt and pepper to taste, then let them cool completely. 5. Toss the shrimp with the feta cheese, tomatoes, olives, olive oil, and vinegar until well incorporated. 6. Divide the salad evenly onto each Bok choy leaf and place them on a serving plate. Scatter the basil and mint leaves on top and serve immediately.

Per Serving:
calories: 129 | fat: 10.7g | protein: 4.9g | carbs: 3.0g | net carbs: 2.4g | fiber: 0.6g

Cayenne Beef Bites

Prep time: 5 minutes | Cook time: 23 minutes | Serves 6

2 tablespoons olive oil
1 pound (454 g) beef steak, cut into cubes
1 cup beef bone broth
¼ cup dry white wine
1 teaspoon cayenne pepper
½ teaspoon dried marjoram
Sea salt and ground black pepper, to taste

1. Set your Instant Pot to Sauté and heat the olive oil. 2. Add the beef and sauté for 2 to 3 minutes, stirring occasionally. 3. Add the remaining ingredients to the Instant Pot and combine well. 4. Lock the lid. Select the Manual mode and set the cooking time for 20 minutes at High Pressure. 5. When the timer beeps, perform a natural pressure release for 10 minutes, then release any remaining pressure. Carefully remove the lid. 6. Remove the beef from the Instant Pot to a platter and serve warm.

Per Serving:
calories: 173 | fat: 10.2g | protein: 18.6g | carbs: 1.0g | net carbs: 0.8g | fiber: 0.2g

Candied Pecans

Prep time: 5 minutes | Cook time: 20 minutes | Serves 10

4 cups raw pecans
1½ teaspoons liquid stevia
½ cup plus 1 tablespoon water, divided
1 teaspoon vanilla extract
1 teaspoon cinnamon
¼ teaspoon nutmeg
⅛ teaspoon ground ginger
⅛ teaspoon sea salt

1. Place the raw pecans, liquid stevia, 1 tablespoon water, vanilla, cinnamon, nutmeg, ground ginger, and sea salt into the inner pot of the Instant Pot. 2. Press the Sauté button on the Instant Pot and sauté the pecans and other ingredients until the pecans are soft. 3. Pour in the ½ cup water and secure the lid to the locked position. Set the vent to sealing. 4. Press Manual and set the Instant Pot for 15 minutes. 5. Preheat the oven to 350°F. 6. When cooking time is up, turn off the Instant Pot, then do a quick release. 7. Spread the pecans onto a greased, lined baking sheet. 8. Bake the pecans for 5 minutes or less in the oven, checking on them frequently so they do not burn.

Per Serving:
calories: 275 | fat: 28g | protein: 4g | carbs: 6g | sugars: 2g | fiber: 4g | sodium: 20mg

Red Wine Mushrooms

Prep time: 5 minutes | Cook time: 15 minutes | Serves 2

8 ounces (227 g) sliced mushrooms
¼ cup dry red wine
2 tablespoons beef broth
½ teaspoon garlic powder
¼ teaspoon Worcestershire sauce
Pinch of salt
Pinch of black pepper
¼ teaspoon xanthan gum

1. Add the mushrooms, wine, broth, garlic powder, Worcestershire sauce, salt, and pepper to the pot. 2. Close the lid and seal the vent. Cook on High Pressure for 13 minutes. Quick release the steam. Press Cancel. 3. Turn the pot to Sauté mode. Add the xanthan gum and whisk until the juices have thickened, 1 to 2 minutes.

Per Serving:
calories: 94 | fat: 1g | protein: 4g | carbs: 8g | net carbs: 6g | fiber: 2g

Zucchini and Cheese Tots

Prep time: 15 minutes | Cook time: 10 minutes | Serves 6

4 ounces (113 g) Parmesan, grated
4 ounces (113 g) Cheddar cheese, grated
1 zucchini, grated
1 egg, beaten
1 teaspoon dried oregano
1 tablespoon coconut oil

1. In the mixing bowl, mix up Parmesan, Cheddar cheese, zucchini, egg, and dried oregano. 2. Make the small tots with the help of the fingertips. 3. Then melt the coconut oil in the instant pot on Sauté mode. 4. Put the prepared zucchini tots in the hot coconut oil and cook them for 3 minutes from each side or until they are light brown. Cool the zucchini tots for 5 minutes.

Per Serving:
calories: 173 | fat: 13g | protein: 12g | carbs: 2g | net carbs: 2g | fiber: 0g

Stuffed Jalapeños with Bacon

Prep time: 10 minutes | Cook time: 6 minutes | Serves 2

1 ounce (28 g) bacon, chopped, fried
2 ounces (57 g) Cheddar cheese, shredded
1 tablespoon coconut cream
1 teaspoon chopped green onions
2 jalapeños, trimmed and seeded

1. Mix together the chopped bacon, cheese, coconut cream, and green onions in a mixing bowl and stir until well incorporated. 2. Stuff the jalapeños evenly with the bacon mixture. 3. Press the Sauté button to heat your Instant Pot. 4. Place the stuffed jalapeños in the Instant Pot and cook each side for 3 minutes until softened. 5. Transfer to a paper towel-lined plate and serve.

Per Serving:
calories: 216 | fat: 17.5g | protein: 12.9g | carbs: 1.7g | net carbs: 1.1g | fiber: 0.6g

Parmesan Chicken Balls with Chives

Prep time: 10 minutes | Cook time: 15 minutes | Serves 4

1 teaspoon coconut oil, softened
1 cup ground chicken
¼ cup chicken broth
1 tablespoon chopped chives
1 teaspoon cayenne pepper
3 ounces (85 g) Parmesan cheese, grated

1. Set your Instant Pot to Sauté and heat the coconut oil. 2. Add the remaining ingredients except the cheese to the Instant Pot and stir to mix well. 3. Secure the lid. Select the Manual mode and set the cooking time for 15 minutes at High Pressure. 4. Once cooking is complete, do a quick pressure release. Carefully open the lid. 5. Add the grated cheese and stir until combined. Form the balls from the cooked chicken mixture and allow to cool for 10 minutes, then serve.

Per Serving:
calories: 154 | fat: 8.7g | protein: 17.5g | carbs: 1.0g | net carbs: 0.9g | fiber: 0.1g

Cheddar Cauliflower Rice

Prep time: 3 minutes | Cook time: 1 minute | Serves 4

1 head fresh cauliflower, chopped into florets
1 cup water
3 tablespoons butter
1 tablespoon heavy cream
1 cup shredded sharp Cheddar cheese
½ teaspoon salt
¼ teaspoon pepper
¼ teaspoon garlic powder

1. Place cauliflower in steamer basket. Pour water into Instant Pot and lower steamer rack into pot. Click lid closed. Press the Steam button and adjust time for 1 minute. When timer beeps, quick-release the pressure. 2. Remove steamer basket and place cauliflower in food processor. Pulse until cauliflower is broken into small pearls. Place cauliflower into large bowl, and add remaining ingredients. Gently fold until fully combined.

Per Serving:
calories: 241 | fat: 18g | protein: 10g | carbs: 8g | net carbs: 5g | fiber: 3g

Deviled Eggs with Tuna

Prep time: 10 minutes | Cook time: 8 minutes | Serves 3

1 cup water
6 eggs
1 (5-ounce / 142-g) can tuna, drained
4 tablespoons mayonnaise
1 teaspoon lemon juice
1 celery stalk, diced finely
¼ teaspoon Dijon mustard
¼ teaspoon chopped fresh dill
¼ teaspoon salt
⅛ teaspoon garlic powder

1. Add water to Instant Pot. Place steam rack or steamer basket inside pot. Carefully put eggs into steamer basket. Click lid closed. Press the Manual button and adjust time for 8 minutes. 2. Add remaining ingredients to medium bowl and mix. 3. When timer beeps, quick-release the steam and remove eggs. Place in bowl of cool water for 10 minutes, then remove shells. 4. Cut eggs in half and remove hard-boiled yolks, setting whites aside. Place yolks in food processor and pulse until smooth, or mash with fork. Add yolks to bowl with tuna and mayo, mixing until smooth. 5. Spoon mixture into egg-white halves. Serve chilled.

Per Serving:
calories: 303 | fat: 22g | protein: 20g | carbs: 2g | net carbs: 2g | fiber: 0g

Thyme Sautéed Radishes

Prep time: 5 minutes | Cook time: 15 minutes | Serves 4

1 pound (454 g) radishes, quartered (remove leaves and ends)
2 tablespoons butter
¼ teaspoon dried thyme
¼ teaspoon minced garlic
⅛ teaspoon salt
⅛ teaspoon garlic powder
⅛ teaspoon dried rosemary

1. Press the Sauté button and then press the Adjust button to lower heat to Less. 2. Place radishes into Instant Pot with butter and seasoning. 3. Sauté, stirring occasionally until tender, about 10 to 15 minutes. Add a couple of teaspoons of water if radishes begin to stick.

Per Serving:
calories: 62 | fat: 5g | protein: 1g | carbs: 3g | net carbs: 2g | fiber: 1g

Jalapeño Poppers with Bacon

Prep time: 10 minutes | Cook time: 3 minutes | Serves 4

6 jalapeños
4 ounces (113 g) cream cheese
¼ cup shredded sharp Cheddar cheese
1 cup water
¼ cup cooked crumbled bacon

1. Cut jalapeños lengthwise and scoop out seeds and membrane, then set aside. 2. In small bowl, mix cream cheese and Cheddar. Spoon into emptied jalapeños. Pour water into Instant Pot and place steamer basket in bottom. 3. Place stuffed jalapeños on steamer rack. Click lid closed. Press the Manual button and adjust time for 3 minutes. When timer beeps, quick-release the pressure. Serve topped with crumbled bacon.

Per Serving:
calories: 185 | fat: 14g | protein: 7g | carbs: 3g | net carbs: 2g | fiber: 1g

Spicy Baked Feta in Foil

Prep time: 10 minutes | Cook time: 6 minutes | Serves 6

12 ounces (340 g) feta cheese
½ tomato, sliced
1 ounce (28 g) bell pepper, sliced
1 teaspoon ground paprika
1 tablespoon olive oil
1 cup water, for cooking

1. Sprinkle the cheese with olive oil and ground paprika and place it on the foil. 2. Then top feta cheese with sliced tomato and bell pepper. Wrap it in the foil well. 3. After this, pour water and insert the steamer rack in the instant pot. 4. Put the wrapped cheese on the rack. Close and seal the lid. 5. Cook the cheese on Manual mode (High Pressure) for 6 minutes. Then make a quick pressure release. 6. Discard the foil and transfer the cheese on the serving plates.

Per Serving:
calories: 178 | fat: 14g | protein: 8g | carbs: 4g | net carbs: 3g | fiber: 1g

Blackberry Baked Brie

Prep time: 5 minutes | Cook time: 15 minutes | Serves 5

8-ounce round Brie
1 cup water
¼ cup sugar-free blackberry preserves
2 teaspoons chopped fresh mint

1. Slice a grid pattern into the top of the rind of the Brie with a knife. 2. In a 7-inch round baking dish, place the Brie, then cover the baking dish securely with foil. 3. Insert the trivet into the inner pot of the Instant Pot; pour in the water. 4. Make a foil sling and arrange it on top of the trivet. Place the baking dish on top of the trivet and foil sling. 5. Secure the lid to the locked position and turn the vent to sealing. 6. Press Manual and set the Instant Pot for 15 minutes on high pressure. 7. When cooking time is up, turn off the Instant Pot and do a quick release of the pressure. 8. When the valve has dropped, remove the lid, then remove the baking dish. 9. Remove the top rind of the Brie and top with the preserves. Sprinkle with the fresh mint.

Per Serving:
calorie: 133 | fat: 10g | protein: 8g | carbs: 4g | sugars: 0g | fiber: 0g | sodium: 238mg

Coconut Cajun Shrimp

Prep time: 10 minutes | Cook time: 6 minutes | Serves 2

4 Royal tiger shrimps
3 tablespoons coconut shred
2 eggs, beaten
½ teaspoon Cajun seasoning
1 teaspoon olive oil

1. Heat up olive oil in the instant pot on Sauté mode. 2. Meanwhile, mix up Cajun seasoning and coconut shred. 3. Dip the shrimps in the eggs and coat in the coconut shred mixture. 4. After this, place the shrimps in the hot olive oil and cook them on Sauté mode for 3 minutes from each side.

Per Serving:
calories: 292 | fat: 54g | protein: 40g | carbs: 2g | net carbs: 1g | fiber: 1g

Spinach and Artichoke Dip

Prep time: 5 minutes | Cook time: 4 minutes | Serves 11

8 ounces low-fat cream cheese
10-ounce box frozen spinach
½ cup no-sodium chicken broth
14-ounce can artichoke hearts, drained
½ cup low-fat sour cream
½ cup low-fat mayo
3 cloves of garlic, minced
1 teaspoon onion powder
16 ounces reduced-fat shredded Parmesan cheese
8 ounces reduced-fat shredded mozzarella

1. Put all ingredients in the inner pot of the Instant Pot, except the Parmesan cheese and the mozzarella cheese. 2. Secure the lid and set vent to sealing. Place on Manual high pressure for 4 minutes. 3. Do a quick release of steam. 4. Immediately stir in the cheeses.

Per Serving:

calories: 288 | fat: 18g | protein: 19g | carbs: 15g | sugars: 3g | fiber: 3g | sodium: 1007mg

Pancetta Pizza Dip

Prep time: 10 minutes | Cook time: 4 minutes | Serves 10

10 ounces (283 g) Pepper Jack cheese
10 ounces (283 g) cream cheese
10 ounces (283 g) pancetta, chopped
1 pound (454 g) tomatoes, puréed
1 cup green olives, pitted and halved
1 teaspoon dried oregano
½ teaspoon garlic powder
1 cup chicken broth
4 ounces (113 g) Mozzarella cheese, thinly sliced

1. Mix together the Pepper Jack cheese, cream cheese, pancetta, tomatoes, olives, oregano, and garlic powder in the Instant Pot. Pour in the chicken broth. 2. Lock the lid. Select the Manual mode and set the cooking time for 4 minutes at High Pressure. 3. When the timer beeps, perform a quick pressure release. Carefully remove the lid. 4. Scatter the Mozzarella cheese on top. Cover and allow to sit in the residual heat. Serve warm.

Per Serving:

calories: 287 | fat: 20.8g | protein: 20.8g | carbs: 3.4g | net carbs: 2.0g | fiber: 1.4g

Creamed Onion Spinach

Prep time: 3 minutes | Cook time: 5 minutes | Serves 6

4 tablespoons butter
¼ cup diced onion
8 ounces (227 g) cream cheese
1 (12-ounce / 340-g) bag frozen spinach
½ cup chicken broth
1 cup shredded whole-milk Mozzarella cheese

1. Press the Sauté button and add butter. Once butter is melted, add onion to Instant Pot and sauté for 2 minutes or until onion begins to turn translucent. 2. Break cream cheese into pieces and add to Instant Pot. Press the Cancel button. Add frozen spinach and broth. Click lid closed. Press the Manual button and adjust time for 5 minutes. When timer beeps, quick-release the pressure and stir in shredded Mozzarella. If mixture is too watery, press the Sauté button and reduce for additional 5 minutes, stirring constantly.

Per Serving:

calories: 273 | fat: 24g | protein: 9g | carbs: 5g | net carbs: 3g | fiber: 2g

Creamy Jalapeño Chicken Dip

Prep time: 5 minutes | Cook time: 12 minutes | Serves 10

1 pound boneless chicken breast
8 ounces low-fat cream cheese
3 jalapeños, seeded and sliced
½ cup water
8 ounces reduced-fat shredded cheddar cheese
¾ cup low-fat sour cream

1. Place the chicken, cream cheese, jalapeños, and water in the inner pot of the Instant Pot. 2. Secure the lid so it's locked and turn the vent to sealing. 3. Press Manual and set the Instant Pot for 12 minutes on high pressure. 4. When cooking time is up, turn off Instant Pot, do a quick release of the remaining pressure, then remove lid. 5. Shred the chicken between 2 forks, either in the pot or on a cutting board, then place back in the inner pot. 6. Stir in the shredded cheese and sour cream.

Per Serving:

calories: 238 | fat: 13g | protein: 24g | carbs: 7g | sugars: 5g | fiber: 1g | sodium: 273mg

Chapter 3 Breakfasts

Spinach and Chicken Casserole

Prep time: 5 minutes | Cook time: 15 minutes | Serves 5

1 tablespoon avocado oil
1 tablespoon coconut oil
1 tablespoon unflavored MCT oil
1 avocado, mashed
½ cup shredded full-fat Cheddar cheese
½ cup chopped spinach
½ teaspoon dried basil
½ teaspoon kosher salt
½ teaspoon freshly ground black pepper
¼ cup sugar-free or low-sugar salsa
¼ cup heavy whipping cream
1 pound (454 g) ground chicken

1. Pour 1 cup of filtered water inside the inner pot of the Instant Pot, then insert the trivet. 2. In a large bowl, combine and mix the avocado oil, coconut oil, MCT oil, avocado, cheese, spinach, basil, salt, black pepper, salsa, and whipping cream. 3. In a greased Instant Pot-safe dish, add the ground chicken in an even layer. Pour the casserole mixture over the chicken and cover with aluminum foil. Using a sling, place this dish on top of the trivet. 4. Close the lid, set the pressure release to Sealing, and select Manual. Set the Instant Pot to 15 minutes on High Pressure, and let cook. 5. Once cooked, carefully switch the pressure release to Venting. Open the Instant Pot, serve, and enjoy!

Per Serving:
calories: 405 | fat: 30g | protein: 30g | carbs: 5g | net carbs: 2g | fiber: 3g

Chocolate Chip Pancake

Prep time: 5 minutes | Cook time: 37 minutes | Serves 5 to 6

4 tablespoons salted grass-fed butter, softened
2 cups blanched almond flour
½ cup Swerve, or more to taste
1 ¼ cups full-fat coconut milk
¼ cup sugar-free chocolate chips
¼ cup organic coconut flour
2 eggs
1 tablespoon chopped walnuts
¼ teaspoon baking soda
½ teaspoon salt
½ cup dark berries, for serving (optional)

1. Grease the bottom and sides of your Instant Pot with the butter. Make sure you coat it very liberally. 2. In a large bowl, mix together the almond flour, Swerve, milk, chocolate chips, coconut flour, eggs, walnuts, baking soda, and salt. Add this mixture to the Instant Pot. Close the lid, set the pressure release to Sealing, and select Multigrain. Set the Instant Pot to 37 minutes on Low Pressure, and let cook. 3. Switch the pressure release to Venting and open the Instant Pot. Confirm your pancake is cooked, then carefully remove it using a spatula. Serve with the berries (if desired), and enjoy!

Per Serving:
calories: 369 | fat: 31g | protein: 7g | carbs: 16g | net carbs: 9g | fiber: 7g

Shredded Potato Omelet

Prep time: 15 minutes | Cook time: 20 minutes | Serves 6

3 slices bacon, cooked and crumbled
2 cups shredded cooked potatoes
¼ cup minced onion
¼ cup minced green bell pepper
1 cup egg substitute
¼ cup fat-free milk
¼ teaspoon salt
⅛ teaspoon black pepper
1 cup 75%-less-fat shredded cheddar cheese
1 cup water

1. With nonstick cooking spray, spray the inside of a round baking dish that will fit in your Instant Pot inner pot. 2. Sprinkle the bacon, potatoes, onion, and bell pepper around the bottom of the baking dish. 3. Mix together the egg substitute, milk, salt, and pepper in mixing bowl. Pour over potato mixture. 4. Top with cheese. 5. Add water, place the steaming rack into the bottom of the inner pot and then place the round baking dish on top. 6. Close the lid and secure to the locking position. Be sure the vent is turned to sealing. Set for 20 minutes on Manual at high pressure. 7. Let the pressure release naturally. 8. Carefully remove the baking dish with the handles of the steaming rack and allow to stand 10 minutes before cutting and serving.

Per Serving:
calories: 130 | fat: 3g | protein: 12g | carbs: 13g | sugars: 2g | fiber: 2g | sodium: 415mg

Bacon Egg Cups

Prep time: 5 minutes | Cook time: 7 minutes | Serves 4

6 large eggs
2 strips cooked bacon, sliced in ¼-inch wide pieces
½ cup Cheddar cheese, divided
¼ teaspoon sea salt
¼ teaspoon black pepper
1 cup water
1 tablespoon chopped fresh flat leaf parsley

1. In a small bowl, beat the eggs. Stir in the cooked bacon, ¼ cup of the cheese, sea salt and pepper. Divide the egg mixture equally among four ramekins and loosely cover with aluminum foil. 2. Pour the water and place the trivet in the Instant Pot. Place two ramekins on the trivet and stack the other two on the top. 3. Lock the lid. Select the Manual mode and set the cooking time for 7 minutes at High Pressure. When the timer goes off, use a natural pressure release for 10 minutes, then release any remaining pressure. Carefully open the lid. 4. Top each ramekin with the remaining ¼ cup of the cheese. Lock the lid and melt the cheese for 2 minutes. Garnish with the chopped parsley and serve immediately.

Per Serving:
calories: 168 | fat: 11.8g | protein: 13.2g | carbs: 1.0g | net carbs: 0.9g | fiber: 0.1g

Streusel Pumpkin Cake

Prep time: 10 minutes | Cook time: 30 minutes | Serves 8

Streusel Topping:
¼ cup Swerve
¼ cup almond flour
2 tablespoons coconut oil or unsalted butter, softened
½ teaspoon ground cinnamon
Cake:
2 large eggs, beaten
2 cups almond flour
1 cup pumpkin purée
¾ cup Swerve
2 teaspoons pumpkin pie spice
2 teaspoons vanilla extract
½ teaspoon fine sea salt
Glaze:
½ cup Swerve
3 tablespoons unsweetened almond milk

1. Set a trivet in the Instant Pot and pour in 1 cup water. Line a baking pan with parchment paper. 2. In a small bowl, whisk together all the ingredients for the streusel topping with a fork. 3. In a medium-sized bowl, stir together all the ingredients for the cake until thoroughly combined. 4. Scoop half of the batter into the prepared baking pan and sprinkle half of the streusel topping on top. Repeat with the remaining batter and topping. 5. Place the baking pan on the trivet in the Instant Pot. 6. Lock the lid, select the Manual mode and set the cooking time for 30 minutes on High Pressure. 7. Meanwhile, whisk together the Swerve and almond milk in a small bowl until it reaches a runny consistency. 8. When the timer goes off, do a natural pressure release for 10 minutes, then release any remaining pressure. Open the lid. 9. Remove the baking pan from the pot. Let cool in the pan for 10 minutes. Transfer the cake onto a plate and peel off the parchment paper. 10. Transfer the cake onto a serving platter. Spoon the glaze over the top of the cake. Serve immediately.

Per Serving:
calories: 238 | fat: 20g | protein: 9.1g | carbs: 9.0g | net carbs: 4.9g | fiber: 4.1g

Cauliflower Nutty Porridge

Prep time: 40 minutes | Cook time: 5 minutes | Serves 4

2½ cups water, divided
½ cup raw cashews
½ cup almond slivers
¼ cup raw pumpkin seeds
¼ head cauliflower, chopped
Sea salt, to taste
¼ cup heavy whipping cream
Topping:
¼ cup hemp seeds
¼ cup chia seeds
1 tablespoon cinnamon

1. In a small bowl, add 2 cups of the water, the cashews, almonds and pumpkin seeds. Soak for 30 minutes. Drain the water and set aside. Reserve a few nuts and pumpkin seeds in a separate bowl to be used as garnish. 2. Pour the remaining ½ cup of the water into the Instant Pot and add the soaked nuts mixture, cauliflower and sea salt. 3. Lock the lid. Select the Manual mode and set the cooking time for 5 minutes at High Pressure. When the timer goes off, use a natural pressure release for 10 minutes, then release any remaining pressure. Carefully open the lid. 4. Transfer the cauliflower and nuts mixture to a food processor, add the heavy cream and pulse until smooth. 5. Season with a pinch of sea salt. Garnish with the reserved nuts, pumpkin seeds, hemp seeds and chia seeds and sprinkle with the cinnamon. Serve immediately.

Per Serving:
calories: 368 | fat: 29.9g | protein: 15.1g | carbs: 15.8g | net carbs: 7.6g | fiber: 8.2g

Gouda Egg Casserole with Canadian Bacon

Prep time: 12 minutes | Cook time: 20 minutes | Serves 4

Nonstick cooking spray
1 slice whole grain bread, toasted
½ cup shredded smoked Gouda cheese
3 slices Canadian bacon, chopped
6 large eggs
¼ cup half-and-half
¼ teaspoon kosher salt
¼ teaspoon freshly ground black pepper
¼ teaspoon dry mustard

1. Spray a 6-inch cake pan with cooking spray, or if the pan is nonstick, skip this step. If you don't have a 6-inch cake pan, any bowl or pan that fits inside your pressure cooker should work. 2. Crumble the toast into the bottom of the pan. Sprinkle with the cheese and Canadian bacon. 3. In a medium bowl, whisk together the eggs, half-and-half, salt, pepper, and dry mustard. 4. Pour the egg mixture into the pan. Loosely cover the pan with aluminum foil. 5. Pour 1½ cups water into the electric pressure cooker and insert a wire rack or trivet. Place the covered pan on top of the rack. 6. Close and lock the lid of the pressure cooker. Set the valve to sealing. 7. Cook on high pressure for 20 minutes. 8. When the cooking is complete, hit Cancel and quick release the pressure. 9. Once the pin drops, unlock and remove the lid. 10. Carefully transfer the pan from the pressure cooker to a cooling rack and let it sit for 5 minutes. 11. Cut into 4 wedges and serve.

Per Serving:
calories: 247 | fat: 15g | protein: 20g | carbs: 8g | sugars: 1g | fiber: 1g | sodium: 717mg

Pumpkin Mug Muffin

Prep time: 5 minutes | Cook time: 9 minutes | Serves 1

½ cup Swerve
½ cup blanched almond flour
2 tablespoons organic pumpkin purée
1 teaspoon sugar-free chocolate chips
1 tablespoon organic coconut flour
1 egg
1 tablespoon coconut oil
½ teaspoon pumpkin pie spice
½ teaspoon ground nutmeg
½ teaspoon ground cinnamon
⅛ teaspoon baking soda

1. Mix the Swerve, almond flour, pumpkin purée, chocolate chips, coconut flour, egg, coconut oil, pumpkin pie spice, nutmeg, cinnamon, and baking soda in a large bowl. Transfer this mixture into a well-greased, Instant Pot-friendly mug. 2. Pour 1 cup of filtered water into the inner pot of the Instant Pot, and insert the trivet. Cover the mug in foil and place on top of the trivet. 3. Close the lid, set the pressure release to Sealing, and select Manual. Set the Instant Pot to 9 minutes on High Pressure. 4. Once cooked, release the pressure immediately by switching the valve to Venting. Be sure your muffin is done by inserting a toothpick into the cake and making sure it comes out clean, as cook times may vary. 5. Remove mug and enjoy!

Per Serving:
calories: 297 | fat: 22g | protein: 9g | carbs: 17g | net carbs: 9g | fiber: 8g

Cauliflower and Cheese Quiche

Prep time: 10 minutes | Cook time: 10 minutes | Serves 2

1 cup chopped cauliflower
¼ cup shredded Cheddar cheese
5 eggs, beaten
1 teaspoon butter
1 teaspoon dried oregano
1 cup water

1. Grease the instant pot baking pan with butter from inside. 2. Pour water in the instant pot. 3. Sprinkle the cauliflower with dried oregano and put it in the prepared baking pan. Flatten the vegetables gently. 4. After this, add eggs and stir the vegetables. 5. Top the quiche with shredded cheese and transfer it in the instant pot. Close and seal the lid. Cook the quiche on Manual mode (High Pressure) for 10 minutes. Make a quick pressure release.

Per Serving:
calories: 246 | fat: 18g | protein: 18g | carbs: 4g | net carbs: 2g | fiber: 2g

Almond Pancakes

Prep time: 10 minutes | Cook time: 15 minutes per batch | Serves 6

4 eggs, beaten
2 cups almond flour
½ cup butter, melted
2 tablespoons granulated erythritol
1 tablespoon avocado oil
1 teaspoon baking powder
1 teaspoon vanilla extract
Pinch of salt
¾ cup water, divided

1. In a blender, combine all the ingredients, except for the ½ cup of the water. Pulse until fully combined and smooth. Let the batter rest for 5 minutes before cooking. 2. Fill each cup with 2 tablespoons of the batter, about two-thirds of the way full. Cover the cups with aluminum foil. 3. Pour the remaining ½ cup of the water and insert the trivet in the Instant Pot. Place the cups on the trivet. 4. Set the lid in place. Select the Manual mode and set the cooking time for 15 minutes on High Pressure. When the timer goes off, do a quick pressure release. Carefully open the lid. 5. Repeat with the remaining batter, until all the batter is used. Add more water to the pot before cooking each batch, if needed. 6. Serve warm.

Per Serving:
3 bites: calories: 423 | fat: 38.7g | protein: 12.3g | carbs: 8.2g | net carbs: 4.0g | fiber: 4.2g

Pork and Quill Egg Cups

Prep time: 15 minutes | Cook time: 15 minutes | Serves 4

10 ounces (283 g) ground pork
1 jalapeño pepper, chopped
1 tablespoon butter, softened
1 teaspoon dried dill
½ teaspoon salt
1 cup water
4 quill eggs

1. In a bowl, stir together all the ingredients, except for the quill eggs and water. Transfer the meat mixture to the silicone muffin molds and press the surface gently. 2. Pour the water and insert the trivet in the Instant Pot. Put the meat cups on the trivet. 3. Crack the eggs over the meat mixture. 4. Set the lid in place. Select the Manual mode and set the cooking time for 15 minutes on High Pressure. When the timer goes off, do a quick pressure release. Carefully open the lid. 5. Serve warm.

Per Serving:
calories: 142 | fat: 6.3g | protein: 20.0g | carbs: 0.3g | net carbs: 0.1g | fiber: 0.2g

Cheddar Broccoli Egg Bites

Prep time: 10 minutes | Cook time: 10 minutes | Serves 7

5 eggs, beaten
3 tablespoons heavy cream
⅛ teaspoon salt
⅛ teaspoon black pepper
1 ounce (28 g) finely chopped broccoli
1 ounce (28 g) shredded Cheddar cheese
½ cup water

1. In a blender, combine the eggs, heavy cream, salt and pepper and pulse until smooth. 2. Divide the chopped broccoli among the egg cups equally. Pour the egg mixture on top of the broccoli, filling the cups about three-fourths of the way full. Sprinkle the Cheddar cheese on top of each cup. 3. Cover the egg cups tightly with aluminum foil. 4. Pour the water and insert the trivet in the Instant Pot. Put the egg cups on the trivet. 5. Lock the lid. Select the Manual mode and set the cooking time for 10 minutes on High Pressure. Once the timer goes off, perform a natural pressure release for 5 minutes, then release any remaining pressure. Carefully open the lid. 6. Serve immediately.

Per Serving:
calories: 89 | fat: 7.0g | protein: 5.8g | carbs: 0.7g | net carbs: 0.5g | fiber: 0.2g

Blueberry Oat Mini Muffins

Prep time: 12 minutes | Cook time: 10 minutes | Serves 7

½ cup rolled oats
¼ cup whole wheat pastry flour or white whole wheat flour
½ tablespoon baking powder
½ teaspoon ground cardamom or ground cinnamon
⅛ teaspoon kosher salt
2 large eggs
½ cup plain Greek yogurt
2 tablespoons pure maple syrup
2 teaspoons extra-virgin olive oil
½ teaspoon vanilla extract
½ cup frozen blueberries (preferably small wild blueberries)

1. In a large bowl, stir together the oats, flour, baking powder, cardamom, and salt. 2. In a medium bowl, whisk together the eggs, yogurt, maple syrup, oil, and vanilla. 3. Add the egg mixture to oat mixture and stir just until combined. Gently fold in the blueberries. 4. Scoop the batter into each cup of the egg bite mold. 5. Pour 1 cup of water into the electric pressure cooker. Place the egg bite mold on the wire rack and carefully lower it into the pot. 6. Close and lock the lid of the pressure cooker. Set the valve to sealing. 7. Cook on high pressure for 10 minutes. 8. When the cooking is complete, allow the pressure to release naturally for 10 minutes, then quick release any remaining pressure. Hit Cancel. 9. Lift the wire rack out of the pot and place on a cooling rack for 5 minutes. Invert the mold onto the cooling rack to release the muffins. 10. Serve the muffins warm or refrigerate or freeze.

Per Serving:
calories: 117 | fat: 4g | protein: 5g | carbs: 15g | sugars: 4g | fiber: 2g | sodium: 89mg

Cynthia's Yogurt

Prep time: 10 minutes | Cook time: 8 hours | Serves 16

1 gallon low-fat milk
¼ cup low-fat plain yogurt with active cultures

1. Pour milk into the inner pot of the Instant Pot. 2. Lock lid, move vent to sealing, and press the yogurt button. Press Adjust till it reads "boil." 3. When boil cycle is complete (about 1 hour), check the temperature. It should be at 185°F. If it's not, use the Sauté function to warm to 185. 4. After it reaches 185°F, unplug Instant Pot, remove inner pot, and cool. You can place on cooling rack and let it slowly cool. If in a hurry, submerge the base of the pot in cool water. Cool milk to 110°F. 5. When mixture reaches 110, stir in the ¼ cup of yogurt. Lock the lid in place and move vent to sealing. 6. Press Yogurt. Use the Adjust button until the screen says 8:00. This will now incubate for 8 hours. 7. After 8 hours (when the cycle is finished), chill yogurt, or go immediately to straining in step 8. 8. After chilling, or following the 8 hours, strain the yogurt using a nut milk bag. This will give it the consistency of Greek yogurt.

Per Serving:
calories: 141 | fat: 5g | protein: 10g | carbs: 14g | sugars: 1g | fiber: 0g | sodium: 145mg

Egg Ham Muffins

Prep time: 10 minutes | Cook time: 6 minutes | Serves 2

2 eggs, beaten
4 ounces (113 g) ham, chopped
½ teaspoon avocado oil
1 cup water, for cooking

1. Pour water in the instant pot. 2. Then brush the muffin molds with avocado oil from inside. 3. In the mixing bowl, mix up ham and beaten eggs. 4. After this, pour the mixture into the muffin molds. 5. Place the muffins in the instant pot. Close and seal the lid. Cook the meal on Manual mode (High Pressure) for 6 minutes. Then make a quick pressure release and remove the muffins.

Per Serving:
calories: 192 | fat: 16g | protein: 8g | carbs: 10g | net carbs: 8g | fiber: 2g

Smoked Salmon and Asparagus Quiche Cups

Prep time: 15 minutes | Cook time: 15 minutes | Serves 2

Nonstick cooking spray
4 asparagus spears, cut into ½-inch pieces
2 tablespoons finely chopped onion
3 ounces (85 g) smoked salmon (skinless and boneless), chopped
3 large eggs
2 tablespoons 2% milk
¼ teaspoon dried dill
Pinch ground white pepper

1. Pour 1½ cups of water into the electric pressure cooker and insert a wire rack or trivet. 2. Lightly spray the bottom and sides of the ramekins with nonstick cooking spray. Divide the asparagus, onion, and salmon between the ramekins. 3. In a measuring cup with a spout, whisk together the eggs, milk, dill, and white pepper. Pour half of the egg mixture into each ramekin. Loosely cover the ramekins with aluminum foil. 4. Carefully place the ramekins inside the pot on the rack. 5. Close and lock the lid of the pressure cooker. Set the valve to sealing. 6. Cook on high pressure for 15 minutes. 7. When the cooking is complete, hit Cancel and quick release the pressure. 8. Once the pin drops, unlock and remove the lid. 9. Carefully remove the ramekins from the pot. Cool, covered, for 5 minutes. 10. Run a small silicone spatula or a knife around the edge of each ramekin. Invert each quiche onto a small plate and serve.

Per Serving:
calories: 180 | fat: 9g | protein: 20g | carbs: 3g | sugars: 1g | fiber: 1g | sodium: 646mg

Keto Cabbage Hash Browns

Prep time: 5 minutes | Cook time: 8 minutes | Serves 3

1 cup shredded white cabbage
3 eggs, beaten
½ teaspoon ground nutmeg
½ teaspoon salt
½ teaspoon onion powder
½ zucchini, grated
1 tablespoon coconut oil

1. In a bowl, stir together all the ingredients, except for the coconut oil. Form the cabbage mixture into medium hash browns. 2. Press the Sauté button on the Instant Pot and heat the coconut oil. 3. Place the hash browns in the hot coconut oil. Cook for 4 minutes on each side, or until lightly browned. 4. Transfer the hash browns to a plate and serve warm.

Per Serving:
calories: 115 | fat: 9.0g | protein: 6.4g | carbs: 3.2g | net carbs: 2.1g | fiber: 1.1g

Potato-Bacon Gratin

Prep time: 20 minutes | Cook time: 40 minutes | Serves 8

1 tablespoon olive oil
6-ounces bag fresh spinach
1 clove garlic, minced
4 large potatoes, peeled or unpeeled, divided
6-ounces Canadian bacon slices, divided
5-ounces reduced-fat grated Swiss cheddar, divided
1 cup lower-sodium, lower-fat chicken broth

1. Set the Instant Pot to Sauté and pour in the olive oil. Cook the spinach and garlic in olive oil just until spinach is wilted (5 minutes or less). Turn off the instant pot. 2. Cut potatoes into thin slices about ¼" thick. 3. In a springform pan that will fit into the inner pot of your Instant Pot, spray it with nonstick spray then layer ⅓ the potatoes, half the bacon, ⅓ the cheese, and half the wilted spinach. 4. Repeat layers ending with potatoes. Reserve ⅓ cheese for later. 5. Pour chicken broth over all. 6. Wipe the bottom of your Instant Pot to soak up any remaining oil, then add in 2 cups of water and the steaming rack. Place the springform pan on top. 7. Close the lid and secure to the locking position. Be sure the vent is turned to sealing. Set for 35 minutes on Manual at high pressure. 8. Perform a quick release. 9. Top with the remaining cheese, then allow to stand 10 minutes before removing from the Instant Pot, cutting and serving.

Per Serving:
calories: 220 | fat: 7g | protein: 14g | carbs: 28g | sugars: 2g | fiber: 3g | sodium: 415mg

Bell Peppers Stuffed with Eggs

Prep time: 5 minutes | Cook time: 14 minutes | Serves 2

2 eggs, beaten
1 tablespoon coconut cream
¼ teaspoon dried oregano
¼ teaspoon salt
1 large bell pepper, cut into halves and deseeded
1 cup water

1. In a bowl, stir together the eggs, coconut cream, oregano and salt. 2. Pour the egg mixture in the pepper halves. 3. Pour the water and insert the trivet in the Instant Pot. Put the stuffed pepper halves on the trivet. 4. Set the lid in place. Select the Manual mode and set the cooking time for 14 minutes on High Pressure. When the timer goes off, do a quick pressure release. Carefully open the lid. 5. Serve warm.

Per Serving:
calories: 99 | fat: 6.2g | protein: 6.4g | carbs: 5.3g | net carbs: 4.2g | fiber: 1.2g

Ground Pork Breakfast Patties

Prep time: 5 minutes | Cook time: 15 minutes | Serves 4

1 pound (454 g) 84% lean ground pork
1 teaspoon dried thyme
½ teaspoon dried sage
½ teaspoon garlic powder
½ teaspoon salt
¼ teaspoon pepper
¼ teaspoon red pepper flakes

1. Mix all ingredients in large bowl. Form into 4 patties based on preference. Press the Sauté button and press the Adjust button to lower heat to Less. 2. Place patties in Instant Pot and allow fat to render while patties begin browning. After 5 minutes, or when a few tablespoons of fat have rendered from meat, press the Cancel button. 3. Press the Sauté button and press the Adjust button to set heat to Normal. Sear each side of patties and allow them to cook fully until no pink remains in centers, approximately 10 additional minutes, depending on thickness.

Per Serving:
calories: 249 | fat: 16g | protein: 20g | carbs: 1g | net carbs: 1g | fiber: 0g

Gruyère Asparagus Frittata

Prep time: 10 minutes | Cook time: 22 minutes | Serves 6

6 eggs
6 tablespoons heavy cream
½ teaspoon salt
½ teaspoon black pepper
1 tablespoon butter
2½ ounces (71 g) asparagus, chopped
1 clove garlic, minced
1¼ cup shredded Gruyère cheese, divided
Cooking spray
3 ounces (85 g) halved cherry tomatoes
½ cup water

1. In a large bowl, stir together the eggs, cream, salt, and pepper. 2. Set the Instant Pot on the Sauté mode and melt the butter. Add the asparagus and garlic to the pot and sauté for 2 minutes, or until the garlic is fragrant. The asparagus should still be crisp. 3. Transfer the asparagus and garlic to the bowl with the egg mixture. Stir in 1 cup of the cheese. Clean the pot. 4. Spritz a baking pan with cooking spray. Spread the tomatoes in a single layer in the pan. Pour the egg mixture on top of the tomatoes and sprinkle with the remaining ¼ cup of the cheese. Cover the pan tightly with aluminum foil. 5. Pour the water in the Instant Pot and insert the trivet. Place the pan on the trivet. 6. Set the lid in place. Select the Manual mode and set the cooking time for 20 minutes on High Pressure. When the timer goes off, perform a quick pressure release. Carefully open the lid. 7. Remove the pan from the pot and remove the foil. Blot off any excess moisture with a paper towel. Let the frittata cool for 5 to 10 minutes before transferring onto a plate.

Per Serving:
calories: 204 | fat: 16.6g | protein: 11.3g | carbs: 2.2g | net carbs: 1.6g | fiber: 0.6g

Instant Pot Hard-Boiled Eggs

Prep time: 10 minutes | Cook time: 5 minutes | Serves 7

1 cup water
6–8 eggs

1. Pour the water into the inner pot. Place the eggs in a steamer basket or rack that came with pot. 2. Close the lid and secure to the locking position. Be sure the vent is turned to sealing. Set for 5 minutes on Manual at high pressure. (It takes about 5 minutes for pressure to build and then 5 minutes to cook.) 3. Let pressure naturally release for 5 minutes, then do quick pressure release. 4. Place hot eggs into cool water to halt cooking process. You can peel cooled eggs immediately or refrigerate unpeeled.

Per Serving:
calories: 72 | fat: 5g | protein: 6g | carbs: 0g | sugars: 0g | fiber: 0g | sodium: 71mg

Easy Quiche

Prep time: 15 minutes | Cook time: 25 minutes | Serves 6

1 cup water
¼ cup chopped onion
¼ cup chopped mushroom, optional
3 ounces 75%-less-fat cheddar cheese, shredded
2 tablespoons bacon bits, chopped ham or browned sausage
4 eggs
¼ teaspoons salt
1½ cups fat-free milk
½ cup whole wheat flour
1 tablespoon trans-fat-free tub margarine

1. Pour water into Instant Pot and place the steaming rack inside. 2. Spray a 6" round cake pan with nonstick spray. 3. Sprinkle the onion, mushroom, shredded cheddar, and meat around in the cake pan. 4. Combine remaining ingredients in medium bowl. Pour over meat and vegetables mixture. 5. Place the cake pan onto the steaming rack, close the lid and secure to the locking position. Be sure the vent is turned to sealing. Set for 25 minutes on Manual at high pressure. 7. Let the pressure release naturally. 8. Carefully remove the cake pan with the handles of the steaming rack and allow to stand 10 minutes before cutting and serving.

Per Serving:
calories: 128 | fat: 5g | protein: 11g | carbs: 10g | sugars: 2g | fiber: 1g | sodium: 302mg

Baked Eggs and Ham

Prep time: 5 minutes | Cook time: 5 minutes | Serves 2

4 large eggs, beaten
4 slices ham, diced
½ cup shredded Cheddar cheese
½ cup heavy cream
½ teaspoon sea salt
Pinch ground black pepper

1. Grease two ramekins. 2. In a large bowl, whisk together all the ingredients. Divide the egg mixture equally between the ramekins. 3. Set a trivet in the Instant Pot and pour in 1 cup water. Place the ramekins on the trivet. 4. Lock the lid. Select the Manual mode and set the cooking time for 5 minutes on High Pressure. When the timer goes off, perform a quick pressure release. Carefully open the lid. 5. Remove the ramekins from the Instant Pot. 6. Serve immediately.

Per Serving:

calories: 591 | fat: 50.8g | protein: 33.2g | carbs: 2.9g | net carbs: 2.7g | fiber: 0.2g

Pulled Pork Hash

Prep time: 10 minutes | Cook time: 15 minutes | Serves 4

4 eggs
10 ounces (283 g) pulled pork, shredded
1 teaspoon coconut oil
1 teaspoon red pepper
1 teaspoon chopped fresh cilantro
1 tomato, chopped
¼ cup water

1. Melt the coconut oil in the instant pot on Sauté mode. 2. Then add pulled pork, red pepper, cilantro, water, and chopped tomato. 3. Cook the ingredients for 5 minutes. 4. Then stir it well with the help of the spatula and crack the eggs over it. 5. Close the lid. 6. Cook the meal on Manual mode (High Pressure) for 7 minutes. Then make a quick pressure release.

Per Serving:

calories: 275 | fat: 18g | protein: 22g | carbs: 6g | net carbs: 5g | fiber: 1g

Coddled Eggs and Smoked Salmon Toasts

Prep time: 5 minutes | Cook time: 10 minutes | Serves 4

2 teaspoons unsalted butter
4 large eggs
4 slices gluten-free or whole-grain rye bread
½ cup plain 2 percent Greek yogurt
4 ounces cold-smoked salmon, or 1 medium avocado, pitted, peeled, and sliced
2 radishes, thinly sliced
1 Persian cucumber, thinly sliced
1 tablespoon chopped fresh chives
¼ teaspoon freshly ground black pepper

1. Pour 1 cup water into the Instant Pot and place a long-handled silicone steam rack into the pot. (If you don't have the long-handled rack, use the wire metal steam rack and a homemade sling) 2. Coat each of four 4-ounce ramekins with ½ teaspoon butter. Crack an egg into each ramekin. Place the ramekins on the steam rack in the pot. 3. Secure the lid and set the Pressure Release to Sealing. Select the Steam setting and set the cooking time for 3 minutes at low pressure. (The pot will take about 5 minutes to come up to pressure before the cooking program begins.) 4. While eggs are cooking, toast the bread in a toaster until golden brown. Spread the yogurt onto the toasted slices, put the toasts onto plates, and then top each toast with the smoked salmon, radishes, and cucumber. 5. When the cooking program ends, let the pressure release naturally for 5 minutes, then move the Pressure Release to Venting to release any remaining steam. Open the pot and, wearing heat-resistant mitts, grasp the handles of the steam rack and lift it out of the pot. 6. Run a knife around the inside edge of each ramekin to loosen the egg and unmold one egg onto each toast. Sprinkle the chives and pepper on top and serve right away. 7. Note 8. The yolks of these eggs are fully cooked through. If you prefer the yolks slightly less solid, perform a quick pressure release rather than letting the pressure release naturally for 5 minutes.

Per Serving:

calories: 275 | fat: 12g | protein: 21g | carbs: 21g | sugars: 4g | fiber: 5g | sodium: 431mg

Bacon Cheddar Bites

Prep time: 15 minutes | Cook time: 3 minutes | Serves 2

2 tablespoons coconut flour
½ cup shredded Cheddar cheese
2 teaspoons coconut cream
2 bacon slices, cooked
½ teaspoon dried parsley
1 cup water, for cooking

1. In the mixing bowl, mix up coconut flour, Cheddar cheese, coconut cream, and dried parsley. 2. Then chop the cooked bacon and add it in the mixture. 3. Stir it well. 4. Pour water and insert the trivet in the instant pot. 5. Line the trivet with baking paper. 6. After this, make the small balls (bites) from the cheese mixture and put them on the prepared trivet. 7. Cook the meal for 3 minutes on Manual mode (High Pressure). 8. Then make a quick pressure release and cool the cooked meal well.

Per Serving:

calories: 260 | fat: 19g | protein: 15g | carbs: 6g | net carbs: 3g | fiber: 3g

Herbed Buttery Breakfast Steak

Prep time: 5 minutes | Cook time: 1 minute | Serves 2

½ cup water
1 pound (454 g) boneless beef sirloin steak
½ teaspoon salt
½ teaspoon black pepper
1 clove garlic, minced
2 tablespoons butter, softened
¼ teaspoon dried rosemary
¼ teaspoon dried parsley
Pinch of dried thyme

1. Pour the water into the Instant Pot and put the trivet in the pot. 2. Rub the steak all over with salt and black pepper. Place the steak on the trivet. 3. In a small bowl, stir together the remaining ingredients. Spread half of the butter mixture over the steak. 4. Set the lid in place. Select the Manual mode and set the cooking time for 1 minute on Low Pressure. When the timer goes off, perform a quick pressure release. Carefully open the lid. 5. Remove the steak from the pot. Top with the remaining half of the butter mixture. Serve hot.

Per Serving:

calories: 426 | fat: 25.1g | protein: 46.8g | carbs: 0.6g | net carbs: 0.4g | fiber: 0.2g

Kale Omelet

Prep time: 5 minutes | Cook time: 10 minutes | Serves 2

2 eggs
1 cup chopped kale
1 teaspoon heavy cream
⅔ teaspoon white pepper
½ teaspoon butter

1. Grease the instant pot pan with butter. 2. Beat the eggs in the separated bowl and whisk them well. 3. After this, add heavy cream and white pepper. Stir it gently. 4. Place the chopped kale in the greased pan and add the whisked eggs. 5. Pour 1 cup of water in the instant pot. 6. Place the trivet in the instant pot and transfer the egg mixture pan on the trivet. 7. Close the instant pot and set the Manual (High Pressure) program and cook the frittata for 5 minutes. Do a natural pressure release for 5 minutes.

Per Serving:

calories: 98 | fat: 6g | protein: 7g | carbs: 5g | net carbs: 4g | fiber: 1g

Mini Chocolate Chip Muffins

Prep time: 5 minutes | Cook time: 20 minutes | Serves 7

1 cup blanched almond flour
2 eggs
¾ cup sugar-free chocolate chips
1 tablespoon vanilla extract
½ cup Swerve, or more to taste
2 tablespoons salted grass-fed butter, softened
½ teaspoon salt
¼ teaspoon baking soda

1. Pour 1 cup of filtered water into the inner pot of the Instant Pot, then insert the trivet. Using an electric mixer, combine flour, eggs, chocolate chips, vanilla, Swerve, butter, salt, and baking soda. Mix thoroughly. Transfer this mixture into a well-greased Instant Pot-friendly muffin (or egg bites) mold. 2. Using a sling if desired, place the pan onto the trivet and cover loosely with aluminum foil. Close the lid, set the pressure release to Sealing, and select Manual. Set the Instant Pot to 20 minutes on High Pressure and let cook. 3. Once cooked, let the pressure naturally disperse from the Instant Pot for about 10 minutes, then carefully switch the pressure release to Venting. 4. Open the Instant Pot and remove the pan. Let cool, serve, and enjoy!

Per Serving:

calories: 204 | fat: 17g | protein: 3g | carbs: 10g | net carbs: 9g | fiber: 1g

Egg Bites with Sausage and Peppers

Prep time: 5 minutes | Cook time: 15 minutes | Serves 7

4 large eggs
¼ cup vegan cream cheese (such as Tofutti brand) or cream cheese
¼ teaspoon fine sea salt
¼ teaspoon freshly ground black pepper
3 ounces lean turkey sausage, cooked and crumbled, or 1 vegetarian sausage (such as Beyond Meat brand), cooked and diced
½ red bell pepper, seeded and chopped
2 green onions, white and green parts, minced, plus more for garnish (optional)
¼ cup vegan cheese shreds or shredded sharp Cheddar cheese

1. In a blender, combine the eggs, cream cheese, salt, and pepper. Blend on medium speed for about 20 seconds, just until combined. Add the sausage, bell pepper, and green onions and pulse for 1 second once or twice. You want to mix in the solid ingredients without grinding them up very much. 2. Pour 1 cup water into the Instant Pot. Generously grease a 7-cup egg-bite mold or seven 2-ounce silicone baking cups with butter or coconut oil, making sure to coat each cup well. Place the prepared mold or cups on a long-handled silicone steam rack. (If you don't have the long-handled rack, use the wire metal steam rack and a homemade sling) 3. Pour ¼ cup of the egg mixture into each prepared mold or cup. Holding the handles of the steam rack, carefully lower the egg bites into the pot. 4. Secure the lid and set the Pressure Release to Sealing. Select the Steam setting and set the cooking time for 8 minutes at low pressure. (The pot will take about 5 minutes to come up to pressure before the cooking program begins.) 5. When the cooking program ends, let the pressure release naturally for 5 minutes, then move the Pressure Release to Venting to release any remaining steam. Open the pot. The egg muffins will have puffed up quite a bit during cooking, but they will deflate and settle as they cool. Wearing heat-resistant mitts, grasp the handles of the steam rack and carefully lift the egg bites out of the pot. Sprinkle the egg bites with the cheese, then let them cool for about 5 minutes, until the cheese has fully melted and you are able to handle the mold or cups comfortably. 6. Pull the sides of the egg mold or cups away from the egg bites, running a butter knife around the edge of each bite to loosen if necessary. Transfer the egg bites to plates, garnish with more green onions (if desired), and serve warm. To store, let cool to room temperature, transfer to an airtight container, and refrigerate for up to 3 days; reheat gently in the microwave for about 1 minute before serving.

Per Serving:

calories: 112 | fat: 8g | protein: 8g | carbs: 3g | sugars: 0g | fiber: 0g | sodium: 297mg

Breakfast Cereal

Prep time: 5 minutes | Cook time: 5 minutes | Serves 4

2 tablespoons coconut oil
1 cup full-fat coconut milk
½ cup chopped cashews
½ cup heavy whipping cream
½ cup chopped pecans
⅓ cup Swerve
¼ cup unsweetened coconut flakes
2 tablespoons flax seeds
2 tablespoons chopped hazelnuts
2 tablespoons chopped macadamia nuts
½ teaspoon ground cinnamon
½ teaspoon ground nutmeg
½ teaspoon ground turmeric

1. Set the Instant Pot to Sauté and melt the coconut oil. Pour in the coconut milk. 2. Add the cashews, whipping cream, pecans, Swerve, coconut flakes, flax seeds, hazelnuts, macadamia nuts, cinnamon, nutmeg, and turmeric to the Instant Pot. Stir thoroughly. 3. Close the lid, set the pressure release to Sealing, and hit Cancel to stop the current program. Select Manual, set the Instant Pot to 5 minutes on High Pressure, and let cook. 4. Once cooked, let the pressure naturally disperse from the Instant Pot for about 10 minutes, then carefully switch the pressure release to Venting. 5. Open the Instant Pot, serve, and enjoy!

Per Serving:

calories: 455 | fat: 45g | protein: 6g | carbs: 13g | net carbs: 8g | fiber: 5g

Bacon and Mushroom Quiche Lorraine

Prep time: 10 minutes | Cook time: 37 minutes | Serves 4

4 strips bacon, chopped
2 cups sliced button mushrooms
½ cup diced onions
8 large eggs
1½ cups shredded Swiss cheese
1 cup unsweetened almond milk
¼ cup sliced green onions
½ teaspoon sea salt
¼ teaspoon ground black pepper
2 tablespoons coconut flour

1. Press the Sauté button on the Instant Pot and add the bacon. Sauté for 4 minutes, or until crisp. Transfer the bacon to a plate lined with paper towel to drain, leaving the drippings in the pot. 2. Add the mushrooms and diced onions to the pot and sauté for 3 minutes, or until the onions are tender. Remove the mixture from the pot to a large bowl. Wipe the Instant Pot clean. 3. Set a trivet in the Instant Pot and pour in 1 cup water. 4. In a medium bowl, stir together the eggs, cheese, almond milk, green onions, salt and pepper. Pour the egg mixture into the bowl with the mushrooms and onions. Stir to combine. Fold in the coconut flour. Pour the mixture into a greased round casserole dish. Spread the cooked bacon on top. 5. Place the casserole dish onto the trivet in the Instant Pot. 6. Lock the lid, select the Manual mode and set the cooking time for 30 minutes on High Pressure. When the timer goes off, do a natural pressure release for 15 minutes, then release any remaining pressure. Open the lid. 7. Remove the casserole dish from the Instant Pot. 8. Let cool for 15 to 30 minutes before cutting into 4 pieces. Serve immediately.

Per Serving:
calories: 433 | fat: 29.1g | protein: 32.0g | carbs: 6.9g | net carbs: 4.8g | fiber: 2.1g

Grain-Free Apple Cinnamon Cake

Prep time: 10 minutes | Cook time: 50 minutes | Serves 8

2 cups almond flour
½ cup Lakanto Monkfruit Sweetener Golden
1½ teaspoons ground cinnamon
1 teaspoon baking powder
½ teaspoon fine sea salt
½ cup plain 2 percent Greek yogurt
2 large eggs
½ teaspoon pure vanilla extract
1 small apple, chopped into small pieces

1. Pour 1 cup water into the Instant Pot. Line the base of a 7 by 3-inch round cake pan with parchment paper. Butter the sides of the pan and the parchment or coat with nonstick cooking spray. 2. In a medium bowl, whisk together the almond flour, sweetener, cinnamon, baking powder, and salt. In a smaller bowl, whisk together the yogurt, eggs, and vanilla until no streaks of yolk remain. Add the wet mixture to the dry mixture and stir just until the dry ingredients are evenly moistened, then fold in the apple. The batter will be very thick. 3. Transfer the batter to the prepared pan and, using a rubber spatula, spread it in an even layer. Cover the pan tightly with aluminum foil. Place the pan on a long-handled silicone steam rack, then, holding the handles of the steam rack, lower it into the Instant Pot. (If you don't have the long-handled rack, use the wire metal steam rack and a homemade sling) 4. Secure the lid and set the Pressure Release to Sealing. Select the Cake, Pressure Cook, or Manual setting and set the cooking time for 40 minutes at high pressure. (The pot will take about 10 minutes to come up to pressure before the cooking program begins.) 5. When the cooking program ends, let the pressure release naturally for 10 minutes, then move the Pressure Release to Venting to release any remaining steam. Open the pot and, wearing heat-resistant mitts, grasp the handles of the steam rack and lift it out of the pot. Uncover the pan, taking care not to get burned by the steam or to drip condensation onto the cake. Let the cake cool in the pan on a cooling rack for about 5 minutes. 6. Run a butter knife around the edge of the pan to loosen the cake from the pan sides. Invert the cake onto the rack, lift off the pan, and peel off the parchment. Let cool for 15 minutes, then invert the cake onto a serving plate. Cut into eight wedges and serve.

Per Serving:
calories: 219 | fat: 16g | protein: 9g | carbs: 20g | sugars: 8g | fiber: 16g | sodium: 154mg

Lettuce Wrapped Chicken Sandwich

Prep time: 10 minutes | Cook time: 15 minutes | Serves 4

1 tablespoon butter
3 ounces (85 g) scallions, chopped
2 cups ground chicken
½ teaspoon ground nutmeg
1 tablespoon coconut flour
1 teaspoon salt
1 cup lettuce

1. Press the Sauté button on the Instant Pot and melt the butter. Add the chopped scallions, ground chicken and ground nutmeg to the pot and sauté for 4 minutes. Add the coconut flour and salt and continue to sauté for 10 minutes. 2. Fill the lettuce with the ground chicken and transfer it on the plate. Serve immediately.

Per Serving:
calories: 176 | fat: 8.5g | protein: 21.2g | carbs: 3.1g | net carbs: 1.5g | fiber: 1.6g

Cinnamon French Toast

Prep time: 10 minutes | Cook time: 20 minutes | Serves 8

3 eggs
2 cups low-fat milk
2 tablespoons maple syrup
15 drops liquid stevia
2 teaspoons vanilla extract
2 teaspoons cinnamon
Pinch salt
16-ounces whole wheat bread, cubed and left out overnight to go stale
1½ cups water

1. In a medium bowl, whisk together the eggs, milk, maple syrup, Stevia, vanilla, cinnamon, and salt. Stir in the cubes of whole wheat bread. 2. You will need a 7-inch round baking pan for this. Spray the inside with nonstick spray, then pour the bread mixture into the pan. 3. Place the trivet in the bottom of the inner pot, then pour in the water. 4. Make foil sling and insert it onto the trivet. Carefully place the 7-inch pan on top of the foil sling/trivet. 5. Secure the lid to the locked position, then make sure the vent is turned to sealing. 6. Press the Manual button and use the "+/-" button to set the Instant Pot for 20 minutes. 7. When cook time is up, let the Instant Pot release naturally for 5 minutes, then quick release the rest

Per Serving:
calories: 75 | fat: 3g | protein: 4g | carbs: 7g | sugars: 6g | fiber: 0g | sodium: 74mg

Blueberry Almond Cereal

Prep time: 5 minutes | Cook time: 2 minutes | Serves 4

⅓ cup crushed roasted almonds
¼ cup almond flour
¼ cup unsalted butter, softened
¼ cup vanilla-flavored egg white protein powder
2 tablespoons Swerve
1 teaspoon blueberry extract
1 teaspoon ground cinnamon

1. Add all the ingredients to the Instant Pot and stir to combine. 2. Lock the lid, select the Manual mode and set the cooking time for 2 minutes on High Pressure. When the timer goes off, do a natural pressure release for 10 minutes, then release any remaining pressure. Open the lid. 3. Stir well and pour the mixture onto a sheet lined with parchment paper to cool. It will be crispy when completely cool. 4. Serve the cereal in bowls.

Per Serving:

calories: 282 | fat: 24.0g | protein: 10.1g | carbs: 6.9g | net carbs: 2.8g | fiber: 4.1g

Poached Eggs

Prep time: 5 minutes | Cook time: 5 minutes | Serves 4

Nonstick cooking spray
4 large eggs

1. Lightly spray 4 cups of a 7-count silicone egg bite mold with nonstick cooking spray. Crack each egg into a sprayed cup. 2. Pour 1 cup of water into the electric pressure cooker. Place the egg bite mold on the wire rack and carefully lower it into the pot. 3. Close and lock the lid of the pressure cooker. Set the valve to sealing. 4. Cook on high pressure for 5 minutes. 5. When the cooking is complete, hit Cancel and quick release the pressure. 6. Once the pin drops, unlock and remove the lid. 7. Run a small rubber spatula or spoon around each egg and carefully remove it from the mold. The white should be cooked, but the yolk should be runny. 8. Serve immediately.

Per Serving:

calories: 78 | fat: 5g | protein: 6g | carbs: 1g | sugars: 0g | fiber: 0g | sodium: 62mg

Eggs Benedict

Prep time: 5 minutes | Cook time: 1 minute | Serves 3

1 teaspoon butter
3 eggs
¼ teaspoon salt
½ teaspoon ground black pepper
1 cup water
3 turkey bacon slices, fried

1. Grease the eggs molds with the butter and crack the eggs inside. Sprinkle with salt and ground black pepper. 2. Pour the water and insert the trivet in the Instant Pot. Put the eggs molds on the trivet. 3. Set the lid in place. Select the Manual mode and set the cooking time for 1 minute on High Pressure. When the timer goes off, do a quick pressure release. Carefully open the lid. 4. Transfer the eggs onto the plate. Top the eggs with the fried bacon slices.

Per Serving:

calories: 94 | fat: 6.1g | protein: 8.7g | carbs: 0.5g | net carbs: 0.4g | fiber: 0.1g

Soft-Scrambled Eggs

Prep time: 5 minutes | Cook time: 7 minutes | Serves 4

6 eggs
2 tablespoons heavy cream
1 teaspoon salt
¼ teaspoon pepper
2 tablespoons butter
2 ounces (57 g) cream cheese, softened

1. In large bowl, whisk eggs, heavy cream, salt, and pepper. Press the Sauté button and then press the Adjust button to set heat to Less. 2. Gently push eggs around pot with rubber spatula. When they begin to firm up, add butter and softened cream cheese. Continue stirring slowly in a figure-8 pattern until eggs are fully cooked, approximately 7 minutes total.

Per Serving:

calories: 232 | fat: 18g | protein: 10g | carbs: 2g | net carbs: 2g | fiber: 0g

Cheesy Vegetable Frittata

Prep time: 10 minutes | Cook time: 10 minutes | Serves 4

4 eggs, beaten
2 ounces (57 g) Pecorino cheese, grated
3 ounces (85 g) okra, chopped
2 ounces (57 g) radish, chopped
1 tablespoon cream cheese
1 teaspoon sesame oil

1. Heat up sesame oil in the instant pot on Sauté mode. 2. Add chopped okra and radish and sauté the vegetables for 4 minutes. 3. Then stir them well and add cream cheese and beaten eggs. 4. Stir the mixture well and top with cheese. 5. Close the lid and cook the frittata on Sauté mode for 6 minutes more.

Per Serving:

calories: 163 | fat: 12g | protein: 12g | carbs: 3g | net carbs: 2g | fiber: 1g

Pecan and Walnut Granola

Prep time: 10 minutes | Cook time: 2 minutes | Serves 12

2 cups chopped raw pecans
1¾ cups vanilla-flavored egg white protein powder
1¼ cups unsalted butter, softened
1 cup sunflower seeds
½ cup chopped raw walnuts
½ cup slivered almonds
½ cup sesame seeds
½ cup Swerve
1 teaspoon ground cinnamon
½ teaspoon sea salt

1. Add all the ingredients to the Instant Pot and stir to combine. 2. Lock the lid, select the Manual mode and set the cooking time for 2 minutes on High Pressure. When the timer goes off, do a natural pressure release for 10 minutes, then release any remaining pressure. Open the lid. 3. Stir well and pour the granola onto a sheet of parchment paper to cool. It will become crispy when completely cool. Serve the granola in bowls.

Per Serving:

calories: 491 | fat: 43.7g | protein: 17.1g | carbs: 8.9g | net carbs: 3.8g | fiber: 5.1g

Cheddar Chicken Casserole

Prep time: 10 minutes | Cook time: 20 minutes | Serves 6

1 cup ground chicken
1 teaspoon olive oil
1 teaspoon chili flakes
1 teaspoon salt
1 cup shredded Cheddar cheese
½ cup coconut cream

1. Press the Sauté button on the Instant Pot and heat the oil. Add the ground chicken, chili flakes and salt to the pot and sauté for 10 minutes. Stir in the remaining ingredients. 2. Set the lid in place. Select the Manual mode and set the cooking time for 10 minutes on High Pressure. When the timer goes off, do a quick pressure release. Carefully open the lid. 3. Let the dish cool for 10 minutes before serving.

Per Serving:
calories: 172 | fat: 13.4g | protein: 12.0g | carbs: 1.3g | net carbs: 0.8g | fiber: 0.5g

Breakfast Millet with Nuts and Strawberries

Prep time: 0 minutes | Cook time: 30 minutes | Serves 8

2 tablespoons coconut oil or unsalted butter
1½ cups millet
2⅔ cups water
½ teaspoon fine sea salt
1 cup unsweetened almond milk or other nondairy milk
1 cup chopped toasted pecans, almonds, or peanuts
4 cups sliced strawberries

1. Select the Sauté setting on the Instant Pot and melt the oil. Add the millet and cook for 4 minutes, until aromatic. Stir in the water and salt, making sure all of the grains are submerged in the liquid. 2. Secure the lid and set the Pressure Release to Sealing. Press the Cancel button to reset the cooking program, then select the Porridge, Pressure Cook, or Manual setting and set the cooking time for 12 minutes at high pressure. (The pot will take about 10 minutes to come up to pressure before the cooking program begins.) 3. When the cooking program ends, let the pressure release naturally for 10 minutes, then move the Pressure Release to Venting to release any remaining steam. Open the pot and use a fork to fluff and stir the millet. 4. Spoon the millet into bowls and top each serving with 2 tablespoons of the almond milk, then sprinkle with the nuts and top with the strawberries. Serve warm.

Per Serving:
calories: 270 | fat: 13g | protein: 6g | carbs: 35g | sugars: 4g | fiber: 6g | sodium: 151mg

Chicken and Egg Sandwich

Prep time: 5 minutes | Cook time: 15 minutes | Serves 1

1 (6-ounce / 170-g) boneless, skinless chicken breast
¼ teaspoon salt
⅛ teaspoon pepper
¼ teaspoon garlic powder
2 tablespoons coconut oil, divided
1 egg
1 cup water
¼ avocado
2 tablespoons mayonnaise
¼ cup shredded white Cheddar
Salt and pepper, to taste

1. Cut chicken breast in half lengthwise. Use meat tenderizer to pound chicken breast until thin. Sprinkle with salt, pepper, and garlic powder, and set aside. 2. Add 1 tablespoon coconut oil to Instant Pot. Press Sauté button, then press Adjust button and set temperature to Less. Once oil is hot, fry the egg, remove, and set aside. Press Cancel button. Press Sauté button, then press Adjust button to set temperature to Normal. Add second tablespoon of coconut oil to Instant Pot and sear chicken on each side for 3 to 4 minutes until golden. 3. Press the Manual button and set time for 8 minutes. While chicken cooks, use fork to mash avocado and then mix in mayo. When timer beeps, quick-release the pressure. Put chicken on plate and pat dry with paper towel. Use chicken pieces to form a sandwich with egg, cheese, and avocado mayo. Season lightly with salt and pepper.

Per Serving:
calories: 760 | fat: 53g | protein: 52g | carbs: 5g | net carbs: 3g | fiber: 2g

Greek Frittata with Peppers, Kale, and Feta

Prep time: 5 minutes | Cook time: 45 minutes | Serves 6

8 large eggs
½ cup plain 2 percent Greek yogurt
Fine sea salt
Freshly ground black pepper
2 cups firmly packed finely shredded kale or baby kale leaves
One 12-ounce jar roasted red peppers, drained and cut into ¼ by 2-inch strips
2 green onions, white and green parts, thinly sliced
1 tablespoon chopped fresh dill
⅓ cup crumbled feta cheese
6 cups loosely packed mixed baby greens
¾ cup cherry or grape tomatoes, halved
2 tablespoons extra-virgin olive oil

1. Pour 1½ cups water into the Instant Pot. Lightly butter a 7-cup round heatproof glass dish or coat with nonstick cooking spray. 2. In a bowl, whisk together the eggs, yogurt, ¼ teaspoon salt, and ¼ teaspoon pepper until well blended, then stir in the kale, roasted peppers, green onions, dill, and feta cheese. 3. Pour the egg mixture into the prepared dish and cover tightly with aluminum foil. Place the dish on a long-handled silicone steam rack, then, holding the handles of the steam rack, lower it into the Instant Pot. (If you don't have the long-handled rack, use the wire metal steam rack and a homemade sling) 4. Secure the lid and set the Pressure Release to Sealing. Select the Pressure Cook or Manual setting and set the cooking time for 30 minutes at high pressure. (The pot will take about 15 minutes to come up to pressure before the cooking program begins.) 5. When the cooking program ends, let the pressure release naturally for 10 minutes, then move the Pressure Release to Venting to release any remaining steam. Open the pot and let the frittata sit for a minute or two, until it deflates and settles into its dish. Then, wearing heat-resistant mitts, grasp the handles of the steam rack and lift it out of the pot. Uncover the dish, taking care not to get burned by the steam or to drip condensation onto the frittata. Let the frittata sit for 10 minutes, giving it time to reabsorb any liquid and set up. 6. In a medium bowl, toss together the mixed greens, tomatoes, and olive oil. Taste and adjust the seasoning with salt and pepper, if needed. 7. Cut the frittata into six wedges and serve warm, with the salad alongside.

Per Serving:
calories: 227 | fat: 13g | protein: 18g | carbs: 8g | sugars: 2g | fiber: 1g | sodium: 153mg

Bacon and Spinach Eggs

Prep time: 5 minutes | Cook time: 9 minutes | Serves 4

2 tablespoons unsalted butter, divided
½ cup diced bacon
⅓ cup finely diced shallots
⅓ cup chopped spinach, leaves only
Pinch of sea salt
Pinch of black pepper
½ cup water
¼ cup heavy whipping cream
8 large eggs
1 tablespoon chopped fresh chives, for garnish

1. Set the Instant Pot on the Sauté mode and melt 1 tablespoon of the butter. Add the bacon to the pot and sauté for about 4 minutes, or until crispy. Using a slotted spoon, transfer the bacon bits to a bowl and set aside. 2. Add the remaining 1 tablespoon of the butter and shallots to the pot and sauté for about 2 minutes, or until tender. Add the spinach leaves and sauté for 1 minute, or until wilted. Season with sea salt and black pepper and stir. Transfer the spinach to a separate bowl and set aside. 3. Drain the oil from the pot into a bowl. Pour in the water and put the trivet inside. 4. With a paper towel, coat four ramekins with the bacon grease. In each ramekin, place 1 tablespoon of the heavy whipping cream, reserved bacon bits and sautéed spinach. Crack two eggs without breaking the yolks in each ramekin. Cover the ramekins with aluminum foil. Place two ramekins on the trivet and stack the other two on top. 5. Lock the lid. Select the Manual mode and set the cooking time for 2 minutes at Low Pressure. When the timer goes off, use a natural pressure release for 5 minutes, then release any remaining pressure. Carefully open the lid. 6. Carefully take out the ramekins and serve garnished with the chives.

Per Serving:
calories: 320 | fat: 25.8g | protein: 17.2g | carbs: 4.0g | net carbs: 3.9g | fiber: 0.1g

Classic Coffee Cake

Prep time: 5 minutes | Cook time: 40 minutes | Serves 5 to 6

Base:
2 eggs
2 tablespoons salted grass-fed butter, softened
1 cup blanched almond flour
1 cup chopped pecans
¼ cup sour cream, at room temperature
¼ cup full-fat cream cheese, softened
½ teaspoon salt
½ teaspoon ground cinnamon
½ teaspoon ground nutmeg
¼ teaspoon baking soda
Topping:
1 cup sugar-free chocolate chips
1 cup chopped pecans
½ cup Swerve, or more to taste
½ cup heavy whipping cream

1. Pour 1 cup of filtered water into the inner pot of the Instant Pot, then insert the trivet. Using an electric mixer, combine the eggs, butter, flour, pecans, sour cream, cream cheese, salt, cinnamon, nutmeg, and baking soda. Mix thoroughly. Transfer this mixture into a well-greased, Instant Pot-friendly pan (or dish). 2. Using a sling if desired, place the pan onto the trivet, and cover loosely with aluminum foil. Close the lid, set the pressure release to Sealing, and select Manual. Set the Instant Pot to 40 minutes on High Pressure and let cook. 3. While cooking, in a large bowl, mix the chocolate chips, pecans, Swerve, and whipping cream thoroughly. Set aside. 4. Once cooked, let the pressure naturally disperse from the Instant Pot for about 10 minutes, then carefully switch the pressure release to Venting. 5. Open the Instant Pot and remove the pan. Evenly sprinkle the topping mixture over the cake. Let cool, serve, and enjoy!

Per Serving:
calories: 267 | fat: 23g | protein: 7g | carbs: 9g | net carbs: 7g | fiber: 2g

Sausage and Cauliflower Breakfast Casserole

Prep time: 5 minutes | Cook time: 10 minutes | Serves 6

1 cup water
½ head cauliflower, chopped into bite-sized pieces
4 slices bacon
1 pound (454 g) breakfast sausage
4 tablespoons melted butter
10 eggs
⅓ cup heavy cream
2 teaspoons salt
1 teaspoon pepper
2 tablespoons hot sauce
2 stalks green onion
1 cup shredded sharp Cheddar cheese

1. Pour water into Instant Pot and place steamer basket in bottom. Add cauliflower. Click lid closed. 2. Press the Steam button and adjust time for 1 minute. When timer beeps, quick-release the pressure and place cauliflower to the side in medium bowl. 3. Drain water from Instant Pot, clean, and replace. Press the Sauté button. Press the Adjust button to set heat to Less. Cook bacon until crispy. Once fully cooked, set aside on paper towels. Add breakfast sausage to pot and brown (still using the Sauté function). 4. While sausage is cooking, whisk butter, eggs, heavy cream, salt, pepper, and hot sauce. 5. When sausage is fully cooked, pour egg mixture into Instant Pot. Gently stir using silicone spatula until eggs are completely cooked and fluffy. Press the Cancel button. Slice green onions. Sprinkle green onions, bacon, and cheese over mixture and let melt. Serve warm.

Per Serving:
calories: 620 | fat: 50g | protein: 30g | carbs: 5g | net carbs: 4g | fiber: 1g

Cranberry Almond Grits

Prep time: 10 minutes | Cook time: 10 minutes | Serves 5

¾ cup stone-ground grits or polenta (not instant)
½ cup unsweetened dried cranberries
Pinch kosher salt
1 tablespoon unsalted butter or ghee (optional)
1 tablespoon half-and-half
¼ cup sliced almonds, toasted

1. In the electric pressure cooker, stir together the grits, cranberries, salt, and 3 cups of water. 2. Close and lock the lid. Set the valve to sealing. 3. Cook on high pressure for 10 minutes. 4. When the cooking is complete, hit Cancel and quick release the pressure. 5. Once the pin drops, unlock and remove the lid. 6. Add the butter (if using) and half-and-half. Stir until the mixture is creamy, adding more half-and-half if necessary. 7. Spoon into serving bowls and sprinkle with almonds.

Per Serving:
calories: 218 | fat: 10g | protein: 5g | carbs: 32g | sugars: 7g | fiber: 4g | sodium: 28mg

Chapter 4 Beef, Pork, and Lamb

Chipotle Pork Chops with Tomatoes

Prep time: 7 minutes | Cook time: 15 minutes | Serves 4

2 tablespoons coconut oil
3 chipotle chilies
2 tablespoons adobo sauce
2 teaspoons cumin
1 teaspoon dried thyme
1 teaspoon salt
4 (5-ounce / 142-g) boneless pork chops
½ medium onion, chopped
2 bay leaves
1 cup chicken broth
½ (7-ounce / 198-g) can fire-roasted diced tomatoes
⅓ cup chopped cilantro

1. Press the Sauté button and add coconut oil to Instant Pot. While it heats, add chilies, adobo sauce, cumin, thyme, and salt to food processor. Pulse to make paste. Rub paste into pork chops. Place in Instant Pot and sear each side 5 minutes or until browned. 2. Press the Cancel button and add onion, bay leaves, broth, tomatoes, and cilantro to Instant Pot. Click lid closed. Press the Manual button and adjust time for 15 minutes. When timer beeps, allow a 10-minute natural release, then quick-release the remaining pressure. Serve warm with additional cilantro as garnish if desired.

Per Serving:
calories: 375 | fat: 24g | protein: 31g | carbs: 5g | net carbs: 3g | fiber: 2g

Beef, Bacon and Cauliflower Rice Casserole

Prep time: 15 minutes | Cook time: 26 minutes | Serves 5

2 cups fresh cauliflower florets
1 pound (454 g) ground beef
5 slices uncooked bacon, chopped
8 ounces (227 g) unsweetened tomato purée
1 cup shredded Cheddar cheese, divided
1 teaspoon garlic powder
½ teaspoon paprika
½ teaspoon sea salt
¼ teaspoon ground black pepper
¼ teaspoon celery seed
1 cup water
1 medium Roma tomato, sliced

1. Spray a round soufflé dish with coconut oil cooking spray. Set aside. 2. Add the cauliflower florets to a food processor and pulse until a riced. Set aside. 3. Select Sauté mode. Once the pot is hot, crumble the ground beef into the pot and add the bacon. Sauté for 6 minutes or until the ground beef is browned and the bacon is cooked through. 4. Transfer the beef, bacon, and rendered fat to a large bowl. 5. Add the cauliflower rice, tomato purée, ½ cup Cheddar cheese, garlic powder, paprika, sea salt, black pepper, and celery seed to the bowl with the beef and bacon. Mix well to combine. 6. Add the mixture to the prepared dish and use a spoon to press and smooth the mixture into an even layer. 7. Place the trivet in the Instant Pot and add the water to the bottom of the pot. Place the dish on top of the trivet. 8. Lock the lid. Select Manual mode and set cooking time for 20 minutes on High Pressure. 9. When cooking is complete, quick release the pressure. 10. Open the lid. Arrange the tomato slices in a single layer on top of the casserole and sprinkle the remaining cheese over top. 11. Secure the lid and let the residual heat melt the cheese for 5 minutes. 12. Open the lid, remove the dish from the pot. 13. Transfer the casserole to a serving plate and slice into 5 equal-sized wedges. Serve warm.

Per Serving:
calories: 350 | fat: 22.7g | protein: 30.0g | carbs: 8.0g | net carbs: 6.0g | fiber: 2.0g

Beef Chili with Kale

Prep time: 10 minutes | Cook time: 10 minutes | Serves 6

2 tablespoons olive oil
1½ pounds (680 g) ground chuck
1 green bell pepper, chopped
1 red bell pepper, chopped
2 red chilies, minced
1 red onion
2 garlic cloves, smashed
1 teaspoon cumin
1 teaspoon Mexican oregano
1 teaspoon cayenne pepper
1 teaspoon smoked paprika
Salt and freshly ground black pepper, to taste
1½ cups puréed tomatoes
4 cups fresh kale

1. Press the Sauté button to heat up the Instant Pot. Then, heat the oil; once hot, cook the ground chuck for 2 minutes, crumbling it with a fork or a wide spatula. 2. Add the pepper, onions, and garlic; cook an additional 2 minutes or until fragrant. Stir in the remaining ingredients, minus kale leaves. 3. Choose the Manual setting and cook for 6 minutes at High Pressure. Once cooking is complete, use a natural pressure release; carefully remove the lid. 4. Add kale, cover with the lid and allow the kale leaves to wilt completely. Bon appétit!

Per Serving:
calories: 238 | fat: 13g | protein: 24g | carbs: 6g | net carbs: 4g | fiber: 2g

Greek Lamb Leg

Prep time: 10 minutes | Cook time: 50 minutes | Serves 4

1 pound (454 g) lamb leg
½ teaspoon dried thyme
1 teaspoon paprika powder
¼ teaspoon cumin seeds
1 tablespoon softened butter
2 garlic cloves
¼ cup water

1. Rub the lamb leg with dried thyme, paprika powder, and cumin seeds on a clean work surface. 2. Brush the leg with softened butter and transfer to the Instant Pot. Add garlic cloves and water. 3. Close the lid. Select Manual mode and set cooking time for 50 minutes on High Pressure. 4. When timer beeps, use a quick pressure release. Open the lid. 5. Serve warm.

Per Serving:
calories: 239 | fat: 11.2g | protein: 32.0g | carbs: 0.6g | net carbs: 0.5g | fiber: 0.1g

Ground Beef Cabbage Casserole

Prep time: 5 minutes | Cook time: 4 minutes | Serves 4

1 pound (454 g) 85% lean ground beef
2 cups shredded white cabbage
1 cup salsa
1 teaspoon salt
1 tablespoon chili powder
½ teaspoon cumin
½ cup water
1 cup shredded Cheddar cheese

1. Press the Sauté button and brown ground beef. Once fully cooked, add remaining ingredients except for cheese. 2. Click lid closed. Press the Manual button and adjust timer for 4 minutes. When timer beeps, quick-release the pressure and stir in Cheddar.

Per Serving:
calories: 393 | fat: 23g | protein: 30g | carbs: 5g | net carbs: 3g | fiber: 2g

Rosemary Pork Belly

Prep time: 10 minutes | Cook time: 75 minutes | Serves 4

10 ounces (283 g) pork belly
1 teaspoon dried rosemary
½ teaspoon dried thyme
¼ teaspoon ground cinnamon
1 teaspoon salt
1 cup water

1. Rub the pork belly with dried rosemary, thyme, ground cinnamon, and salt and transfer in the instant pot bowl. 2. Add water, close and seal the lid. 3. Cook the pork belly on Manual mode (High Pressure) for 75 minutes. 4. Remove the cooked pork belly from the instant pot and slice it into servings.

Per Serving:
calories: 329 | fat: 19g | protein: 33g | carbs: 0g | net carbs: 0g | fiber: 0g

Salisbury Steak with Mushroom Sauce

Prep time: 10 minutes | Cook time: 15 minutes | Serves 4

1 pound (454 g) 85% lean ground beef
1 teaspoon steak seasoning
1 egg
2 tablespoons butter
½ medium onion, thinly sliced
½ cup sliced button mushrooms
1 cup beef broth
2 ounces (57 g) cream cheese
¼ cup heavy cream
¼ teaspoon xanthan gum

1. In large bowl mix ground beef, steak seasoning, and egg. Form 4 patties and set aside. 2. Press the Sauté button and add butter, onion, and mushrooms to Instant Pot. Sauté 3 to 5 minutes or until onions are translucent and fragrant. Press the Cancel button. 3. Add broth, beef patties, and cream cheese to Instant Pot. Click lid closed. Press the Manual button and adjust time for 15 minutes. 4. When timer beeps, allow a 10-minute natural release. Quick-release the remaining pressure. Carefully remove patties and set aside. Add heavy cream and xanthan gum. Whisk until fully mixed. Press the Sauté button and reduce gravy until desired thickness, about 5 to 10 minutes. Press the Cancel button and add patties back to Instant Pot until ready to serve.

Per Serving:
calories: 420 | fat: 30g | protein: 25g | carbs: 3g | net carbs: 2g | fiber: 1g

Beef and Red Cabbage Stew

Prep time: 10 minutes | Cook time: 20 minutes | Serves 4

2 tablespoons butter, at room temperature
1 onion, chopped
2 garlic cloves, minced
1½ pounds (680 g) beef stew meat, cubed
2½ cups beef stock
8 ounces (227 g) sugar-free tomato sauce
2 cups shredded red cabbage
1 tablespoon coconut aminos
2 bay leaves
1 teaspoon dried parsley flakes
½ teaspoon crushed red pepper flakes
Sea salt and ground black pepper, to taste

1. Press the Sauté button to heat up the Instant Pot. Then, melt the butter. Cook the onion and garlic until softened. 2. Add beef stew meat and cook an additional 3 minutes or until browned. Stir the remaining ingredients into the Instant Pot. 3. Secure the lid. Choose Manual mode and High Pressure; cook for 15 minutes. Once cooking is complete, use a quick pressure release; carefully remove the lid. 4. Discard bay leaves and ladle into individual bowls. Enjoy!

Per Serving:
calories: 320 | fat: 16g | protein: 39g | carbs: 7g | net carbs: 5g | fiber: 2g

Spicy Beef Stew with Butternut Squash

Prep time: 15 minutes | Cook time: 30 minutes | Serves 8

1½ tablespoons smoked paprika
2 teaspoons ground cinnamon
1½ teaspoons kosher salt
1 teaspoon ground ginger
1 teaspoon red pepper flakes
½ teaspoon freshly ground black pepper
2 pounds beef shoulder roast, cut into 1-inch cubes
2 tablespoons avocado oil, divided
1 cup low-sodium beef or vegetable broth
1 medium red onion, cut into wedges
8 garlic cloves, minced
1 (28-ounce) carton or can no-salt-added diced tomatoes
2 pounds butternut squash, peeled and cut into 1-inch pieces
Chopped fresh cilantro or parsley, for serving

1. In a zip-top bag or medium bowl, combine the paprika, cinnamon, salt, ginger, red pepper, and black pepper. Add the beef and toss to coat. 2. Set the electric pressure cooker to the Sauté setting. When the pot is hot, pour in 1 tablespoon of avocado oil. 3. Add half of the beef to the pot and cook, stirring occasionally, for 3 to 5 minutes or until the beef is no longer pink. Transfer it to a plate, then add the remaining 1 tablespoon of avocado oil and brown the remaining beef. Transfer to the plate. Hit Cancel. 4. Stir in the broth and scrape up any brown bits from the bottom of the pot. Return the beef to the pot and add the onion, garlic, tomatoes and their juices, and squash. Stir well. 5. Close and lock lid of pressure cooker. Set the valve to sealing. 6. Cook on high pressure for 30 minutes. 7. When cooking is complete, hit Cancel. Allow the pressure to release naturally for 10 minutes, then quick release any remaining pressure. 8. Unlock and remove lid. 9. Spoon into serving bowls, sprinkle with cilantro or parsley, and serve.

Per Serving:
calorie: 275 | fat: 9g | protein: 28g | carbs: 24g | sugars: 7g | fiber: 6g | sodium: 512mg

Cuban Pork Shoulder

Prep time: 20 minutes | Cook time: 35 minutes | Serves 3

9 ounces (255 g) pork shoulder, boneless, chopped
1 tablespoon avocado oil
1 teaspoon ground cumin
½ teaspoon ground black pepper
¼ cup apple cider vinegar
1 cup water

1. In the mixing bowl, mix up avocado oil, ground cumin, ground black pepper, and apple cider vinegar. 2. Mix up pork shoulder and spice mixture together and transfer on the foil. Wrap the meat mixture. 3. Pour water and insert the steamer rack in the instant pot. 4. Put the wrapped pork shoulder on the rack. Close and seal the lid. 5. Cook the Cuban pork for 35 minutes. 6. Then allow the natural pressure release for 10 minutes.

Per Serving:
calories: 262 | fat: 19g | protein: 20g | carbs: 1g | net carbs: 1g | fiber: 0g

Bone Broth Brisket with Tomatoes

Prep time: 5 minutes | Cook time: 75 minutes | Serves 4 to 5

2 tablespoons coconut oil
½ teaspoon garlic salt
½ teaspoon crushed red pepper
½ teaspoon dried basil
½ teaspoon kosher salt
½ teaspoon freshly ground black pepper
1 (14-ounce / 397-g) can sugar-free or low-sugar diced tomatoes
1 cup grass-fed bone broth
1 pound (454 g) beef brisket, chopped

1. Set the Instant Pot to Sauté and melt the oil. Mix the garlic salt, red pepper, basil, kosher salt, black pepper, and tomatoes in a medium bowl. 2. Pour bone broth into the Instant Pot, then add the brisket, and top with the premixed sauce. Close the lid, set the pressure release to Sealing, and hit Cancel to stop the current program. Select Manual, set the Instant Pot to 75 minutes on High Pressure, and let cook. 3. Once cooked, carefully switch the pressure release to Venting. Open the Instant Pot, and serve. You can pour remaining sauce over brisket, if desired.

Per Serving:
calories: 240 | fat: 11g | protein: 29g | carbs: 5g | net carbs: 3g | fiber: 2g

Blade Pork with Sauerkraut

Prep time: 15 minutes | Cook time: 37 minutes | Serves 6

2 pounds (907 g) blade pork steaks
Sea salt and ground black pepper, to taste
½ teaspoon cayenne pepper
½ teaspoon dried parsley flakes
1 tablespoon butter
1½ cups water
2 cloves garlic, thinly sliced
2 pork sausages, casing removed and sliced
4 cups sauerkraut

1. Season the blade pork steaks with salt, black pepper, cayenne pepper, and dried parsley. 2. Press the Sauté button to heat up the Instant Pot. Melt the butter and sear blade pork steaks for 5 minutes or until browned on all sides. 3. Clean the Instant Pot. Add water and trivet to the bottom of the Instant Pot. 4. Place the blade pork steaks on the trivet. Make small slits over entire pork with a knife. Insert garlic pieces into each slit. 5. Secure the lid. Choose the Meat/Stew mode and set cooking time for 30 minutes on High pressure. 6. Once cooking is complete, use a natural pressure release for 15 minutes, then release any remaining pressure. Carefully remove the lid. 7. Add the sausage and sauerkraut. Press the Sauté button and cook for 2 minutes more or until heated through. 8. Serve immediately

Per Serving:
calories: 471 | fat: 27.3g | protein: 47.7g | carbs: 8.4g | net carbs: 2.0g | fiber: 6.4g

Zesty Swiss Steak

Prep time: 35 minutes | Cook time: 35 minutes | Serves 6

3–4 tablespoons flour
½ teaspoon salt
¼ teaspoon pepper
1½ teaspoons dry mustard
1½–2 pounds round steak, trimmed of fat
1 tablespoon canola oil
1 cup sliced onions
1 pound carrots, sliced
14½-ounce can whole tomatoes
⅓ cup water
1 tablespoon brown sugar
1½ tablespoons Worcestershire sauce

1. Combine flour, salt, pepper, and dry mustard. 2. Cut steak in serving pieces. Dredge in flour mixture. 3. Set the Instant Pot to Sauté and add in the oil. Brown the steak pieces on both sides in the oil. Press Cancel. 4. Add onions and carrots into the Instant Pot. 5. Combine the tomatoes, water, brown sugar, and Worcestershire sauce. Pour into the Instant Pot. 6. Secure the lid and make sure the vent is set to sealing. Press Manual and set the time for 35 minutes. 7. When cook time is up, let the pressure release naturally for 15 minutes, then perform a quick release.

Per Serving:
calories: 236 | fat: 8g | protein: 23g | carbs: 18g | sugars: 9g | fiber: 3g | sodium: 426mg

Pork Meatballs with Thyme

Prep time: 15 minutes | Cook time: 16 minutes | Serves 8

2 cups ground pork
1 teaspoon dried thyme
½ teaspoon chili flakes
½ teaspoon garlic powder
¼ cup water
1 tablespoon coconut oil
¼ teaspoon ground ginger
3 tablespoons almond flour

1. In the mixing bowl, mix up ground pork, dried thyme, chili flakes, garlic powder, ground ginger, and almond flour. 2. Make the meatballs. 3. Melt the coconut oil in the instant pot on Sauté mode. 4. Arrange the meatballs in the instant pot in one layer and cook them for 3 minutes from each side. 5. Then add water and cook the meatballs for 10 minutes.

Per Serving:
calories: 264 | fat: 19g | protein: 20g | carbs: 1g | net carbs: 1g | fiber: 0g

Coconut Pork Muffins

Prep time: 5 minutes | Cook time: 9 minutes | Serves 2

1 egg, beaten
2 tablespoons coconut flour
1 teaspoon parsley
¼ teaspoon salt
1 tablespoon coconut cream
4 ounces (113 g) ground pork, fried
1 cup water

1. Whisk together the egg, coconut flour, parsley, salt, and coconut cream. Add the fried ground pork. Mix the the mixture until homogenous. 2. Pour the mixture into a muffin pan. 3. Pour the water in the Instant Pot and place in the trivet. 4. Lower the muffin pan on the trivet and close the Instant Pot lid. 5. Set the Manual mode and set cooking time for 4 minutes on High Pressure. 6. When timer beeps, perform a natural pressure release for 5 minutes, then release any remaining pressure. Open the lid. 7. Serve warm.

Per Serving:
calories: 160 | fat: 6.7g | protein: 18.8g | carbs: 5.6g | net carbs: 2.4g | fiber: 3.2g

Golden Bacon Sticks

Prep time: 5 minutes | Cook time: 6 minutes | Serves 4

6 ounces (170 g) bacon, sliced
2 tablespoons almond flour
1 tablespoon water
¾ teaspoon chili pepper

1. Sprinkle the sliced bacon with the almond flour and drizzle with water. Add the chili pepper. 2. Put the bacon in the Instant Pot. 3. Cook on Sauté mode for 3 minutes per side. Serve immediately.
Per Serving:
calories: 251 | fat: 19.4g | protein: 16.5g | carbs: 1.5g | net carbs: 1.1g | fiber: 0.4g

Pork Chops Pomodoro

Prep time: 0 minutes | Cook time: 30 minutes | Serves 6

2 pounds boneless pork loin chops, each about 5⅓ ounces and ½ inch thick
¾ teaspoon fine sea salt
½ teaspoon freshly ground black pepper
2 tablespoons extra-virgin olive oil
2 garlic cloves, chopped
½ cup low-sodium chicken broth or vegetable broth
½ teaspoon Italian seasoning
1 tablespoon capers, drained
2 cups cherry tomatoes
2 tablespoons chopped fresh basil or flat-leaf parsley
Spiralized zucchini noodles, cooked cauliflower "rice," or cooked whole-grain pasta for serving
Lemon wedges for serving

1. Pat the pork chops dry with paper towels, then season them all over with the salt and pepper. 2. Select the Sauté setting on the Instant Pot and heat 1 tablespoon of the oil for 2 minutes. Swirl the oil to coat the bottom of the pot. Using tongs, add half of the pork chops in a single layer and sear for about 3 minutes, until lightly browned on the first side. Flip the chops and sear for about 3 minutes more, until lightly browned on the second side. Transfer the chops to a plate. Repeat with the remaining 1 tablespoon oil and pork chops. 3. Add the garlic to the pot and sauté for about 1 minute, until bubbling but not browned. Stir in the broth, Italian seasoning, and capers, using a wooden spoon to nudge any browned bits from the bottom of the pot and working quickly so not too much liquid evaporates. Using the tongs, transfer the pork chops to the pot. Add the tomatoes in an even layer on top of the chops. 4. Secure the lid and set the Pressure Release to Sealing. Press the Cancel button to reset the cooking program, then select the Pressure Cook or Manual setting and set the cooking time for 10 minutes at high pressure. (The pot will take about 5 minutes to come up to pressure before the cooking program begins.) 5. When the cooking program ends, let the pressure release naturally for at least 10 minutes, then move the Pressure Release to Venting to release any remaining steam. Open the pot and, using the tongs, transfer the pork chops to a serving dish. 6. Spoon the tomatoes and some of the cooking liquid on top of the pork chops. Sprinkle with the basil and serve right away, with zucchini noodles and lemon wedges on the side.

Per Serving:
calorie: 265 | fat: 13g | protein: 31g | carbs: 3g | sugars: 2g | fiber: 1g | sodium: 460mg

Low Carb Pork Tenderloin

Prep time: 15 minutes | Cook time: 30 minutes | Serves 2

9 ounces (255 g) pork tenderloin
1 teaspoon erythritol
½ teaspoon dried dill
½ teaspoon white pepper
1 garlic clove, minced
3 tablespoons butter
¼ cup water

1. Rub the pork tenderloin with erythritol, dried dill, white pepper, and minced garlic. 2. Then melt the butter in the instant pot on Sauté mode. 3. Add pork tenderloin and cook it for 8 minutes from each side (use Sauté mode). 4. Then add water and close the lid. 5. Cook the meat on Sauté mode for 10 minutes. 6. Cool the cooked tenderloin for 10 to 15 minutes and slice.

Per Serving:
calories: 339 | fat: 22g | protein: 34g | carbs: 4g | net carbs: 4g | fiber: 0g

Cinnamon Beef with Blackberries

Prep time: 15 minutes | Cook time: 30 minutes | Serves 2

15 ounces (425 g) beef loin, chopped
1 tablespoon blackberries
1 cup water
½ teaspoon ground cinnamon
⅓ teaspoon ground black pepper
½ teaspoon salt
1 tablespoon butter

1. Pour water in the instant pot bowl. 2. Add chopped beef loin, blackberries, ground cinnamon, salt, and ground black pepper. Add butter. 3. Close the instant pot lid and set the Meat/Stew mode. 4. Cook the meat for 30 minutes. Then remove the meat from the instant pot. Blend the remaining blackberry mixture. 5. Pour it over the meat.

Per Serving:
calories: 372 | fat: 21g | protein: 39g | carbs: 4g | net carbs: 3g | fiber: 1g

Beef Burgundy

Prep time: 30 minutes | Cook time: 30 minutes | Serves 6

2 tablespoons olive oil
2 pounds stewing meat, cubed, trimmed of fat
2½ tablespoons flour
5 medium onions, thinly sliced
½ pound fresh mushrooms, sliced
1 teaspoon salt
¼ teaspoon dried marjoram
¼ teaspoon dried thyme
⅛ teaspoon pepper
¾ cup beef broth
1½ cups burgundy

1. Press Sauté on the Instant pot and add in the olive oil. 2. Dredge meat in flour, then brown in batches in the Instant Pot. Set aside the meat. Sauté the onions and mushrooms in the remaining oil and drippings for about 3–4 minutes, then add the meat back in. Press Cancel. 3. Add the salt, marjoram, thyme, pepper, broth, and wine to the Instant Pot. 4. Secure the lid and make sure the vent is set to sealing. Press the Manual button and set to 30 minutes. 5. When cook time is up, let the pressure release naturally for 15 minutes, then perform a quick release. 6. Serve over cooked noodles.

Per Serving:
calories: 358 | fat: 11g | protein: 37g | carbs: 15g | sugars: 5g | fiber: 2g | sodium: 472mg

Pork Adobo

Prep time: 10 minutes | Cook time: 30 minutes | Serves 6

1 pound (454 g) pork belly, chopped
1 bay leaf
1 teaspoon salt
2 tablespoons apple cider vinegar
1 teaspoon cayenne pepper
1 garlic clove, peeled
2 cups water

1. Put all ingredients in the instant pot. 2. Close and seal the lid. 3. Cook Adobo pork for 30 minutes on Manual mode (High Pressure). 4. When the cooking time is finished, make a quick pressure release and transfer the pork belly in the bowls. 5. Add 1 ladle of the pork gravy.

Per Serving:
calories: 352 | fat: 20g | protein: 35g | carbs: 0g | net carbs: 0g | fiber: 0g

Braised Tri-Tip Steak

Prep time: 20 minutes | Cook time: 54 minutes | Serves 4

2 pounds (907 g) tri-tip steak, patted dry
2 teaspoons coarse sea salt
3 tablespoons avocado oil
½ medium onion, diced
2 cloves garlic, smashed
1 tablespoon unsweetened tomato purée
1½ cups dry red wine
½ tablespoon dried thyme
2 bay leaves
1 Roma (plum) tomato, diced
1 stalk celery, including leaves, chopped
1 small turnip, chopped
½ cup water

1. Season the tri-tip with the coarse salt. Set the Instant Pot to Sauté mode and heat the avocado oil until shimmering. 2. Cook the steak in the pot for 2 minutes per side or until well browned. Remove the steak from the pot and place it in a shallow bowl. Set aside. 3. Add the onion to the pot and sauté for 3 minutes. Add the garlic and sauté for 1 minute. Add the unsweetened tomato purée and cook for 1 minute, stirring constantly. 4. Pour in the red wine. Stir in the thyme and bay leaves. 5. Return the tri-tip steak to the pot. Scatter the tomato, celery, and turnip around the steak. Pour in the water. 6. Secure the lid. Press the Manual button and set cooking time for 35 minutes on High Pressure. 7. When timer beeps, allow the pressure to release naturally for 20 minutes, then release any remaining pressure. Open the lid. Discard the bay leaves. 8. Remove the steak and place in a dish. Press the Sauté button and bring the braising liquid to a boil. Cook for 10 minutes or until the liquid is reduced by about half. 9. Slice the steak thinly and serve with braising liquid over.

Per Serving:
calories: 726 | fat: 45.1g | protein: 68.7g | carbs: 3.5g | net carbs: 2.6g | fiber: 0.9g

Beef Big Mac Salad

Prep time: 10 minutes | Cook time: 9 minutes | Serves 2

5 ounces (142 g) ground beef
1 teaspoon ground black pepper
1 tablespoon sesame oil
1 cup lettuce, chopped
¼ cup Monterey Jack cheese, shredded
2 ounces (57 g) dill pickles, sliced
1 ounce (28 g) scallions, chopped
1 tablespoon heavy cream

1. In a mixing bowl, combine the ground beef and ground black pepper.shape the mixture into mini burgers. 2. Pour the sesame oil in the Instant Pot and heat for 3 minutes on Sauté mode. 3. Place the mini hamburgers in the hot oil and cook for 3 minutes on each side. 4. Meanwhile, in a salad bowl, mix the chopped lettuce, shredded cheese, dill pickles, scallions, and heavy cream. Toss to mix well. 5. Top the salad with cooked mini burgers. Serve immediately.

Per Serving:
calories: 284 | fat: 18.5g | protein: 25.7g | carbs: 3.5g | net carbs: 2.3g | fiber: 1.2g

Romano-Crusted Pork Chops

Prep time: 10 minutes | Cook time: 18 minutes | Serves 3

3 pork chops
4 ounces (113 g) Romano cheese, grated
½ teaspoon Cajun seasoning
1 egg, beaten
1 tablespoon cream cheese
⅓ cup almond flour
3 tablespoons avocado oil

1. Rub the pork chops with Cajun seasoning. 2. After this, in the mixing bowl mix up grated Romano cheese and almond flour. 3. In the separated bow mix up eggs and cream cheese. 4. Dip the pork chops in the egg mixture and then coat in the cheese mixture. 5. Repeat the step one more time. 6. Pour avocado oil in the instant pot. Preheat it on Sauté mode for 2 minutes. 7. Add the pork chops and cook them for 8 minutes per side.

Per Serving:
calories: 528 | fat: 40g | protein: 35g | carbs: 5g | net carbs: 3g | fiber: 2g

Spanish Pork Shoulder

Prep time: 10 minutes | Cook time: 40 minutes | Serves 3

12 ounces (340 g) pork shoulder
½ cup chili verde
1 tablespoon butter
¼ cup beef broth
¾ teaspoon ground black pepper
½ teaspoon salt

1. Chop the pork shoulder and sprinkle the meat with the ground black pepper and salt. 2. Toss the butter in the instant pot and sauté it for 1 minute or until it is melted. 3. After this, add pork shoulder and sauté it for 10 minutes. 4. After this, add beef broth and chili Verde. 5. Lock the instant pot lid and seal it. 6. Set the Bean/Chili mode and set the timer on 30 minutes (High Pressure). 7. When the time is over, make a natural pressure release. 8. Serve it!

Per Serving:
calories: 370 | fat: 28g | protein: 27g | carbs: 0g | net carbs: 0g | fiber: 0g

Ground Beef Tacos

Prep time: 0 minutes | Cook time: 25 minutes | Serves 6

Filling
1 tablespoon cold-pressed avocado oil or other neutral oil
2 garlic cloves, minced
1 yellow onion, diced
1½ pounds 95 percent lean ground beef
2 tablespoons chili powder
½ cup low-sodium roasted beef bone broth
Fine sea salt
1 tablespoon tomato paste
Twelve 7-inch corn tortillas, warmed
1 cup chopped white onion
1 cup chopped tomatoes
2 tablespoons chopped fresh cilantro
1 large avocado, pitted, peeled, and sliced
Hot sauce (such as Cholula or Tapatío) for serving

1. To make the filling: Select the Sauté setting on the Instant Pot and heat the oil and garlic for 2 minutes, until the garlic is bubbling but not browned. Add the yellow onion and sauté for about 3 minutes, until it begins to soften. Add the ground beef and sauté, using a wooden spoon or spatula to break up the meat as it cooks for about 3 minutes more; it's fine if some streaks of pink remain, the beef does not need to be cooked through. Stir in the chili powder, bone broth, and ½ teaspoon salt. Dollop the tomato paste on top. Do not stir it in. 2. Secure the lid and set the Pressure Release to Sealing. Press the Cancel button to reset the cooking program, then select the Pressure Cook or Manual setting and set the cooking time for 10 minutes at high pressure. (The pot will take about 5 minutes to come up to pressure before the cooking program begins.) 3. When the cooking program ends, you can either perform a quick pressure release by moving the Pressure Release to Venting, or you can let the pressure release naturally and leave the pot on the Keep Warm setting for up to 10 hours. Open the pot and give the meat a stir. Taste for seasoning and add more salt, if needed. 4. Using a slotted spoon, spoon the meat onto the tortillas. Top with the white onion, tomatoes, cilantro, and avocado and serve right away. Pass the hot sauce at the table.

Per Serving:
calories: 353 | fat: 13g | protein: 28g | carbs: 28g | sugars: 3g | fiber: 6g | sodium: 613mg

Pork Taco Casserole

Prep time: 15 minutes | Cook time: 30 minutes | Serves 6

½ cup water
2 eggs
3 ounces (85 g) Cottage cheese, at room temperature
¼ cup heavy cream
1 teaspoon taco seasoning
6 ounces (170 g) Cotija cheese, crumbled
¾ pound (340 g) ground pork
½ cup tomatoes, puréed
1 tablespoon taco seasoning
3 ounces (85 g) chopped green chilies
6 ounces (170 g) Queso Manchego cheese, shredded

1. Add the water in the Instant Pot and place in the trivet. 2. In a mixing bowl, combine the eggs, Cottage cheese, heavy cream, and taco seasoning. 3. Lightly grease a casserole dish. Spread the Cotija cheese over the bottom. Stir in the egg mixture. 4. Lower the casserole dish onto the trivet. 5. Secure the lid. Choose Manual mode and set cooking time for 20 minutes on High Pressure. 6. Once cooking is complete, use a quick pressure release. Carefully remove the lid. 7. In the meantime, heat a skillet over a medium-high heat. Brown the ground pork, crumbling with a fork. 8. Add the tomato purée, taco seasoning, and green chilies. Spread the mixture over the prepared cheese crust. 9. Top with shredded Queso Manchego. 10. Secure the lid. Choose Manual mode and set cooking time for 10 minutes on High Pressure. 11. Once cooking is complete, use a quick pressure release. Carefully remove the lid. Serve immediately.

Per Serving:
calories: 409 | fat: 31.6g | protein: 25.7g | carbs: 4.7g | net carbs: 2.7g | fiber: 2.0g

Cheesesteak Stuffed Peppers

Prep time: 10 minutes | Cook time: 8 minutes | Serves 4

1 tablespoon butter
1 pound (454 g) shaved beef
4 ounces (113 g) mushrooms, coarsely chopped
2½ ounces (71 g) sliced onion
1 tablespoon Worcestershire sauce
1 teaspoon seasoned salt
¼ teaspoon salt
¼ teaspoon black pepper
4 large bell peppers (any color)
½ cup water
4 slices provolone cheese

1. Heat the broiler. 2. Turn the pot to Sauté mode and add the butter. Once melted, add the beef, mushrooms, and onion. Sauté until softened, 2 to 3 minutes. Add the Worcestershire sauce, seasoned salt, salt, and black pepper. Stir to evenly combine. Press Cancel. 3. Slice the tops off the bell peppers and remove the cores and seeds. Fill each pepper with 4¼ ounces (120 g) of the meat mixture. Rinse out the pot. 4. Place the pot back into the base. Add the water and the trivet. Place the peppers on top of the trivet. 5. Close the lid and seal the vent. Cook on High Pressure for 5 minutes. Quick release the steam. 6. Carefully remove the trivet from the pot. Transfer the peppers to a baking sheet. Place one slice of provolone cheese on top of each pepper and broil for about 1 minute to melt the cheese.

Per Serving:
calories: 294 | fat: 18g | protein: 26g | carbs: 5g | net carbs: 4g | fiber: 1g

Garlic Butter Italian Sausages

Prep time: 15 minutes | Cook time: 20 minutes | Serves 4

1 teaspoon garlic powder
1 cup water
1 teaspoon butter
12 ounces (340 g) Italian sausages, chopped
½ teaspoon Italian seasoning

1. Sprinkle the chopped Italian sausages with Italian seasoning and garlic powder and place in the instant pot. 2. Add butter and cook the sausages on Sauté mode for 10 minutes. Stir them from time to time with the help of the spatula. 3. Then add water and close the lid. 4. Cook the sausages on Manual mode (High Pressure) for 10 minutes. 5. Allow the natural pressure release for 10 minutes more.

Per Serving:
calories: 307 | fat: 28g | protein: 12g | carbs: 1g | net carbs: 1g | fiber: 0g

Carnitas Burrito Bowls

Prep time: 10 minutes | Cook time: 1 hour | Serves 6

Carnitas
1 tablespoon chili powder
½ teaspoon garlic powder
1 teaspoon ground coriander
1 teaspoon fine sea salt
½ cup water
¼ cup fresh lime juice
One 2-pound boneless pork shoulder butt roast, cut into 2-inch cubes
Rice and Beans
1 cup Minute brand brown rice (see Note)
1½ cups drained cooked black beans, or one 15-ounce can black beans, rinsed and drained
Pico de Gallo
8 ounces tomatoes (see Note), diced
½ small yellow onion, diced
1 jalapeño chile, seeded and finely diced
1 tablespoon chopped fresh cilantro
1 teaspoon fresh lime juice
Pinch of fine sea salt
¼ cup sliced green onions, white and green parts
2 tablespoons chopped fresh cilantro
3 hearts romaine lettuce, cut into ¼-inch-wide ribbons
2 large avocados, pitted, peeled, and sliced
Hot sauce (such as Cholula or Tapatío) for serving

1. To make the carnitas: In a small bowl, combine the chili powder, garlic powder, coriander, and salt and mix well. 2. Pour the water and lime juice into the Instant Pot. Add the pork, arranging the pieces in a single layer. Sprinkle the chili powder mixture evenly over the pork. 3. Secure the lid and set the Pressure Release to Sealing. Select the Meat/Stew setting and set the cooking time for 30 minutes at high pressure. (The pot will take about 10 minutes to come up to pressure before the cooking program begins.) 4. When the cooking program ends, let the pressure release naturally for at least 15 minutes, then move the Pressure Release to Venting to release any remaining steam. Open the pot and, using tongs, transfer the pork to a plate or cutting board. 5. While the pressure is releasing, preheat the oven to 400°F. 6. Wearing heat-resistant mitts, lift out the inner pot and pour the cooking liquid into a fat separator. Pour the defatted cooking liquid into a liquid measuring cup and discard the fat. (Alternatively, use a ladle or large spoon to skim the fat off the surface of the liquid.) Add water as needed to the cooking liquid to total 1 cup (you may have enough without adding water). 7. To make the rice and beans: Pour the 1 cup cooking liquid into the Instant Pot and add the rice, making sure it is in an even layer. Place a tall steam rack into the pot. Add the black beans to a 1½-quart stainless-steel bowl and place the bowl on top of the rack. (The bowl should not touch the lid once the pot is closed.) 8. Secure the lid and set the Pressure Release to Sealing. Press the Cancel button to reset the cooking program, then select the Pressure Cook or Manual setting and set the cooking time for 15 minutes at high pressure. (The pot will take about 5 minutes to come to pressure before the cooking program begins.) 9. While the rice and beans are cooking, using two forks, shred the meat into bite-size pieces. Transfer the pork to a sheet pan, spreading it out in an even layer. Place in the oven for 20 minutes, until crispy and browned. 10. To make the pico de gallo: While the carnitas, rice, and beans are cooking, in a medium bowl, combine the tomatoes, onion, jalapeño, cilantro, lime juice, and salt and mix well. Set aside. 11. When the cooking program ends, let the pressure release naturally for 5 minutes, then move the Pressure Release to Venting to release any remaining steam. Open the pot and, wearing heat-resistant mitts, remove the bowl of beans and then the steam rack from the pot. Then remove the inner pot. Add the green onions and cilantro to the rice and, using a fork, fluff the rice and mix in the green onions and cilantro. 12. Divide the rice, beans, carnitas, pico de gallo, lettuce, and avocados evenly among six bowls. Serve warm, with the hot sauce on the side.

Per Serving:
calories: 447 | fat: 20g | protein: 31g | carbs: 35g | sugars: 4g | fiber: 9g | sodium: 653mg

Aromatic Pork Steak Curry

Prep time: 15 minutes | Cook time: 8 minutes | Serves 6

½ teaspoon mustard seeds
1 teaspoon fennel seeds
1 teaspoon cumin seeds
2 chili peppers, deseeded and minced
½ teaspoon ground bay leaf
1 teaspoon mixed peppercorns
1 tablespoon sesame oil
1½ pounds (680 g) pork steak, sliced
2 cloves garlic, finely minced
2 tablespoons scallions, chopped
1 teaspoon fresh ginger, grated
1 teaspoon curry powder
1 cup chicken broth
2 tablespoons balsamic vinegar
3 tablespoons coconut cream
¼ teaspoon red pepper flakes, crushed
Sea salt, to taste
¼ teaspoon ground black pepper

1. Heat a skillet over medium-high heat. Once hot, roast the mustard seeds, fennel seeds, cumin seeds, chili peppers, ground bay leaf, and peppercorns for 1 or 2 minutes or until aromatic. 2. Press the Sauté button to heat up the Instant Pot. Heat the sesame oil until sizzling. Sear pork steak for 5 minutes or until browned. 3. Add the remaining ingredients, including roasted seasonings. Stir to mix well. 4. Secure the lid. Choose the Manual mode and set cooking time for 8 minutes on High pressure. 5. Once cooking is complete, use a quick pressure release. Carefully remove the lid. Serve immediately.

Per Serving:
calories: 362 | fat: 25.2g | protein: 29.6g | carbs: 2.2g | net carbs: 0.9g | fiber: 1.3g

Rosemary Lamb Chops

Prep time: 25 minutes | Cook time: 2 minutes | Serves 4

1½ pounds lamb chops (4 small chops)
1 teaspoon kosher salt
Leaves from 1 (6-inch) rosemary sprig
2 tablespoons avocado oil
1 shallot, peeled and cut in quarters
1 tablespoon tomato paste
1 cup beef broth

1. Place the lamb chops on a cutting board. Press the salt and rosemary leaves into both sides of the chops. Let rest at room temperature for 15 to 30 minutes. 2. Set the electric pressure cooker to Sauté/More setting. When hot, add the avocado oil. 3. Brown the lamb chops, about 2 minutes per side. (If they don't all fit in a single layer, brown them in batches.) 4. Transfer the chops to a plate. In the pot, combine the shallot, tomato paste, and broth. Cook for about a minute, scraping up the brown bits from the bottom. Hit Cancel. 5. Add the chops and any accumulated juices back to the pot. 6. Close and lock the lid of the pressure cooker. Set the valve to sealing. 7. Cook on high pressure for 2 minutes. 8. When the cooking is complete, hit Cancel and quick release the pressure. 9. Once the pin drops, unlock and remove the lid. 10. Place the lamb chops on plates and serve immediately.

Per Serving:

calorie: 352 | fat: 20g | protein: 37g | carbs: 7g | sugars: 1g | fiber: 0g | sodium: 440mg

BBQ Ribs and Broccoli Slaw

Prep time: 10 minutes | Cook time: 50 minutes | Serves 6

BBQ Ribs
4 pounds baby back ribs
1 teaspoon fine sea salt
1 teaspoon freshly ground black pepper
Broccoli Slaw
½ cup plain 2 percent Greek yogurt
1 tablespoon olive oil
1 tablespoon fresh lemon juice
½ teaspoon fine sea salt
¼ teaspoon freshly ground black pepper
1 pound broccoli florets (or florets from 2 large crowns), chopped
10 radishes, halved and thinly sliced
1 red bell pepper, seeded and cut lengthwise into narrow strips
1 large apple (such as Fuji, Jonagold, or Gala), thinly sliced
½ red onion, thinly sliced
¾ cup low-sugar or unsweetened barbecue sauce

1. To make the ribs: Pat the ribs dry with paper towels, then cut the racks into six sections (three to five ribs per section, depending on how big the racks are). Season the ribs all over with the salt and pepper. 2. Pour 1 cup water into the Instant Pot and place the wire metal steam rack into the pot. Place the ribs on top of the wire rack (it's fine to stack them up). 3. Secure the lid and set the Pressure Release to Sealing. Select the Pressure Cook or Manual setting and set the cooking time for 20 minutes at high pressure. (The pot will take about 15 minutes to come up to pressure before the cooking program begins.) 4. To make the broccoli slaw: While the ribs are cooking, in a small bowl, stir together the yogurt, oil, lemon juice, salt, and pepper, mixing well. In a large bowl, combine the broccoli, radishes, bell pepper, apple, and onion. Drizzle with the yogurt mixture and toss until evenly coated. 5. When the ribs have about 10 minutes left in their cooking time, preheat the oven to 400°F. Line a sheet pan with aluminum foil. 6. When the cooking program ends, perform a quick pressure release by moving the Pressure Release to Venting. Open the pot and, using tongs, transfer the ribs in a single layer to the prepared sheet pan. Brush the barbecue sauce onto both sides of the ribs, using 2 tablespoons of sauce per section of ribs. Bake, meaty-side up, for 15 to 20 minutes, until lightly browned. 7. Serve the ribs warm, with the slaw on the side.

Per Serving:

calories: 392 | fat: 15g | protein: 45g | carbs: 19g | sugars: 9g | fiber: 4g | sodium: 961mg

Korean Short Rib Lettuce Wraps

Prep time: 7 minutes | Cook time: 25 minutes | Serves 4

¼ cup coconut aminos, or 1 tablespoon wheat-free tamari
2 tablespoons coconut vinegar
2 tablespoons sesame oil
3 green onions, thinly sliced, plus more for garnish
2 teaspoons peeled and grated fresh ginger
2 teaspoons minced garlic
½ teaspoon fine sea salt
½ teaspoon red pepper flakes, plus more for garnish
1 pound (454 g) boneless beef short ribs, sliced ½ inch thick
For Serving:
1 head radicchio, thinly sliced
Butter lettuce leaves

1. Place the coconut aminos, vinegar, sesame oil, green onions, ginger, garlic, salt, and red pepper flakes in the Instant Pot and stir to combine. Add the short ribs and toss to coat well. 2. Seal the lid, press Manual, and set the timer for 20 minutes. Once finished, let the pressure release naturally. 3. Remove the ribs from the Instant Pot and set aside on a warm plate, leaving the sauce in the pot. 4. Press Sauté and cook the sauce, whisking often, until thickened to your liking, about 5 minutes. 5. Put the sliced radicchio on a serving platter, then lay the short ribs on top. Pour the thickened sauce over the ribs. Garnish with more sliced green onions and red pepper flakes. Serve wrapped in lettuce leaves.

Per Serving:

calories: 547 | fat: 48g | protein: 18g | carbs: 9g | net carbs: 0g | fiber: 9g

Beef Burgers with Kale and Cheese

Prep time: 6 minutes | Cook time: 6 minutes | Serves 6

1 pound (454 g) ground beef
½ pound (227 g) beef sausage, crumbled
1½ cups chopped kale
¼ cup chopped scallions
2 garlic cloves, minced
½ cup grated Romano cheese
⅓ cup crumbled blue cheese
Salt and ground black pepper, to taste
1 teaspoon crushed dried sage
½ teaspoon oregano
½ teaspoon dried basil
1 tablespoon olive oil

1. Place 1½ cups of water and a steamer basket in your Instant Pot. 2. Mix all ingredients until everything is well incorporated. 3. Shape the mixture into 6 equal sized patties. Place the burgers on the steamer basket. 4. Secure the lid. Choose Manual mode and High Pressure; cook for 6 minutes. Once cooking is complete, use a quick pressure release; carefully remove the lid. Bon appétit!

Per Serving:

calories: 323 | fat: 20g | protein: 30g | carbs: 6g | net carbs: 5g | fiber: 1g

Cilantro Lime Shredded Pork

Prep time: 5 minutes | Cook time: 30 minutes | Serves 4

1 tablespoon chili adobo sauce
1 tablespoon chili powder
2 teaspoons salt
1 teaspoon garlic powder
1 teaspoon cumin
½ teaspoon pepper
1 (2½ to 3 pounds / 1.1 to 1.4 kg) cubed pork butt
1 tablespoon coconut oil
2 cups beef broth
1 lime, cut into wedges
¼ cup chopped cilantro

1. In a small bowl, mix adobo sauce, chili powder, salt, garlic powder, cumin, and pepper. 2. Press the Sauté button on Instant Pot and add coconut oil to pot. Rub spice mixture onto cubed pork butt. Place pork into pot and sear for 3 to 5 minutes per side. Add broth. 3. Press the Cancel button. Lock Lid. Press the Manual button and adjust time to 30 minutes. 4. When timer beeps, let pressure naturally release until the float valve drops, and unlock lid. 5. Shred pork with fork. Pork should easily fall apart. For extra-crispy pork, place single layer in skillet on stove over medium heat. Cook for 10 to 15 minutes or until water has cooked out and pork becomes brown and crisp. Serve warm with fresh lime wedges and cilantro garnish.

Per Serving:
calories: 570 | fat: 36g | protein: 55g | carbs: 3g | net carbs: 2g | fiber: 1g

Marjoram Beef Ribs

Prep time: 10 minutes | Cook time: 40 minutes | Serves 2

10 ounces (283 g) beef ribs
¾ cup water
2 tablespoons coconut oil
1 teaspoon dried marjoram
½ teaspoon salt
½ cup chicken broth

1. Rub the beef ribs with the dried marjoram and salt. 2. Place the beef ribs in the instant pot bowl. 3. Add chicken broth and water. 4. Then add coconut oil. 5. Close the lid and set the Meat/Stew mode. Cook the ribs for 40 minutes.

Per Serving:
calories: 391 | fat: 23g | protein: 44g | carbs: 0g | net carbs: 0g | fiber: 0g

Lamb Chops with Shaved Zucchini Salad

Prep time: 20 minutes | Cook time: 40 minutes | Serves 4

4 (8- to 12-ounce/ 227- to 340-g) lamb shoulder chops (blade or round bone), about ¾ inch thick, trimmed
¾ teaspoon table salt, divided
¾ teaspoon pepper, divided
2 tablespoons extra-virgin olive oil, divided
1 onion, chopped
5 garlic cloves, minced
½ cup chicken broth
1 bay leaf
4 zucchini (6 ounces / 170 g each), sliced lengthwise into ribbons
1 teaspoon grated lemon zest plus 1 tablespoon juice
2 ounces (57 g) goat cheese, crumbled (½ cup)
¼ cup chopped fresh mint
2 tablespoons raisins

1. Pat lamb chops dry with paper towels and sprinkle with ½ teaspoon salt and ½ teaspoon pepper. Using highest sauté function, heat 1½ teaspoons oil in Instant Pot for 5 minutes (or until just smoking). Brown half of chops on both sides, 6 to 8 minutes; transfer to plate. Repeat with 1½ teaspoons oil and remaining chops; transfer to plate. 2. Add onion to fat left in pot and cook, using highest sauté function, until softened, about 5 minutes. Stir in garlic and cook until fragrant, about 30 seconds. Stir in broth and bay leaf, scraping up any browned bits. Return chops to pot along with any accumulated juices (chops will overlap). Lock lid in place and close pressure release valve. Select high pressure cook function and cook for 20 minutes. 3. Turn off Instant Pot and let pressure release naturally for 15 minutes. Quick-release any remaining pressure, then carefully remove lid, allowing steam to escape away from you. Transfer chops to serving dish. Gently toss zucchini with lemon zest and juice, remaining 1 tablespoon oil, remaining ¼ teaspoon salt, and remaining ¼ teaspoon pepper in bowl. Arrange zucchini on serving dish with lamb, and sprinkle with goat cheese, mint, and raisins. Serve.

Per Serving:
calories: 390 | fat: 20g | protein: 38g | carbs: 14g | fiber: 2g | sodium: 720mg

French Dip Chuck Roast

Prep time: 5 minutes | Cook time: 70 minutes | Serves 6

2 tablespoons avocado oil
2 to 2½ pounds (907 g to 1.1 kg) chuck roast
2 cups beef broth
2 tablespoons dried rosemary
3 cloves garlic, minced
1 teaspoon salt
½ teaspoon black pepper
¼ teaspoon dried thyme
½ onion, quartered
2 bay leaves

1. Turn the pot to Sauté mode. Once hot, add the avocado oil. Add the roast and sear it on each side. This should take about 5 minutes. Press Cancel. 2. Add the broth to the pot. 3. Add the rosemary, garlic, salt, pepper, and thyme to the top of the roast. Add the onion and bay leaves. 4. Close the lid and seal the vent. Cook on High Pressure for 50 minutes. Let the steam naturally release for 15 minutes before Manually releasing. 5. Remove the roast to a plate and shred with two forks. Strain the jus though a fine-mesh sieve. Serve the roast au jus for dipping.

Per Serving:
calories: 548 | fat: 34g | protein: 55g | carbs: 2g | net carbs: 1g | fiber: 1g

Peppercorn Pork with Salsa Verde

Prep time: 10 minutes | Cook time: 40 minutes | Serves 3

12 ounces (340 g) pork shoulder, sliced
½ cup salsa verde
½ cup water
¾ teaspoon peppercorns
½ teaspoon salt

1. Toss the butter in the instant pot and sauté it for 1 minute or until it is melted. 2. After this, add pork shoulder, salt, and peppercorns; sauté the ingredients for 10 minutes. 3. After this, add water and salsa verde. 4. Set the Bean/Chili mode and set the timer on 30 minutes (High Pressure). 5. When the time is over, make a natural pressure release.

Per Serving:
calories: 342 | fat: 24g | protein: 27g | carbs: 2g | net carbs: 2g | fiber: 0g

Smothered Pork Chops with Leeks and Mustard

Prep time: 15 minutes | Cook time: 35 minutes | Serves 4

4 (8- to 10-ounce/ 227- to 283-g) bone-in blade-cut pork chops, about ¾ inch thick, trimmed
½ teaspoon table salt
½ teaspoon pepper
4 teaspoons extra-virgin olive oil, divided
2 ounces (57 g) pancetta, chopped fine
1 tablespoon all-purpose flour
¾ cup dry white wine
1½ pounds (680 g) leeks, ends trimmed, halved lengthwise, sliced into 3-inch lengths, and washed thoroughly
1 tablespoon Dijon mustard
2 tablespoons chopped fresh parsley

1. Pat pork chops dry with paper towels. Using sharp knife, cut 2 slits, about 2 inches apart, through fat on edge of each chop. Sprinkle with salt and pepper. Using highest sauté function, heat 2 teaspoons oil in Instant Pot for 5 minutes (or until just smoking). Brown 2 chops on both sides, 6 to 8 minutes; transfer to plate. Repeat with remaining 2 teaspoons oil and remaining chops; transfer to plate. 2. Add pancetta to fat left in pot and cook, using highest sauté function, until softened and lightly browned, about 2 minutes. Stir in flour and cook for 30 seconds. Stir in wine, scraping up any browned bits and smoothing any lumps. Stir in leeks and cook until softened, about 3 minutes. Nestle chops into pot (chops will overlap) and add any accumulated juices. Lock lid in place and close pressure release valve. Select high pressure cook function and cook for 10 minutes. 3. Turn off Instant Pot and let pressure release naturally for 15 minutes. Quick-release any remaining pressure, then carefully remove lid, allowing steam to escape away from you. Transfer chops to serving platter, tent with aluminum foil, and let rest while finishing leeks. 4. Using highest sauté function, bring leek mixture to simmer. Stir in mustard and cook until slightly thickened, about 5 minutes. Season with salt and pepper to taste. Spoon leek mixture over chops and sprinkle with parsley. Serve.

Per Serving:
calories: 390 | fat: 17g | protein: 35g | carbs: 13g | fiber: 1g | sodium: 780mg

Bacon Cheddar Cheese Stuffed Burgers

Prep time: 10 minutes | Cook time: 9 minutes | Serves 4

1 pound (454 g) ground beef
6 ounces (170 g) shredded Cheddar cheese
5 slices bacon, coarsely chopped
2 teaspoons Worcestershire sauce
1 teaspoon salt
½ teaspoon liquid smoke
½ teaspoon black pepper
½ teaspoon garlic powder
1 cup water

1. In a large bowl, add the beef, cheese, bacon, Worcestershire sauce, salt, liquid smoke, pepper, and garlic powder. Gently work everything into the meat. Do not overwork the meat, or it will become tough when it cooks. 2. Separate the meat into four equal portions. Use a food scale to measure evenly. 3. Shape each piece into a ball. Use your thumb to make a crater in the middle of the patty but make sure the round shape is retained. 4. Wrap each patty loosely in aluminum foil. Place them on top of the trivet in the pot. They will overlap. 5. Add the water to the bottom of the pot. Close the lid and seal the vent. Cook on High Pressure for 9 minutes. Quick release the steam. Remove the foil packets from the pot and set them on a large plate. Carefully unwrap the burgers. There will be juices in the bottom of the foil.

Per Serving:
calories: 454 | fat: 33g | protein: 39g | carbs: 2g | net carbs: 0g | fiber: 2g

Bavarian Beef

Prep time: 35 minutes | Cook time: 1 hour 15 minutes | Serves 8

1 tablespoon canola oil
3-pound boneless beef chuck roast, trimmed of fat
3 cups sliced carrots
3 cups sliced onions
2 large kosher dill pickles, chopped
1 cup sliced celery
½ cup dry red wine or beef broth
⅓ cup German-style mustard
2 teaspoons coarsely ground black pepper
2 bay leaves
¼ teaspoon ground cloves
1 cup water
⅓ cup flour

1. Press Sauté on the Instant Pot and add in the oil. Brown roast on both sides for about 5 minutes. Press Cancel. 2. Add all of the remaining ingredients, except for the flour, to the Instant Pot. 3. Secure the lid and make sure the vent is set to sealing. Press Manual and set the time to 1 hour and 15 minutes. Let the pressure release naturally. 4. Remove meat and vegetables to large platter. Cover to keep warm. 5. Remove 1 cup of the liquid from the Instant Pot and mix with the flour. Press Sauté on the Instant Pot and add the flour/ broth mixture back in, whisking. Cook until the broth is smooth and thickened. 6. Serve over noodles or spaetzle.

Per Serving:
calories: 251 | fat: 8g | protein: 26g | carbs: 17g | sugars: 7g | fiber: 4g | sodium: 525mg

Machaca Beef

Prep time: 15 minutes | Cook time: 10 to 12 hours | Serves 12

1½-pound beef roast
1 large onion, sliced
4-ounce can chopped green chilies
2 beef bouillon cubes
1½ teaspoons dry mustard
½ teaspoon garlic powder
1 teaspoon seasoning salt
½ teaspoon pepper
1 cup water
1 cup salsa

1. Combine all ingredients except salsa in the Instant Pot inner pot. 2. Secure the lid and make sure the vent is set to sealing. Press the Slow Cook button and set on low for 12 hours, or until beef is tender. Drain and reserve liquid. 3. Shred beef using two forks to pull it apart. 4. Combine beef, salsa, and enough of the reserved liquid to make desired consistency. 5. Use this filling for burritos, chalupas, quesadillas, or tacos.

Per Serving:
calories: 69 | fat: 2g | protein: 9g | carbs: 3g | sugars: 2g | fiber: 1g | sodium: 392mg

Beery Boston-Style Butt

Prep time: 10 minutes | Cook time: 1 hour 1 minutes | Serves 4

1 tablespoon butter
1 pound (454 g) Boston-style butt
½ cup leeks, chopped
¼ cup beer
½ cup chicken stock
Pinch of grated nutmeg
Sea salt, to taste
¼ teaspoon ground black pepper
¼ cup water

1. Press the Sauté button to heat up the Instant Pot. Once hot, melt the butter. 2. Cook the Boston-style butt for 3 minutes on each side. Remove from the pot and reserve. 3. Sauté the leeks for 5 minutes or until fragrant. Add the remaining ingredients and stir to combine. 4. Secure the lid. Choose the Manual mode and set cooking time for 50 minutes on High pressure. 5. Once cooking is complete, use a natural pressure release for 20 minutes, then release any remaining pressure. Carefully remove the lid. 6. Serve immediately.

Per Serving:
calories: 330 | fat: 13.1g | protein: 48.4g | carbs: 2.1g | net carbs: 0.4g | fiber: 1.7g

Herbed Lamb Shank

Prep time: 15 minutes | Cook time: 35 minutes | Serves 2

2 lamb shanks
1 rosemary spring
1 teaspoon coconut flour
¼ teaspoon onion powder
¼ teaspoon chili powder
¾ teaspoon ground ginger
½ cup beef broth
½ teaspoon avocado oil

1. Put all ingredients in the Instant Pot. Stir to mix well. 2. Close the lid. Select Manual mode and set cooking time for 35 minutes on High Pressure. 3. When timer beeps, use a natural pressure release for 15 minutes, then release any remaining pressure. Open the lid. 4. Discard the rosemary sprig and serve warm.

Per Serving:
calories: 179 | fat: 7.0g | protein: 25.4g | carbs: 2.0g | net carbs: 1.2g | fiber: 0.8g

Wine-Braised Short Ribs with Potatoes

Prep time: 20 minutes | Cook time: 1 hour 20 minutes | Serves 4

2 pounds (907 g) bone-in English-style beef short ribs, trimmed
¾ teaspoon table salt, divided
¼ teaspoon pepper
1 tablespoon extra-virgin olive oil
1 onion, chopped fine
6 garlic cloves, minced
2 tablespoons tomato paste
1 tablespoon minced fresh oregano or 1 teaspoon dried
1 (14½-ounce / 411-g) can whole peeled tomatoes, drained with ¼ cup juice reserved, chopped coarse
½ cup dry red wine
1 pound (454 g) small red potatoes, unpeeled, halved
2 tablespoons minced fresh parsley

1. Pat short ribs dry with paper towels and sprinkle with ½ teaspoon salt and pepper. Using highest sauté function, heat oil in Instant Pot for 5 minutes (or until just smoking). Brown short ribs on all sides, 6 to 8 minutes; transfer to plate. 2. Add onion and remaining ¼ teaspoon salt to fat left in pot and cook, using highest sauté function, until onion is softened, about 3 minutes. Stir in garlic, tomato paste, and oregano and cook until fragrant, about 30 seconds. Stir in tomatoes and reserved juice and wine, scraping up any browned bits. Nestle short ribs meat side down into pot and add any accumulated juices. Lock lid in place and close pressure release valve. Select high pressure cook function and cook for 60 minutes. 3. Turn off Instant Pot and let pressure release naturally for 15 minutes. Quick-release any remaining pressure, then carefully remove lid, allowing steam to escape away from you. Transfer short ribs to serving dish, tent with aluminum foil, and let rest while preparing potatoes. 4. Strain braising liquid through fine-mesh strainer into fat separator; transfer solids to now-empty pot. Let braising liquid settle for 5 minutes, then pour 1½ cups defatted liquid and any accumulated juices into pot with solids; discard remaining liquid. Add potatoes. Lock lid in place and close pressure release valve. Select high pressure cook function and cook for 4 minutes. Turn off Instant Pot and quick-release pressure. Carefully remove lid, allowing steam to escape away from you. 5. Using slotted spoon, transfer potatoes to serving dish. Season sauce with salt and pepper to taste. Spoon sauce over short ribs and potatoes and sprinkle with parsley. Serve.

Per Serving:
calories: 340 | fat: 13g | protein: 21g | carbs: 29g | fiber: 3g | sodium: 700mg

Pork Steaks with Pico de Gallo

Prep time: 15 minutes | Cook time: 12 minutes | Serves 6

1 tablespoon butter
2 pounds (907 g) pork steaks
1 bell pepper, deseeded and sliced
½ cup shallots, chopped
2 garlic cloves, minced
¼ cup dry red wine
1 cup chicken bone broth
¼ cup water
Salt, to taste
¼ teaspoon freshly ground black pepper, or more to taste
Pico de Gallo:
1 tomato, chopped
1 chili pepper, seeded and minced
½ cup red onion, chopped
2 garlic cloves, minced
1 tablespoon fresh cilantro, finely chopped
Sea salt, to taste

1. Press the Sauté button to heat up the Instant Pot. Melt the butter and sear the pork steaks about 4 minutes or until browned on both sides. 2. Add bell pepper, shallot, garlic, wine, chicken bone broth, water, salt, and black pepper to the Instant Pot. 3. Secure the lid. Choose the Manual mode and set cooking time for 8 minutes at High pressure. 4. Meanwhile, combine the ingredients for the Pico de Gallo in a small bowl. Refrigerate until ready to serve. 5. Once cooking is complete, use a quick pressure release. Carefully remove the lid. 6. Serve warm pork steaks with the chilled Pico de Gallo on the side.

Per Serving:
calories: 448 | fat: 29g | protein: 39g | carbs: 4g | net carbs: 2g | fiber: 2g

Basic Nutritional Values

Prep time: 20 minutes | Cook time: 2 hours | Serves 4 to 6

2 pounds beef roast, boneless
¼ teaspoon salt
¼ teaspoon pepper
1 tablespoon olive oil
2 stalks celery, chopped
4 tablespoons margarine
2 cups low-sodium tomato juice
2 cloves garlic, finely chopped, or 1 teaspoon garlic powder
1 teaspoon thyme
1 bay leaf
4 carrots, chopped
1 medium onion, chopped
4 medium potatoes, chopped

1. Pat beef dry with paper towels; season on all sides with salt and pepper. 2. Select Sauté function on the Instant Pot and adjust heat to more. Put the oil in the inner pot, then cook the beef in oil for 6 minutes, until browned, turning once. Set on plate. 3. Add celery and margarine to the inner pot; cook 2 minutes. Stir in tomato juice, garlic, thyme, and bay leaf. Hit Cancel to turn off Sauté function. 4. Place beef on top of the contents of the inner pot and press into sauce. Cover and lock lid and make sure vent is at sealing. Select Manual and cook at high pressure for 1 hour 15 minutes. 5. Once cooking is complete, release pressure by using natural release function. Transfer beef to cutting board. Discard bay leaf. 6. Skim off any excess fat from surface. Choose Sauté function and adjust heat to more. Cook 18 minutes, or until reduced by about half (2½ cups). Hit Cancel to turn off Sauté function. 7. Add carrots, onion, and potatoes. Cover and lock lid and make sure vent is at sealing. Select Manual and cook at high pressure for 10 minutes. 8. Once cooking is complete, release pressure by using a quick release. Using Sauté function, keep at a simmer. 9. Season with more salt and pepper to taste.

Per Serving:
calories: 391 | fat: 19 g | protein: 34g | carbs: 22g | sugars: 6g | fiber: 4g | sodium: 395mg

Beef Shawarma and Veggie Salad Bowls

Prep time: 10 minutes | Cook time: 19 minutes | Serves 4

2 teaspoons olive oil
1½ pounds (680 g) beef flank steak, thinly sliced
Sea salt and freshly ground black pepper, to taste
1 teaspoon cayenne pepper
½ teaspoon ground bay leaf
½ teaspoon ground allspice
½ teaspoon cumin, divided
½ cup Greek yogurt
2 tablespoons sesame oil
1 tablespoon fresh lime juice
2 English cucumbers, chopped
1 cup cherry tomatoes, halved
1 red onion, thinly sliced
½ head romaine lettuce, chopped

1. Press the Sauté button to heat up the Instant Pot. Then, heat the olive oil and cook the beef for about 4 minutes. 2. Add all seasonings, 1½ cups of water, and secure the lid. 3. Choose Manual mode. Set the cook time for 15 minutes on High Pressure. 4. Once cooking is complete, use a natural pressure release. Carefully remove the lid. 5. Allow the beef to cool completely. 6. To make the dressing, whisk Greek yogurt, sesame oil, and lime juice in a mixing bowl. 7. Then, divide cucumbers, tomatoes, red onion, and romaine lettuce among four serving bowls. Dress the salad and top with the reserved beef flank steak. Serve warm.

Per Serving:
calories: 367 | fat: 19.1g | protein: 39.5g | carbs: 8.4g | net carbs: 5.0g | fiber: 3.4g

Chapter 5 Fish and Seafood

Snapper in Spicy Tomato Sauce

Prep time: 5 minutes | Cook time: 5 minutes | Serves 6

2 teaspoons coconut oil, melted
1 teaspoon celery seeds
½ teaspoon fresh grated ginger
½ teaspoon cumin seeds
1 yellow onion, chopped
2 cloves garlic, minced
1½ pounds (680 g) snapper fillets
¾ cup vegetable broth
1 (14-ounce / 113-g) can fire-roasted diced tomatoes
1 bell pepper, sliced
1 jalapeño pepper, minced
Sea salt and ground black pepper, to taste
¼ teaspoon chili flakes
½ teaspoon turmeric powder

1. Set the Instant Pot to Sauté. Add and heat the sesame oil until hot. Sauté the celery seeds, fresh ginger, and cumin seeds. 2. Add the onion and continue to sauté until softened and fragrant. 3. Mix in the minced garlic and continue to cook for 30 seconds. Add the remaining ingredients and stir well. 4. Lock the lid. Select the Manual mode and set the cooking time for 3 minutes at Low Pressure. 5. When the timer beeps, perform a quick pressure release. Carefully remove the lid. 6. Serve warm

Per Serving:
calories: 177 | fat: 5.9g | protein: 25.8g | carbs: 5.1g | net carbs: 3.7g | fiber: 1.4g

Cod with Warm Beet and Arugula Salad

Prep time: 15 minutes | Cook time: 8 minutes | Serves 4

¼ cup extra-virgin olive oil, divided, plus extra for drizzling
1 shallot, sliced thin
2 garlic cloves, minced
1½ pounds (680 g) small beets, scrubbed, trimmed, and cut into ½-inch wedges
½ cup chicken or vegetable broth
1 tablespoon dukkah, plus extra for sprinkling
¼ teaspoon table salt
4 (6-ounce / 170-g) skinless cod fillets, 1½ inches thick
1 tablespoon lemon juice
2 ounces (57 g) baby arugula

1. Using highest sauté function, heat 1 tablespoon oil in Instant Pot until shimmering. Add shallot and cook until softened, about 2 minutes. Stir in garlic and cook until fragrant, about 30 seconds. Stir in beets and broth. Lock lid in place and close pressure release valve. Select high pressure cook function and cook for 3 minutes. Turn off Instant Pot and quick-release pressure. Carefully remove lid, allowing steam to escape away from you. 2. Fold sheet of aluminum foil into 16 by 6-inch sling. Combine 2 tablespoons oil, dukkah, and salt in bowl, then brush cod with oil mixture. Arrange cod skinned side down in center of sling. Using sling, lower cod into Instant Pot; allow narrow edges of sling to rest along sides of insert. Lock lid in place and close pressure release valve. Select high pressure cook function and cook for 2 minutes. 3. Turn off Instant Pot and quick-release pressure. Carefully remove lid, allowing steam to escape away from you. Using sling, transfer cod to large plate. Tent with foil and let rest while finishing beet salad. 4. Combine lemon juice and remaining 1 tablespoon oil in large bowl. Using slotted spoon, transfer beets to bowl with oil mixture. Add arugula and gently toss to combine. Season with salt and pepper to taste. 5 Serve cod with salad, sprinkling individual portions with extra dukkah and drizzling with extra oil.

Per Serving:
calories: 340 | fat: 16g | protein: 33g | carbs: 14g | fiber: 4g | sodium: 460mg

Baked Flounder with Artichoke

Prep time: 10 minutes | Cook time: 10 minutes | Serves 2

8 ounces (227 g) flounder fillet
1 lemon slice, chopped
1 teaspoon ground black pepper
¼ teaspoon salt
½ large artichoke, chopped
1 tablespoon sesame oil
1 cup water, for cooking

1. Brush the round baking pan with sesame oil. 2. Then place the chopped artichoke in the baking pan and flatten it. 3. Sprinkle the flounder fillet with ground black pepper and salt and put over the artichoke. 4. Add chopped lemon. 5. Pour water and insert the steamer rack in the instant pot. 6. Place the pan with fish in the steamer. Close and seal the lid. 7. Cook the meal on Manual (High Pressure) for 10 minutes. Make a quick pressure release.

Per Serving:
calories: 216 | fat: 9g | protein: 29g | carbs: 5g | net carbs: 2g | fiber: 3g

Caprese Salmon

Prep time: 10 minutes | Cook time: 15 minutes | Serves 2

10 ounces (283 g) salmon fillet (2 fillets)
4 ounces (113 g) Mozzarella, sliced
4 cherry tomatoes, sliced
1 teaspoon erythritol
1 teaspoon dried basil
½ teaspoon ground black pepper
1 tablespoon apple cider vinegar
1 tablespoon butter
1 cup water, for cooking

1. Grease the mold with butter and put the salmon inside. 2. Sprinkle the fish with erythritol, dried basil, ground black pepper, and apple cider vinegar. 3. Then top the salmon with tomatoes and Mozzarella. 4. Pour water and insert the steamer rack in the instant pot. 5. Put the fish on the rack. 6. Close and seal the lid. 7. Cook the meal on Manual mode at High Pressure for 15 minutes. Make a quick pressure release.

Per Serving:
calories: 447 | fat: 25g | protein: 46g | carbs: 15g | net carbs: 12g | fiber: 3g

Dill Salmon Cakes

Prep time: 15 minutes | Cook time: 10 minutes | Serves 4

1 pound (454 g) salmon fillet, chopped
1 tablespoon chopped dill
2 eggs, beaten
½ cup almond flour
1 tablespoon coconut oil

1. Put the chopped salmon, dill, eggs, and almond flour in the food processor. 2. Blend the mixture until it is smooth. 3. Then make the small balls (cakes) from the salmon mixture. 4. After this, heat up the coconut oil on Sauté mode for 3 minutes. 5. Put the salmon cakes in the instant pot in one layer and cook them on Sauté mode for 2 minutes from each side or until they are light brown.

Per Serving:
calories: 297 | fat: 19g | protein: 28g | carbs: 4g | net carbs: 2g | fiber: 2g

Basil Cod Fillets

Prep time: 5 minutes | Cook time: 12 minutes | Serves 4

½ cup water
4 frozen cod fillets (about 6 ounces / 170 g each)
1 teaspoon dried basil
Pinch of salt
Pinch of black pepper
4 lemon slices
¼ cup heavy cream
2 tablespoons butter, softened
1 ounce (28 g) cream cheese, softened
2 teaspoons lemon juice
1½ teaspoons chopped fresh basil, plus more for garnish (optional)
Lemon wedges, for garnish (optional)

1. Place the trivet inside the pot and add the water. Lay a piece of aluminum foil on top of the trivet and place the cod on top. 2. Sprinkle the fish with the dried basil, salt, and pepper. Set a lemon slice on top of each fillet. 3. Close the lid and seal the vent. Cook on High Pressure for 9 minutes. Quick release the steam. Press Cancel. 4. Remove the trivet and fish from the pot. Rinse the pot if needed and turn to Sauté mode. 5. Add the cream and butter and whisk as the butter melts and the cream warms up. Add the cream cheese and whisk until thickened, 2 to 3 minutes. Add the lemon juice and another pinch of salt and pepper. Once the sauce is thickened and well combined, 1 to 2 minutes, press Cancel and add the fresh basil. 6. Pour the sauce over the fish. Garnish with fresh basil or a lemon wedge, if desired.

Per Serving:
calories: 221 | fat: 11g | protein: 27g | carbs: 1g | net carbs: 1g | fiber: 0g

Rosemary Catfish

Prep time: 10 minutes | Cook time: 20 minutes | Serves 4

16 ounces (454 g) catfish fillet
1 tablespoon dried rosemary
1 teaspoon garlic powder
1 tablespoon avocado oil
1 teaspoon salt
1 cup water, for cooking

1. Cut the catfish fillet into 4 steaks. 2. Then sprinkle them with dried rosemary, garlic powder, avocado oil, and salt. 3. Place the fish steak in the baking mold in one layer. 4. After this, pour water and insert the steamer rack in the instant pot. 5. Put the baking mold with fish on the rack. Close and seal the lid. 6. Cook the meal on Manual (High Pressure) for 20 minutes. Make a quick pressure release.

Per Serving:
calories: 163 | fat: 9g | protein: 18g | carbs: 1g | net carbs: 1g | fiber: 0g

Italian Salmon

Prep time: 10 minutes | Cook time: 4 minutes | Serves 2

10 ounces (283 g) salmon fillet
1 teaspoon Italian seasoning
1 cup water

1. Pour water and insert the trivet in the instant pot. 2. Then rub the salmon fillet with Italian seasoning and wrap in the foil. 3. Place the wrapped fish on the trivet and close the lid. 4. Cook the meal on Manual mode (High Pressure) for 4 minutes. 5. Make a quick pressure release and remove the fish from the foil. 6. Cut it into servings.

Per Serving:
calories: 195 | fat: 10g | protein: 27g | carbs: 0g | net carbs: 0g | fiber: 0g

Turmeric Salmon

Prep time: 10 minutes | Cook time: 4 minutes | Serves 3

1 pound (454 g) salmon fillet
1 teaspoon ground black pepper
½ teaspoon salt
1 teaspoon ground turmeric
1 teaspoon lemon juice
1 cup water

1. In the shallow bowl, mix up salt, ground black pepper, and ground turmeric. 2. Sprinkle the salmon fillet with lemon juice and rub with the spice mixture. 3. Then pour water in the instant pot and insert the steamer rack. 4. Wrap the salmon fillet in the foil and place it on the rack. 5. Close and seal the lid. 6. Cook the fish on Manual mode (High Pressure) for 4 minutes. 7. Make a quick pressure release and cut the fish on servings.

Per Serving:
calories: 205 | fat: 9g | protein: 30g | carbs: 1g | net carbs: 1g | fiber: 0g

Almond Milk Curried Fish

Prep time: 10 minutes | Cook time: 3 minutes | Serves 2

8 ounces (227 g) cod fillet, chopped
1 teaspoon curry paste
1 cup organic almond milk

1. Mix up curry paste and almond milk and pour the liquid in the instant pot. 2. Add chopped cod fillet and close the lid. 3. Cook the fish curry on Manual mode (High Pressure) for 3 minutes. 4. Then make the quick pressure release for 5 minutes.

Per Serving:
calories: 138 | fat: 4g | protein: 21g | carbs: 5g | net carbs: 5g | fiber: 0g

Mussels with Fennel and Leeks

Prep time: 20 minutes | Cook time: 6 minutes | Serves 4

1 tablespoon extra-virgin olive oil, plus extra for drizzling
1 fennel bulb, 1 tablespoon fronds minced, stalks discarded, bulb halved, cored, and sliced thin
1 leek, ends trimmed, leek halved lengthwise, sliced 1 inch thick, and washed thoroughly
4 garlic cloves, minced
3 sprigs fresh thyme
¼ teaspoon red pepper flakes
½ cup dry white wine
3 pounds (1.4 kg) mussels, scrubbed and debearded

1. Using highest sauté function, heat oil in Instant Pot until shimmering. Add fennel and leek and cook until softened, about 5 minutes. Stir in garlic, thyme sprigs, and pepper flakes and cook until fragrant, about 30 seconds. Stir in wine, then add mussels. 2. Lock lid in place and close pressure release valve. Select high pressure cook function and set cook time for 0 minutes. Once Instant Pot has reached pressure, immediately turn off pot and quick-release pressure. Carefully remove lid, allowing steam to escape away from you. 3. Discard thyme sprigs and any mussels that have not opened. Transfer mussels to individual serving bowls, sprinkle with fennel fronds, and drizzle with extra oil. Serve.

Per Serving:
calories: 384 | fat: 11g | protein: 42g | carbs: 23g | fiber: 2g | sodium: 778mg

Ginger Cod

Prep time: 10 minutes | Cook time: 20 minutes | Serves 2

1 teaspoon ginger paste
8 ounces (227 g) cod fillet, chopped
1 tablespoon coconut oil
¼ cup coconut milk

1. Melt the coconut oil in the instant pot on Sauté mode. 2. Then add ginger paste and coconut milk and bring the mixture to boil. 3. Add chopped cod and sauté the meal for 12 minutes. Stir the fish cubes with the help of the spatula from time to time.

Per Serving:
calories: 222 | fat: 15g | protein: 21g | carbs: 2g | net carbs: 1g | fiber: 1g

Louisiana Shrimp Gumbo

Prep time: 10 minutes | Cook time: 4 minutes | Serves 6

1 pound (454 g) shrimp
¼ cup chopped celery stalk
1 chili pepper, chopped
¼ cup chopped okra
1 tablespoon coconut oil
2 cups chicken broth
1 teaspoon sugar-free tomato paste

1. Put all ingredients in the instant pot and stir until you get a light red color. 2. Then close and seal the lid. 3. Cook the meal on Manual mode (High Pressure) for 4 minutes. 4. When the time is finished, allow the natural pressure release for 10 minutes.

Per Serving:
calories: 126 | fat: 4g | protein: 19g | carbs: 2g | net carbs: 2g | fiber: 0g

Steamed Halibut with Lemon

Prep time: 10 minutes | Cook time: 9 minutes | Serves 3

3 halibut fillet
½ lemon, sliced
½ teaspoon white pepper
½ teaspoon ground coriander
1 tablespoon avocado oil
1 cup water, for cooking

1. Pour water and insert the steamer rack in the instant pot. 2. Rub the fish fillets with white pepper, ground coriander, and avocado oil. 3. Place the fillets in the steamer rack. 4. Then top the halibut with sliced lemon. Close and seal the lid. 5. Cook the meal on High Pressure for 9 minutes. Make a quick pressure release.

Per Serving:
calories: 328 | fat: 7g | protein: 60g | carbs: 1g | net carbs: 1g | fiber: 0g

Salmon with Wild Rice and Orange Salad

Prep time: 20 minutes | Cook time: 18 minutes | Serves 4

1 cup wild rice, picked over and rinsed
3 tablespoons extra-virgin olive oil, divided
1½ teaspoon table salt, for cooking rice
2 oranges, plus ⅛ teaspoon grated orange zest
4 (6-ounce / 170-g) skinless salmon fillets, 1½ inches thick
1 teaspoon ground dried Aleppo pepper
½ teaspoon table salt
1 small shallot, minced
1 tablespoon red wine vinegar
2 teaspoons Dijon mustard
1 teaspoon honey
2 carrots, peeled and shredded
¼ cup chopped fresh mint

1. Combine 6 cups water, rice, 1 tablespoon oil, and 1½ teaspoons salt in Instant Pot. Lock lid in place and close pressure release valve. Select high pressure cook function and cook for 15 minutes. Turn off Instant Pot and let pressure release naturally for 15 minutes. Quick-release any remaining pressure, then carefully remove lid, allowing steam to escape away from you. Drain rice and set aside to cool slightly. Wipe pot clean with paper towels. 2. Add ½ cup water to now-empty Instant Pot. Fold sheet of aluminum foil into 16 by 6-inch sling. Slice 1 orange ¼ inch thick and shingle widthwise in 3 rows across center of sling. Sprinkle flesh side of salmon with Aleppo pepper and ½ teaspoon salt, then arrange skinned side down on top of orange slices. Using sling, lower salmon into Instant Pot; allow narrow edges of sling to rest along sides of insert. Lock lid in place and close pressure release valve. Select high pressure cook function and cook for 3 minutes. 3. Meanwhile, cut away peel and pith from remaining 1 orange. Quarter orange, then slice crosswise into ¼-inch pieces. Whisk remaining 2 tablespoons oil, shallot, vinegar, mustard, honey, and orange zest together in large bowl. Add rice, orange pieces, carrots, and mint, and gently toss to combine. Season with salt and pepper to taste. 4. Turn off Instant Pot and quick-release pressure. Carefully remove lid, allowing steam to escape away from you. Using sling, transfer salmon to large plate. Gently lift and tilt fillets with spatula to remove orange slices. Serve salmon with salad.

Per Serving:
calories: 690 | fat: 34g | protein: 43g | carbs: 51g | fiber: 5g | sodium: 770mg

Parmesan Salmon Loaf

Prep time: 15 minutes | Cook time: 25 minutes | Serves 6

12 ounces (340 g) salmon, boiled and shredded
3 eggs, beaten
½ cup almond flour
1 teaspoon garlic powder
¼ cup grated Parmesan
1 teaspoon butter, softened
1 cup water, for cooking

1. Pour water in the instant pot. 2. Mix up the rest of the ingredients in the mixing bowl and stir until smooth. 3. After this, transfer the salmon mixture in the loaf pan and flatten; insert the pan in the instant pot. Close and seal the lid. 4. Cook the meal on Manual mode (High Pressure) for 25 minutes. 5. When the cooking time is finished, make a quick pressure release and cool the loaf well before serving.

Per Serving:
calories: 172 | fat: 10g | protein: 19g | carbs: 2g | net carbs: 2g | fiber: 0g

Aromatic Monkfish Stew

Prep time: 5 minutes | Cook time: 6 minutes | Serves 6

Juice of 1 lemon
1 tablespoon fresh basil
1 tablespoon fresh parsley
1 tablespoon olive oil
1 teaspoon garlic, minced
1½ pounds (680 g) monkfish
1 tablespoon butter
1 bell pepper, chopped
1 onion, sliced
½ teaspoon cayenne pepper
½ teaspoon mixed peppercorns
¼ teaspoon turmeric powder
¼ teaspoon ground cumin
Sea salt and ground black pepper, to taste
2 cups fish stock
½ cup water
¼ cup dry white wine
2 bay leaves
1 ripe tomato, crushed

1. Stir together the lemon juice, basil, parsley, olive oil, and garlic in a ceramic dish. Add the monkfish and marinate for 30 minutes. 2. Set your Instant Pot to Sauté. Add and melt the butter. Once hot, cook the bell pepper and onion until fragrant. 3. Stir in the remaining ingredients. 4. Lock the lid. Select the Manual mode and set the cooking time for 6 minutes at High Pressure. 5. When the timer beeps, perform a quick pressure release. Carefully remove the lid. 6. Discard the bay leaves and divide your stew into serving bowls. Serve hot.

Per Serving:
calories: 153 | fat: 6.9g | protein: 18.9g | carbs: 3.8g | net carbs: 3.0g | fiber: 0.8g

Mahi-Mahi Fillets with Peppers

Prep time: 10 minutes | Cook time: 3 minutes | Serves 3

2 sprigs fresh rosemary
2 sprigs dill, tarragon
1 sprig fresh thyme
1 cup water
1 lemon, sliced
3 mahi-mahi fillets
2 tablespoons coconut oil, melted
Sea salt and ground black pepper, to taste
1 serrano pepper, seeded and sliced
1 green bell pepper, sliced
1 red bell pepper, sliced

1. Add the herbs, water, and lemon slices to the Instant Pot and insert a steamer basket. 2. Arrange the mahi-mahi fillets in the steamer basket. 3. Drizzle the melted coconut oil over the top and season with the salt and black pepper. 4. Lock the lid. Select the Manual mode and set the cooking time for 3 minutes at Low Pressure. 5. When the timer beeps, perform a natural pressure release for 10 minutes, then release any remaining pressure. Carefully remove the lid. 6. Place the peppers on top. Select the Sauté mode and let it simmer for another 1 minute. 7. Serve immediately.

Per Serving:
calories: 454 | fat: 14.7g | protein: 76.4g | carbs: 4.1g | net carbs: 3.5g | fiber: 0.6g

Rosemary Baked Haddock

Prep time: 7 minutes | Cook time: 10 minutes | Serves 2

2 eggs, beaten
12 ounces (340 g) haddock fillet, chopped
1 tablespoon cream cheese
¾ teaspoon dried rosemary
2 ounces (57 g) Parmesan, grated
1 teaspoon butter

1. Whisk the beaten eggs until homogenous. Add the cream cheese, dried rosemary, and dill. 2. Grease the springform with the butter and place the haddock inside. 3. Pour the egg mixture over the fish and add sprinkle with Parmesan. 4. Set the Manual mode (High Pressure) and cook for 5 minutes. Then make a natural release pressure for 5 minutes.

Per Serving:
calories: 380 | fat: 16g | protein: 56g | carbs: 18g | net carbs: 18g | fiber: 0g

Rainbow Trout with Mixed Greens

Prep time: 5 minutes | Cook time: 12 minutes | Serves 4

1 cup water
1½ (680 g) pounds rainbow trout fillets
4 tablespoons melted butter, divided
Sea salt and ground black pepper, to taste
1 pound (454 g) mixed greens, trimmed and torn into pieces
1 bunch of scallions
½ cup chicken broth
1 tablespoon apple cider vinegar
1 teaspoon cayenne pepper

1. Pour the water into your Instant Pot and insert a steamer basket. 2. Add the fish to the basket. Drizzle with 1 tablespoon of the melted butter and season with the salt and black pepper. 3. Lock the lid. Select the Manual mode and set the cooking time for 12 minutes at Low pressure. 4. When the timer beeps, perform a quick pressure release. Carefully remove the lid. 5. Wipe down the Instant Pot with a damp cloth. 6. Add and warm the remaining 3 tablespoons of butter. Once hot, add the greens, scallions, broth, vinegar, and cayenne pepper and cook until the greens are wilted, stirring occasionally. 7. Serve the prepared trout fillets with the greens on the side.

Per Serving:
calories: 349 | fat: 18.1g | protein: 38.9g | carbs: 7.7g | net carbs: 3.3g | fiber: 4.4g

Salmon Fillets and Bok Choy

Prep time: 5 minutes | Cook time: 8 minutes | Serves 4

1½ cups water
2 tablespoons unsalted butter
4 (1-inch thick) salmon fillets
½ teaspoon cayenne pepper
Sea salt and freshly ground pepper, to taste
2 cups Bok choy, sliced
1 cup chicken broth
3 cloves garlic, minced
1 teaspoon grated lemon zest
½ teaspoon dried dill weed

1. Pour the water into your Instant Pot and insert a trivet. 2. Brush the salmon with the melted butter and season with the cayenne pepper, salt, and black pepper on all sides. 3. Lock the lid. Select the Manual mode and set the cooking time for 3 minutes at Low Pressure. 4. When the timer beeps, perform a quick pressure release. Carefully remove the lid. 5. Add the remaining ingredients. 6. Lock the lid. Select the Manual mode and set the cooking time for 5 minutes at High Pressure. 7. When the timer beeps, perform a quick pressure release. Carefully remove the lid. 8. Serve the poached salmon with the veggies on the side.

Per Serving:
calories: 209 | fat: 11.3g | protein: 23.9g | carbs: 2.1g | net carbs: 1.6g | fiber: 0.5g

Shrimp Louie Salad with Thousand Island Dressing

Prep time: 5 minutes | Cook time: 20 minutes | Serves 4

2 cups water
1½ teaspoons fine sea salt
1 pound medium shrimp, peeled and deveined
4 large eggs
Thousand island Dressing
¼ cup no-sugar-added ketchup
¼ cup mayonnaise
1 tablespoon fresh lemon juice
1 teaspoon Worcestershire sauce
⅛ teaspoon cayenne pepper
Freshly ground black pepper
2 green onions, white and green parts, sliced thinly
2 hearts romaine lettuce or 1 head iceberg lettuce, shredded
1 English cucumber, sliced
8 radishes, sliced
1 cup cherry tomatoes, sliced
1 large avocado, pitted, peeled, and sliced

1. Combine the water and salt in the Instant Pot and stir to dissolve the salt. 2. Secure the lid and set the Pressure Release to Sealing. Select the Steam setting and set the cooking time for 0 (zero) minutes at low pressure. (The pot will take about 10 minutes to come up to pressure before the cooking program begins.) 3. Meanwhile, prepare an ice bath. 4. When the cooking program ends, perform a quick release by moving the Pressure Release to Venting. Open the pot and stir in the shrimp, using a wooden spoon to nudge them all down into the water. Cover the pot and leave the shrimp for 2 minutes on the Keep Warm setting. The shrimp will gently poach and cook through. Uncover the pot and, wearing heat-resistant mitts, lift out the inner pot and drain the shrimp in a colander. Transfer them to the ice bath to cool for 5 minutes, then drain them in the colander and set aside in the refrigerator. 5. Rinse out the inner pot and return it to the housing. Pour in 1 cup water and place the wire metal steam rack into the pot. Place the eggs on top of the steam rack. 6. Secure the lid and set the Pressure Release to Sealing. Press the Cancel button to reset the cooking program, then select the Egg, Pressure Cook, or Manual setting and set the cooking time for 5 minutes at high pressure. (The pot will take about 5 minutes to come up to pressure before the cooking program begins.) 7. While the eggs are cooking, prepare another ice bath. 8. When the cooking program ends, let the pressure release naturally for 5 minutes, then move the Pressure Release to Venting to release any remaining steam. Using tongs, transfer the eggs to the ice bath and let cool for 5 minutes. 9. To make the dressing: In a small bowl, stir together the ketchup, mayonnaise, lemon juice, Worcestershire sauce, cayenne, ¼ teaspoon black pepper, and green onions. 10. Arrange the lettuce, cucumber, radishes, tomatoes, and avocado on individual plates or in large, shallow individual bowls. Mound the cooked shrimp in the center of each salad. Peel the eggs, quarter them lengthwise, and place the quarters around the shrimp. 11. Spoon the dressing over the salads and top with additional black pepper. Serve right away.

Per Serving:
calories: 407 | fat: 23g | protein: 35g | carbs: 16g | sugars: 10g | fiber: 6g | sodium: 1099mg

Cod Fillet with Olives

Prep time: 15 minutes | Cook time: 10 minutes | Serves 2

8 ounces (227 g) cod fillet
¼ cup sliced olives
1 teaspoon olive oil
¼ teaspoon salt
1 cup water, for cooking

1. Pour water and insert the steamer rack in the instant pot. 2. Then cut the cod fillet into 2 servings and sprinkle with salt and olive oil. 3. Then place the fish on the foil and top with the sliced olives. Wrap the fish and transfer it in the steamer rack. 4. Close and seal the lid. Cook the fish on Manual mode (High Pressure) for 10 minutes. 5. Allow the natural pressure release for 5 minutes.

Per Serving:
calories: 130 | fat: 5g | protein: 20g | carbs: 1g | net carbs: 1g | fiber: 0g

Tuna Fillets with Lemon Butter

Prep time: 5 minutes | Cook time: 3 minutes | Serves 4

1 cup water
⅓ cup lemon juice
2 sprigs fresh thyme
2 sprigs fresh parsley
2 sprigs fresh rosemary
1 pound (454 g) tuna fillets
4 cloves garlic, pressed
Sea salt, to taste
¼ teaspoon black pepper, or more to taste
2 tablespoons butter, melted
1 lemon, sliced

1. Pour the water into your Instant Pot. Add the lemon juice, thyme, parsley, and rosemary and insert a steamer basket. 2. Put the tuna fillets in the basket. Top with the garlic and season with the salt and black pepper. 3. Drizzle the melted butter over the fish fillets and place the lemon slices on top. 4. Lock the lid. Select the Manual mode and set the cooking time for 3 minutes at Low Pressure. 5. When the timer beeps, perform a quick pressure release. Carefully remove the lid. Serve immediately.

Per Serving:
calories: 178 | fat: 7.0g | protein: 25.4g | carbs: 3.5g | net carbs: 3.2g | fiber: 0.3g

Cod with Warm Tabbouleh Salad

Prep time: 10 minutes | Cook time: 6 minutes | Serves 4

1 cup medium-grind bulgur, rinsed
1 teaspoon table salt, divided
1 lemon, sliced ¼ inch thick, plus 2 tablespoons juice
4 (6-ounce / 170-g) skinless cod fillets, 1½ inches thick
3 tablespoons extra-virgin olive oil, divided, plus extra for drizzling
¼ teaspoon pepper
1 small shallot, minced
10 ounces (283 g) cherry tomatoes, halved
1 cup chopped fresh parsley
½ cup chopped fresh mint

1. Arrange trivet included with Instant Pot in base of insert and add ½ cup water. Fold sheet of aluminum foil into 16 by 6-inch sling, then rest 1½-quart round soufflé dish in center of sling. Combine 1 cup water, bulgur, and ½ teaspoon salt in dish. Using sling, lower soufflé dish into pot and onto trivet; allow narrow edges of sling to rest along sides of insert. 2. Lock lid in place and close pressure release valve. Select high pressure cook function and cook for 3 minutes. Turn off Instant Pot and quick-release pressure. Carefully remove lid, allowing steam to escape away from you. Using sling, transfer soufflé dish to wire rack; set aside to cool. Remove trivet; do not discard sling or water in pot. 3. Arrange lemon slices widthwise in 2 rows across center of sling. Brush cod with 1 tablespoon oil and sprinkle with remaining ½ teaspoon salt and pepper. Arrange cod skinned side down in even layer on top of lemon slices. Using sling, lower cod into Instant Pot; allow narrow edges of sling to rest along sides of insert. Lock lid in place and close pressure release valve. Select high pressure cook function and cook for 3 minutes. 4. Meanwhile, whisk remaining 2 tablespoons oil, lemon juice, and shallot together in large bowl. Add bulgur, tomatoes, parsley, and mint, and gently toss to combine. Season with salt and pepper to taste. 5. Turn off Instant Pot and quick-release pressure. Carefully remove lid, allowing steam to escape away from you. Using sling, transfer cod to large plate. Gently lift and tilt fillets with spatula to remove lemon slices. Serve cod with salad, drizzling individual portions with extra oil.

Per Serving:
calories: 380 | fat: 12g | protein: 36g | carbs: 32g | fiber: 6g | sodium: 690mg

Herb-Crusted Cod Steaks

Prep time: 5 minutes | Cook time: 4 minutes | Serves 4

1½ cups water
2 tablespoons garlic-infused oil
4 cod steaks, 1½-inch thick
Sea salt, to taste
½ teaspoon mixed peppercorns, crushed
2 sprigs thyme
1 sprig rosemary
1 yellow onion, sliced

1. Pour the water into your Instant Pot and insert a trivet. 2. Rub the garlic-infused oil into the cod steaks and season with the salt and crushed peppercorns. 3. Lower the cod steaks onto the trivet, skin-side down. Top with the thyme, rosemary, and onion. 4. Lock the lid. Select the Manual mode and set the cooking time for 4 minutes at High Pressure. 5. When the timer beeps, perform a quick pressure release. Carefully remove the lid. 6. Serve immediately.

Per Serving:
calories: 149 | fat: 7.3g | protein: 18.0g | carbs: 2.0g | net carbs: 1.5g | fiber: 0.5g

Salmon with Lemon-Garlic Mashed Cauliflower

Prep time: 15 minutes | Cook time: 10 minutes | Serves 4

2 tablespoons extra-virgin olive oil
4 garlic cloves, peeled and smashed
½ cup chicken or vegetable broth
¾ teaspoon table salt, divided
1 large head cauliflower (3 pounds / 1.4 kg), cored and cut into 2-inch florets
4 (6-ounce / 170-g) skinless salmon fillets, 1½ inches thick
½ teaspoon ras el hanout
½ teaspoon grated lemon zest
3 scallions, sliced thin
1 tablespoon sesame seeds, toasted

1. Using highest sauté function, cook oil and garlic in Instant Pot until garlic is fragrant and light golden brown, about 3 minutes. Turn off Instant Pot, then stir in broth and ¼ teaspoon salt. Arrange cauliflower in pot in even layer. 2. Fold sheet of aluminum foil into 16 by 6-inch sling. Sprinkle flesh side of salmon with ras el hanout and remaining ½ teaspoon salt, then arrange skinned side down in center of sling. Using sling, lower salmon into Instant Pot on top of cauliflower; allow narrow edges of sling to rest along sides of insert. Lock lid in place and close pressure release valve. Select high pressure cook function and cook for 2 minutes. 3. Turn off Instant Pot and quick-release pressure. Carefully remove lid, allowing steam to escape away from you. Using sling, transfer salmon to large plate. Tent with foil and let rest while finishing cauliflower. 4. Using potato masher, mash cauliflower mixture until no large chunks remain. Using highest sauté function, cook cauliflower, stirring often, until slightly thickened, about 3 minutes. Stir in lemon zest and season with salt and pepper to taste. Serve salmon with cauliflower, sprinkling individual portions with scallions and sesame seeds.

Per Serving:
calories: 480 | fat: 31g | protein: 38g | carbs: 9g | fiber: 3g | sodium: 650mg

Poached Salmon

Prep time: 10 minutes | Cook time: 5 minutes | Serves 4

1 lemon, sliced ¼ inch thick
4 (6-ounce / 170-g) skinless salmon fillets, 1½ inches thick
½ teaspoon table salt
¼ teaspoon pepper

1. Add ½ cup water to Instant Pot. Fold sheet of aluminum foil into 16 by 6-inch sling. Arrange lemon slices widthwise in 2 rows across center of sling. Sprinkle flesh side of salmon with salt and pepper, then arrange skinned side down on top of lemon slices. 2. Using sling, lower salmon into Instant Pot; allow narrow edges of sling to rest along sides of insert. Lock lid in place and close pressure release valve. Select high pressure cook function and cook for 3 minutes. 3. Turn off Instant Pot and quick-release pressure. Carefully remove lid, allowing steam to escape away from you. Using sling, transfer salmon to large plate. Gently lift and tilt fillets with spatula to remove lemon slices. Serve.

Per Serving:
calories: 350 | fat: 23g | protein: 35g | carbs: 0g | fiber: 0g | sodium: 390mg

Cayenne Cod

Prep time: 10 minutes | Cook time: 10 minutes | Serves 2

2 cod fillets
¼ teaspoon chili powder
½ teaspoon cayenne pepper
½ teaspoon dried oregano
1 tablespoon lime juice
2 tablespoons avocado oil

1. Rub the cod fillets with chili powder, cayenne pepper, dried oregano, and sprinkle with lime juice. 2. Then pour the avocado oil in the instant pot and heat it up on Sauté mode for 2 minutes. 3. Put the cod fillets in the hot oil and cook for 5 minutes. 4. Then flip the fish on another side and cook for 5 minutes more.

Per Serving:
calories: 144 | fat: 3g | protein: 20g | carbs: 2g | net carbs: 1g | fiber: 1g

Lemon Butter Mahi Mahi

Prep time: 10 minutes | Cook time: 9 minutes | Serves 4

1 pound (454 g) mahi-mahi fillet
1 teaspoon grated lemon zest
1 tablespoon lemon juice
1 tablespoon butter, softened
½ teaspoon salt
1 cup water, for cooking

1. Cut the fish on 4 servings and sprinkle with lemon zest, lemon juice, salt, and rub with softened butter. 2. Then put the fish in the baking pan in one layer. 3. Pour water and insert the steamer rack in the instant pot. 4. Put the mold with fish on the rack. Close and seal the lid. 5. Cook the Mahi Mahi on Manual mode (High Pressure) for 9 minutes. Make a quick pressure release.

Per Serving:
calories: 128 | fat: 4g | protein: 21g | carbs: 0g | net carbs: 0g | fiber: 0g

Mediterranean Salmon with Whole-Wheat Couscous

Prep time: 5 minutes | Cook time: 30 minutes | Serves 4

Couscous
1 cup whole-wheat couscous
1 cup water
1 tablespoon extra-virgin olive oil
1 teaspoon dried basil
¼ teaspoon fine sea salt
1 pint cherry or grape tomatoes, halved
8 ounces zucchini, halved lengthwise, then sliced crosswise ¼ inch thick

Salmon
1 pound skinless salmon fillet
2 teaspoons extra-virgin olive oil
1 tablespoon fresh lemon juice
1 garlic clove, minced
¼ teaspoon dried oregano
¼ teaspoon fine sea salt
¼ teaspoon freshly ground black pepper
1 tablespoon capers, drained
Lemon wedges for serving

1. Pour 1 cup water into the Instant Pot. Have ready two-tier stackable stainless-steel containers. 2. To make the couscous: In one of the containers, stir together the couscous, water, oil, basil, and salt. Sprinkle the tomatoes and zucchini over the top. 3. To make the salmon: Place the salmon fillet in the second container. In a small bowl, whisk together the oil, lemon juice, garlic, oregano, salt, pepper, and capers. Spoon the oil mixture over the top of the salmon. 4. Place the container with the couscous and vegetables on the bottom and the salmon container on top. Cover the top container with its lid and then latch the containers together. Grasping the handle, lower the containers into the Instant Pot. 5. Secure the lid and set the Pressure Release to Sealing. Select the Pressure Cook or Manual setting and set the cooking time for 20 minutes at high pressure. (The pot will take about 10 minutes to come up to pressure before the cooking program begins.) 6. When the cooking program ends, let the pressure release naturally for 5 minutes, then move the Pressure Release to Venting to release any remaining steam. Open the pot and, wearing heat-resistant mitts, lift out the stacked containers. Unlatch, unstack, and open the containers, taking care not to get burned by the steam. 7. Using a fork, fluff the couscous and mix in the vegetables. Spoon the couscous onto plates, then use a spatula to cut the salmon into four pieces and place a piece on top of each couscous serving. Serve right away, with lemon wedges on the side.

Per Serving:
calories: 427 | fat: 18g | protein: 28g | carbs: 36g | sugars: 2g | fiber: 6g | sodium: 404mg

Braised Striped Bass with Zucchini and Tomatoes

Prep time: 20 minutes | Cook time: 16 minutes | Serves 4

2 tablespoons extra-virgin olive oil, divided, plus extra for drizzling
3 zucchini (8 ounces / 227 g each), halved lengthwise and sliced ¼ inch thick
1 onion, chopped
¾ teaspoon table salt, divided
3 garlic cloves, minced
1 teaspoon minced fresh oregano or ¼ teaspoon dried
¼ teaspoon red pepper flakes
1 (28-ounce / 794-g) can whole peeled tomatoes, drained with juice reserved, halved
1½ pounds (680 g) skinless striped bass, 1½ inches thick, cut into 2-inch pieces
¼ teaspoon pepper
2 tablespoons chopped pitted kalamata olives
2 tablespoons shredded fresh mint

1. Using highest sauté function, heat 1 tablespoon oil in Instant Pot for 5 minutes (or until just smoking). Add zucchini and cook until tender, about 5 minutes; transfer to bowl and set aside. 2. Add remaining 1 tablespoon oil, onion, and ¼ teaspoon salt to now-empty pot and cook, using highest sauté function, until onion is softened, about 5 minutes. Stir in garlic, oregano, and pepper flakes and cook until fragrant, about 30 seconds. Stir in tomatoes and reserved juice. 3. Sprinkle bass with remaining ½ teaspoon salt and pepper. Nestle bass into tomato mixture and spoon some of cooking liquid on top of pieces. Lock lid in place and close pressure release valve. Select high pressure cook function and set cook time for 0 minutes. Once Instant Pot has reached pressure, immediately turn off pot and quick-release pressure. Carefully remove lid, allowing steam to escape away from you. 4. Transfer bass to plate, tent with aluminum foil, and let rest while finishing vegetables. Stir zucchini into pot and let sit until heated through, about 5 minutes. Stir in olives and season with salt and pepper to taste. Serve bass with vegetables, sprinkling individual portions with mint and drizzling with extra oil.

Per Serving:
calories: 302 | fat: 12g | protein: 34g | carbs: 15g | fiber: 6g | sodium: 618mg

Clam Chowder with Bacon and Celery

Prep time: 10 minutes | Cook time: 4 minutes | Serves 2

5 ounces (142 g) clams
1 ounce (28 g) bacon, chopped
3 ounces (85 g) celery, chopped
½ cup water
½ cup heavy cream

1. Cook the bacon on Sauté mode for 1 minute. 2. Then add clams, celery, water, and heavy cream. 3. Close and seal the lid. 4. Cook the seafood on steam mode (High Pressure) for 3 minutes. Make a quick pressure release. 5. Ladle the clams with the heavy cream mixture in the bowls.

Per Serving:
calories: 221 | fat: 17g | protein: 7g | carbs: 10g | net carbs: 9g | fiber: 1g

Perch Fillets with Red Curry

Prep time: 5 minutes | Cook time: 6 minutes | Serves 4

1 cup water
2 sprigs rosemary
1 large-sized lemon, sliced
1 pound (454 g) perch fillets
1 teaspoon cayenne pepper
Sea salt and ground black pepper, to taste
1 tablespoon red curry paste
1 tablespoons butter

1. Add the water, rosemary, and lemon slices to the Instant Pot and insert a trivet. 2. Season the perch fillets with the cayenne pepper, salt, and black pepper. Spread the red curry paste and butter over the fillets. 3. Arrange the fish fillets on the trivet. 4. Lock the lid. Select the Manual mode and set the cooking time for 6 minutes at Low Pressure. 5. When the timer beeps, perform a quick pressure release. Carefully remove the lid. Serve with your favorite keto sides.

Per Serving:
calories: 142 | fat: 4.3g | protein: 22.5g | carbs: 3.2g | net carbs: 1.6g | fiber: 1.6g

Garlic Tuna Casserole

Prep time: 7 minutes | Cook time: 9 minutes | Serves 4

1 cup grated Parmesan or shredded Cheddar cheese, plus more for topping
1 (8-ounce / 227-g) package cream cheese (1 cup), softened
½ cup chicken broth
1 tablespoon unsalted butter
½ small head cauliflower, cut into 1-inch pieces
1 cup diced onions
2 cloves garlic, minced, or more to taste
2 (4-ounce / 113-g) cans chunk tuna packed in water, drained
1½ cups cold water
For Garnish:
Chopped fresh flat-leaf parsley
Sliced green onions
Cherry tomatoes, halved
Ground black pepper

1. In a blender, add the Parmesan cheese, cream cheese, and broth and blitz until smooth. Set aside. 2. Set your Instant Pot to Sauté. Add and melt the butter. Add the cauliflower and onions and sauté for 4 minutes, or until the onions are softened. Fold in the garlic and sauté for an additional 1 minute. 3. Place the cheese sauce and tuna in a large bowl. Mix in the veggies and stir well. Transfer the mixture to a casserole dish. 4. Place a trivet in the bottom of your Instant Pot and add the cold water. Use a foil sling, lower the casserole dish onto the trivet. Tuck in the sides of the sling. 5. Lock the lid. Select the Manual mode and set the cooking time for 5 minutes for al dente cauliflower or 8 minutes for softer cauliflower at High Pressure. 6. Once cooking is complete, do a quick pressure release. Carefully open the lid. 7. Serve topped with the cheese and garnished with the parsley, green onions, cherry tomatoes, and freshly ground pepper.

Per Serving:
calories: 378 | fat: 26.8g | protein: 23.8g | carbs: 10.5g | net carbs: 9.3g | fiber: 1.2g

Foil-Pack Haddock with Spinach

Prep time: 15 minutes | Cook time: 15 minutes | Serves 4

12 ounces (340 g) haddock fillet
1 cup spinach
1 tablespoon avocado oil
1 teaspoon minced garlic
½ teaspoon ground coriander
1 cup water, for cooking

1. Blend the spinach until smooth and mix up with avocado oil, ground coriander, and minced garlic. 2. Then cut the haddock into 4 fillets and place on the foil. 3. Top the fish fillets with spinach mixture and place them on the rack. 4. Pour water and insert the rack in the instant pot. 5. Close and seal the lid and cook the haddock on Manual (High Pressure) for 15 minutes. 6. Do a quick pressure release.

Per Serving:
calories: 103 | fat: 1g | protein: 21g | carbs: 1g | net carbs: 1g | fiber: 0g

Lemony Fish and Asparagus

Prep time: 5 minutes | Cook time: 3 minutes | Serves 4

2 lemons
2 cups cold water
2 tablespoons extra-virgin olive oil
4 (4-ounce / 113-g) white fish fillets, such as cod or haddock
1 teaspoon fine sea salt
1 teaspoon ground black pepper
1 bundle asparagus, ends trimmed
2 tablespoons lemon juice
Fresh dill, for garnish

1. Grate the zest off the lemons until you have about 1 tablespoon and set the zest aside. Slice the lemons into ⅛-inch slices. 2. Pour the water into the Instant Pot. Add 1 tablespoon of the olive oil to each of two stackable steamer pans. 3. Sprinkle the fish on all sides with the lemon zest, salt, and pepper. 4. Arrange two fillets in each steamer pan and top each with the lemon slices and then the asparagus. Sprinkle the asparagus with the salt and drizzle the lemon juice over the top. 5. Stack the steamer pans in the Instant Pot. Cover the top steamer pan with its lid. 6. Lock the lid. Select the Manual mode and set the cooking time for 3 minutes at High Pressure. 7. Once cooking is complete, do a natural pressure release for 7 minutes, then release any remaining pressure. Carefully open the lid. 8. Lift the steamer pans out of the Instant Pot. 9. Transfer the fish and asparagus to a serving plate. Garnish with the lemon slices and dill. 10. Serve immediately.

Per Serving:
calories: 163 | fat: 5.8g | protein: 23.7g | carbs: 7.1g | net carbs: 4.1g | fiber: 3.0g

Salade Niçoise with Oil-Packed Tuna

Prep time: 5 minutes | Cook time: 20 minutes | Serves 4

8 ounces small red potatoes, quartered
8 ounces green beans, trimmed
4 large eggs
french vinaigrette
2 tablespoons extra-virgin olive oil
2 tablespoons cold-pressed avocado oil
2 tablespoons white wine vinegar
1 tablespoon water
1 teaspoon Dijon mustard
½ teaspoon dried oregano
¼ teaspoon fine sea salt
1 tablespoon minced shallot
2 hearts romaine lettuce, leaves separated and torn into bite-size pieces
½ cup grape tomatoes, halved
¼ cup pitted Niçoise or Greek olives
One 7-ounce can oil-packed tuna, drained and flaked
Freshly ground black pepper
1 tablespoon chopped fresh flat-leaf parsley

1. Pour 1 cup water into the Instant Pot and place a steamer basket into the pot. Add the potatoes, green beans, and eggs to the basket. 2. Secure the lid and set the Pressure Release to Sealing. Select the Steam setting and set the cooking time for 3 minutes at high pressure. (The pot will take about 15 minutes to come up to pressure before the cooking program begins.) 3. To make the vinaigrette: While the vegetables and eggs are steaming, in a small jar or other small container with a tight-fitting lid, combine the olive oil, avocado oil, vinegar, water, mustard, oregano, salt, and shallot and shake vigorously to emulsify. Set aside. 4. Prepare an ice bath. 5. When the cooking program ends, perform a quick release by moving the Pressure Release to Venting. Open the pot and, wearing heat-resistant mitts, lift out the steamer basket. Using tongs, transfer the eggs and green beans to the ice bath, leaving the potatoes in the steamer basket. 6. While the eggs and green beans are cooling, divide the lettuce, tomatoes, olives, and tuna among four shallow individual bowls. Drain the eggs and green beans. Peel and halve the eggs lengthwise, then arrange them on the salads along with the green beans and potatoes. 7. Spoon the vinaigrette over the salads and sprinkle with the pepper and parsley. Serve right away.

Per Serving:
calories: 367 | fat: 23g | protein: 20g | carbs: 23g | sugars: 7g | fiber: 4g | sodium: 268mg

Lemon Shrimp Skewers

Prep time: 10 minutes | Cook time: 2 minutes | Serves 4

1 tablespoon lemon juice
1 teaspoon coconut aminos
12 ounces (340 g) shrimp, peeled
1 teaspoon olive oil
1 cup water

1. Put the shrimp in the mixing bowl. 2. Add lemon juice, coconut aminos, and olive oil. 3. Then string the shrimp on the skewers. 4. Pour water in the instant pot. 5. Then insert the trivet. 6. Put the shrimp skewers on the trivet. 7. Close the lid and cook the seafood on Manual mode (High Pressure) for 2 minutes. 8. When the time is finished, make a quick pressure release.

Per Serving:
calories: 113 | fat: 3g | protein: 19g | carbs: 2g | net carbs: 2g | fiber: 0g

Cod Fillets with Cherry Tomatoes

Prep time: 2 minutes | Cook time: 15 minutes | Serves 4

2 tablespoons butter
¼ cup diced onion
1 clove garlic, minced
1 cup cherry tomatoes, halved
¼ cup chicken broth
¼ teaspoon dried thyme
¼ teaspoon salt
⅛ teaspoon pepper
4 (4-ounce / 113-g) cod fillets
1 cup water
¼ cup fresh chopped Italian parsley

1. Set your Instant Pot to Sauté. Add and melt the butter. Once hot, add the onions and cook until softened. Add the garlic and cook for another 30 seconds. 2. Add the tomatoes, chicken broth, thyme, salt, and pepper. Continue to cook for 5 to 7 minutes, or until the tomatoes start to soften. 3. Pour the sauce into a glass bowl. Add the fish fillets. Cover with foil. 4. Pour the water into the Instant Pot and insert a trivet. Place the bowl on top. 5. Lock the lid. Select the Manual mode and set the cooking time for 3 minutes at Low Pressure. 6. Once cooking is complete, do a quick pressure release. Carefully open the lid. 7. Sprinkle with the fresh parsley and serve.

Per Serving:
calories: 159 | fat: 7.9g | protein: 21.7g | carbs: 3.0g | net carbs: 2.1g| fiber: 0.9g

Cajun Cod Fillet

Prep time: 10 minutes | Cook time: 4 minutes | Serves 2

10 ounces (283 g) cod fillet
1 tablespoon olive oil
1 teaspoon Cajun seasoning
2 tablespoons coconut aminos

1. Sprinkle the cod fillet with coconut aminos and Cajun seasoning. 2. Then heat up olive oil in the instant pot on Sauté mode. 3. Add the spiced cod fillet and cook it for 4 minutes from each side. 4. Then cut it into halves and sprinkle with the oily liquid from the instant pot.

Per Serving:
calories: 189 | fat: 8g | protein: 25g | carbs: 3g | net carbs: 3g | fiber: 0g

Salmon with Dill Butter

Prep time: 7 minutes | Cook time: 8 minutes | Serves 2

1 teaspoon salt
2 tablespoons chopped fresh dill
10 ounces (283 g) salmon fillet
¼ cup butter
½ cup water

1. Put butter and salt in the baking pan. 2. Add salmon fillet and dill. Cover the pan with foil. 3. Pour water in the instant pot and insert the baking pan with fish inside. 4. Set the Steam mode and cook the salmon for 8 minutes. 5. Unwrap the cooked salmon and serve!

Per Serving:
calories: 399 | fat: 32g | protein: 28g | carbs: 2g | net carbs: 2g | fiber: 0g

Salmon Steaks with Garlicky Yogurt

Prep time: 2 minutes | Cook time: 4 minutes | Serves 4

1 cup water
2 tablespoons olive oil
4 salmon steaks
Coarse sea salt and ground black pepper, to taste
Garlicky Yogurt:
1 (8-ounce / 227-g) container full-fat Greek yogurt
2 cloves garlic, minced
2 tablespoons mayonnaise
⅓ teaspoon Dijon mustard

1. Pour the water into the Instant Pot and insert a trivet. 2. Rub the olive oil into the fish and sprinkle with the salt and black pepper on all sides. Put the fish on the trivet. 3. Lock the lid. Select the Manual mode and set the cooking time for 4 minutes at High Pressure. 4. When the timer beeps, perform a quick pressure release. Carefully remove the lid. 5. Meanwhile, stir together all the ingredients for the garlicky yogurt in a bowl. 6. Serve the salmon steaks alongside the garlicky yogurt.

Per Serving:
calories: 128 | fat: 11.2g | protein: 2.5g | carbs:4.9g | net carbs: 4.7g | fiber: 0.2g

Fish Tagine

Prep time: 25 minutes | Cook time: 12 minutes | Serves 4

2 tablespoons extra-virgin olive oil, plus extra for drizzling
1 large onion, halved and sliced ¼ inch thick
1 pound (454 g) carrots, peeled, halved lengthwise, and sliced ¼ inch thick
2 (2-inch) strips orange zest, plus 1 teaspoon grated zest
¾ teaspoon table salt, divided
2 tablespoons tomato paste
4 garlic cloves, minced, divided
1¼ teaspoons paprika
1 teaspoon ground cumin
¼ teaspoon red pepper flakes
¼ teaspoon saffron threads, crumbled
1 (8-ounce / 227-g) bottle clam juice
1½ pounds (680 g) skinless halibut fillets, 1½ inches thick, cut into 2-inch pieces
¼ cup pitted oil-cured black olives, quartered
2 tablespoons chopped fresh parsley
1 teaspoon sherry vinegar

1. Using highest sauté function, heat oil in Instant Pot until shimmering. Add onion, carrots, orange zest strips, and ¼ teaspoon salt, and cook until vegetables are softened and lightly browned, 10 to 12 minutes. Stir in tomato paste, three-quarters of garlic, paprika, cumin, pepper flakes, and saffron and cook until fragrant, about 30 seconds. Stir in clam juice, scraping up any browned bits. 2. Sprinkle halibut with remaining ½ teaspoon salt. Nestle halibut into onion mixture and spoon some of cooking liquid on top of pieces. Lock lid in place and close pressure release valve. Select high pressure cook function and set cook time for 0 minutes. Once Instant Pot has reached pressure, immediately turn off pot and quick-release pressure. 3. Discard orange zest. Gently stir in olives, parsley, vinegar, grated orange zest, and remaining garlic. Season with salt and pepper to taste. Drizzle extra oil over individual portions before serving.

Per Serving:
calories: 310 | fat: 15g | protein: 34g | carbs: 18g | fiber: 4g | sodium: 820mg

Steamed Lobster Tails with Thyme

Prep time: 10 minutes | Cook time: 4 minutes | Serves 4

4 lobster tails
1 tablespoon butter, softened
1 teaspoon dried thyme
1 cup water

1. Pour water and insert the steamer rack in the instant pot. 2. Put the lobster tails on the rack and close the lid. 3. Cook the meal on Manual mode (High Pressure) for 4 minutes. Make a quick pressure release. 4. After this, mix up butter and dried thyme. Peel the lobsters and rub them with thyme butter.

Per Serving:
calories: 126 | fat: 3g | protein: 24g | carbs: 0g | net carbs: 0g | fiber: 0g

Mascarpone Tilapia with Nutmeg

Prep time: 10 minutes | Cook time: 20 minutes | Serves 2

10 ounces (283 g) tilapia
½ cup mascarpone
1 garlic clove, diced
1 teaspoon ground nutmeg
1 tablespoon olive oil
½ teaspoon salt

1. Pour olive oil in the instant pot. 2. Add diced garlic and sauté it for 4 minutes. 3. Add tilapia and sprinkle it with ground nutmeg. Sauté the fish for 3 minutes per side. 4. Add mascarpone and close the lid. 5. Sauté tilapia for 10 minutes.

Per Serving:
calories: 293 | fat: 17g | protein: 33g | carbs: 3g | net carbs: 2g | fiber: 1g

Tuna Salad with Tomatoes and Peppers

Prep time: 10 minutes | Cook time: 4 minutes | Serves 4

1½ cups water
1 pound (454 g) tuna steaks
1 green bell pepper, sliced
1 red bell pepper, sliced
2 Roma tomatoes, sliced
1 head lettuce
1 red onion, chopped
2 tablespoons Kalamata olives, pitted and halved
2 tablespoons extra-virgin olive oil
2 tablespoons balsamic vinegar
½ teaspoon chili flakes
Sea salt, to taste

1. Add the water to the Instant Pot and insert a steamer basket. 2. Arrange the tuna steaks in the basket. Put the bell peppers and tomato slices on top. 3. Lock the lid. Select the Manual mode and set the cooking time for 4 minutes at High Pressure. 4. When the timer beeps, perform a quick pressure release. Carefully remove the lid. 5. Flake the fish with a fork. 6. Divide the lettuce leaves among 4 serving plates to make a bed for your salad. Add the onion and olives. Drizzle with the olive oil and balsamic vinegar. 7. Season with the chili flakes and salt. Place the prepared fish, tomatoes, and bell peppers on top. 8. Serve immediately.

Per Serving:
calories: 170 | fat: 4.8g | protein: 23.9g | carbs: 7.6g | net carbs: 6.0g | fiber: 1.6g

Coconut Milk-Braised Squid

Prep time: 10 minutes | Cook time: 20 minutes | Serves 3

1 pound (454 g) squid, sliced
1 teaspoon sugar-free tomato paste
1 cup coconut milk
1 teaspoon cayenne pepper
½ teaspoon salt

1. Put all ingredients from the list above in the instant pot. 2. Close and seal the lid and cook the squid on Manual (High Pressure) for 20 minutes. 3. When the cooking time is finished, do the quick pressure release. 4. Serve the squid with coconut milk gravy.

Per Serving:
calories: 326 | fat: 21g | protein: 25g | carbs: 10g | net carbs: 8g | fiber: 2g

Haddock and Veggie Foil Packets

Prep time: 5 minutes | Cook time: 10 minutes | Serves 4

1½ cups water
1 lemon, sliced
2 bell peppers, sliced
1 brown onion, sliced into rings
4 sprigs parsley
2 sprigs thyme
2 sprigs rosemary
4 haddock fillets
Sea salt, to taste
⅓ teaspoon ground black pepper, or more to taste
2 tablespoons extra-virgin olive oil

1. Pour the water and lemon into your Instant Pot and insert a steamer basket. 2. Assemble the packets with large sheets of heavy-duty foil. 3. Place the peppers, onion rings, parsley, thyme, and rosemary in the center of each foil. Place the fish fillets on top of the veggies. 4. Sprinkle with the salt and black pepper and drizzle the olive oil over the fillets. Place the packets in the steamer basket. 5. Lock the lid. Select the Manual mode and set the cooking time for 10 minutes at Low Pressure. 6. When the timer beeps, perform a quick pressure release. Carefully remove the lid. 7. Serve warm.

Per Serving:
calories: 218 | fat: 7.7g | protein: 32.3g | carbs: 4.8g | net carbs: 4.0g | fiber: 0.8g

Trout Casserole

Prep time: 5 minutes | Cook time: 10 minutes | Serves 3

1½ cups water
1½ tablespoons olive oil
3 plum tomatoes, sliced
½ teaspoon dried oregano
1 teaspoon dried basil
3 trout fillets
½ teaspoon cayenne pepper, or more to taste
⅓ teaspoon black pepper
Salt, to taste
1 bay leaf
1 cup shredded Pepper Jack cheese

1. Pour the water into your Instant Pot and insert a trivet. 2. Grease a baking dish with the olive oil. Add the tomatoes slices to the baking dish and sprinkle with the oregano and basil. 3. Add the fish fillets and season with the cayenne pepper, black pepper, and salt. Add the bay leaf. Lower the baking dish onto the trivet. 4. Lock the lid. Select the Manual mode and set the cooking time for 10 minutes at High Pressure. 5. When the timer beeps, perform a quick pressure release. Carefully remove the lid. 6. Scatter the Pepper Jack cheese on top, lock the lid, and allow the cheese to melt. 7. Serve warm.

Per Serving:
calories: 361 | fat: 23.5g | protein: 25.2g | carbs: 12.1g | net carbs: 11.3g | fiber: 0.8g

Halibut Stew with Bacon and Cheese

Prep time: 10 minutes | Cook time: 10 minutes | Serves 4

1½ cups water
Cooking spray
4 slices bacon, chopped
1 celery, chopped
½ cup chopped shallots
1 teaspoon garlic, smashed
1 pound (454 g) halibut
2 cups fish stock
1 tablespoon coconut oil, softened
¼ teaspoon ground allspice
Sea salt and crushed black peppercorns, to taste
1 cup Cottage cheese, at room temperature
1 cup heavy cream

1. Set the Instant Pot to Sauté. Cook the bacon until crispy. 2. Add the celery, shallots, and garlic and sauté for another 2 minutes, or until the vegetables are just tender. 3. Mix in the halibut, stock, coconut oil, allspice, salt, and black peppercorns. Stir well. 4. Lock the lid. Select the Manual mode and set the cooking time for 7 minutes at Low Pressure. 5. When the timer beeps, perform a natural pressure release for 10 minutes, then release any remaining pressure. Carefully remove the lid. 6. Stir in the cheese and heavy cream. Select the Sauté mode again and let it simmer for a few minutes until heated through. Serve immediately.

Per Serving:
calories: 531 | fat: 43.6g | protein: 29.1g | carbs: 5.7g | net carbs: 5.1g | fiber: 0.6g

Fish Packets with Pesto and Cheese

Prep time: 8 minutes | Cook time: 6 minutes | Serves 4

1½ cups cold water.
4 (4-ounce / 113-g) white fish fillets, such as cod or haddock
1 teaspoon fine sea salt
½ teaspoon ground black pepper
1 (4-ounce / 113-g) jar pesto
½ cup shredded Parmesan cheese (about 2 ounces / 57 g)
Halved cherry tomatoes, for garnish

1. Pour the water into your Instant Pot and insert a steamer basket. 2. Sprinkle the fish on all sides with the salt and pepper. Take four sheets of parchment paper and place a fillet in the center of each sheet. 3. Dollop 2 tablespoons of the pesto on top of each fillet and sprinkle with 2 tablespoons of the Parmesan cheese. 4. Wrap the fish in the parchment by folding in the edges and folding down the top like an envelope to close tightly. 5. Stack the packets in the steamer basket, seam-side down. 6. Lock the lid. Select the Manual mode and set the cooking time for 6 minutes at Low Pressure. 7. Once cooking is complete, do a natural pressure release for 10 minutes, then release any remaining pressure. Carefully open the lid. 8. Remove the fish packets from the pot. Transfer to a serving plate and garnish with the cherry tomatoes. 9. Serve immediately.

Per Serving:
calories: 257 | fat: 17.8g | protein: 23.7g | carbs: 2.3g | net carbs: 1.3g | fiber: 1.0g

Greek Shrimp with Tomatoes and Feta

Prep time: 10 minutes | Cook time: 2 minutes | Serves 6

3 tablespoons unsalted butter
1 tablespoon garlic
½ teaspoon red pepper flakes, or more as needed
1½ cups chopped onion
1 (14½-ounce / 411-g) can diced tomatoes, undrained
1 teaspoon dried oregano
1 teaspoon salt
1 pound (454 g) frozen shrimp, peeled
1 cup crumbled feta cheese
½ cup sliced black olives
¼ cup chopped parsley

1. Preheat the Instant Pot by selecting Sauté and adjusting to high heat. When the inner cooking pot is hot, add the butter and heat until it foams. Add the garlic and red pepper flakes, and cook just until fragrant, about 1 minute. 2. Add the onion, tomatoes, oregano, and salt, and stir to combine. 3. Add the frozen shrimp. 4. Lock the lid into place. Select Manual and adjust the pressure to Low. Cook for 1 minute. When the cooking is complete, quick-release the pressure. Unlock the lid. 5. Mix the shrimp in with the lovely tomato broth. 6. Allow the mixture to cool slightly. Right before serving, sprinkle with the feta cheese, olives, and parsley. This dish makes a soupy broth, so it's great over mashed cauliflower.

Per Serving:
calories: 361 | fat: 22g | protein: 30g | carbs: 13g | net carbs: 11g | fiber: 2g

Asian Cod with Brown Rice, Asparagus, and Mushrooms

Prep time: 5 minutes | Cook time: 25 minutes | Serves 2

¾ cup Minute brand brown rice
½ cup water
Two 5-ounce skinless cod fillets
1 tablespoon soy sauce or tamari
1 tablespoon fresh lemon juice
½ teaspoon peeled and grated fresh ginger
1 tablespoon extra-virgin olive oil or 1 tablespoon unsalted butter, cut into 8 pieces
2 green onions, white and green parts, thinly sliced
12 ounces asparagus, trimmed
4 ounces shiitake mushrooms, stems removed and sliced
⅛ teaspoon fine sea salt
⅛ teaspoon freshly ground black pepper
Lemon wedges for serving

1. Pour 1 cup water into the Instant Pot. Have ready two-tier stackable stainless-steel containers. 2. In one of the containers, combine the rice and ½ cup water, then gently shake the container to spread the rice into an even layer, making sure all of the grains are submerged. Place the fish fillets on top of the rice. In a small bowl, stir together the soy sauce, lemon juice, and ginger. Pour the soy sauce mixture over the fillets. Drizzle 1 teaspoon olive oil on each fillet (or top with two pieces of the butter), and sprinkle the green onions on and around the fish. 3. In the second container, arrange the asparagus in the center in as even a layer as possible. Place the mushrooms on either side of the asparagus. Drizzle with the remaining 2 teaspoons olive oil (or put the remaining six pieces butter on top of the asparagus, spacing them evenly). Sprinkle the salt and pepper evenly over the vegetables. 4. Place the container with the rice and fish on the bottom and the vegetable container on top. Cover the top container with its lid and then latch the containers together. Grasping the handle, lower the containers into the Instant Pot. 5. Secure the lid and set the Pressure Release to Sealing. Select the Pressure Cook or Manual setting and set the cooking time for 15 minutes at high pressure. (The pot will take about 10 minutes to come up to pressure before the cooking program begins.) 6. When the cooking program ends, let the pressure release naturally for 5 minutes, then move the Pressure Release to Venting to release any remaining steam. Open the pot and, wearing heat-resistant mitts, lift out the stacked containers. Unlatch, unstack, and open the containers, taking care not to get burned by the steam. 7. Transfer the vegetables, rice, and fish to plates and serve right away, with the lemon wedges on the side.

Per Serving:
calories: 344 | fat: 11g | protein: 27g | carbs: 46g | sugars: 6g | fiber: 7g | sodium: 637mg

Chunky Fish Soup with Tomatoes

Prep time: 10 minutes | Cook time: 8 minutes | Serves 4

2 teaspoons olive oil
1 yellow onion, chopped
1 bell pepper, sliced
1 celery, diced
2 garlic cloves, minced
3 cups fish stock
2 ripe tomatoes, crushed
¾ pound (340 g) haddock fillets
1 cup shrimp
1 tablespoon sweet Hungarian paprika
1 teaspoon hot Hungarian paprika
½ teaspoon caraway seeds

1. Set the Instant Pot to Sauté. Add and heat the oil. Once hot, add the onions and sauté until soft and fragrant. 2. Add the pepper, celery, and garlic and continue to sauté until soft. 3. Stir in the remaining ingredients. 4. Lock the lid. Select the Manual mode and set the cooking time for 5 minutes at High Pressure. 5. When the timer beeps, perform a quick pressure release. Carefully remove the lid. 6. Divide into serving bowls and serve hot.

Per Serving:
calories: 177 | fat: 4.7g | protein: 25.8g | carbs: 8.0g | net carbs: 5.6g | fiber: 2.4g

Shrimp Zoodle Alfredo

Prep time: 10 minutes | Cook time: 10 minutes | Serves 4

10 ounces (283 g) salmon fillet (2 fillets)
4 ounces (113 g) Mozzarella, sliced
4 cherry tomatoes, sliced
1 teaspoon erythritol
1 teaspoon dried basil
½ teaspoon ground black pepper
1 tablespoon apple cider vinegar
1 tablespoon butter
1 cup water, for cooking

1. Melt the butter on Sauté mode and add shrimp. 2. Sprinkle them with seafood seasoning and sauté then for 2 minutes. 3. After this, spiralizer the zucchini with the help of the spiralizer and add in the shrimp. 4. Add coconut cream and close the lid. Cook the meal on Sauté mode for 8 minutes.

Per Serving:
calories: 213 | fat: 16g | protein: 12g | carbs: 7g | net carbs: 5g | fiber: 2g

Tilapia Fillets with Arugula

Prep time: 5 minutes | Cook time: 4 minutes | Serves 4

1 lemon, juiced
1 cup water
1 pound (454 g) tilapia fillets
½ teaspoon cayenne pepper, or more to taste
2 teaspoons butter, melted
Sea salt and ground black pepper, to taste
½ teaspoon dried basil
2 cups arugula

1. Pour the fresh lemon juice and water into your Instant Pot and insert a steamer basket. 2. Brush the fish fillets with the melted butter. 3. Sprinkle with the cayenne pepper, salt, and black pepper. Place the tilapia fillets in the basket. Sprinkle the dried basil on top. 4. Lock the lid. Select the Manual mode and set the cooking time for 4 minutes at Low Pressure. 5. When the timer beeps, perform a quick pressure release. Carefully remove the lid. 6. Serve with the fresh arugula.

Per Serving:
calories: 134 | fat: 4.0g | protein: 23.2g | carbs: 1.4g | net carbs: 1.1g | fiber: 0.3g

Flounder Meuniere

Prep time: 15 minutes | Cook time: 10 minutes | Serves 4

16 ounces (454 g) flounder fillet
½ teaspoon ground black pepper
½ teaspoon salt
½ cup almond flour
2 tablespoons olive oil
1 tablespoon lemon juice
1 teaspoon chopped fresh parsley

1. Cut the fish fillets into 4 servings and sprinkle with salt, ground black pepper, and lemon juice. 2. Heat up the instant pot on Sauté mode for 2 minutes and add olive oil. 3. Coat the flounder fillets in the almond flour and put them in the hot olive oil. 4. Sauté the fish fillets for 4 minutes and then flip on another side. 5. Cook the meal for 3 minutes more or until it is golden brown. 6. Sprinkle the cooked flounder with the fresh parsley.

Per Serving:
calories: 214 | fat: 10g | protein: 28g | carbs: 1g | net carbs: 1g | fiber: 0g

Tuna Stuffed Poblano Peppers

Prep time: 15 minutes | Cook time: 12 minutes | Serves 4

7 ounces (198 g) canned tuna, shredded
1 teaspoon cream cheese
¼ teaspoon minced garlic
2 ounces (57 g) Provolone cheese, grated
4 poblano pepper
1 cup water, for cooking

1. Remove the seeds from poblano peppers. 2. In the mixing bowl, mix up shredded tuna, cream cheese, minced garlic, and grated cheese. 3. Then fill the peppers with tuna mixture and put it in the baking pan. 4. Pour water and insert the baking pan in the instant pot. 5. Cook the meal on Manual mode (High Pressure) for 12 minutes. Then make a quick pressure release.

Per Serving:
calories: 153 | fat: 8g | protein: 17g | carbs: 2g | net carbs: 1g | fiber: 1g

Coconut Shrimp Curry

Prep time: 10 minutes | Cook time: 4 minutes | Serves 5

15 ounces (425 g) shrimp, peeled
1 teaspoon chili powder
1 teaspoon garam masala
1 cup coconut milk
1 teaspoon olive oil
½ teaspoon minced garlic

1. Heat up the instant pot on Sauté mode for 2 minutes. 2. Then add olive oil. Cook the ingredients for 1 minute. 3. Add shrimp and sprinkle them with chili powder, garam masala, minced garlic, and coconut milk. 4. Carefully stir the ingredients and close the lid. 5. Cook the shrimp curry on Manual mode for 1 minute. Make a quick pressure release.

Per Serving:
calories: 222 | fat: 14g | protein: 21g | carbs: 4g | net carbs: 3g | fiber: 1g

Chapter 6 Poultry

Chicken and Bacon Ranch Casserole

Prep time: 5 minutes | Cook time: 30 minutes | Serves 4

4 slices bacon
4 (6-ounce / 170-g) boneless, skinless chicken breasts, cut into 1-inch cubes
½ teaspoon salt
¼ teaspoon pepper
1 tablespoon coconut oil
½ cup chicken broth
½ cup ranch dressing
½ cup shredded Cheddar cheese
2 ounces (57 g) cream cheese

1. Press the Sauté button to heat your Instant Pot. 2. Add the bacon slices and cook for about 7 minutes until crisp, flipping occasionally. 3. Remove from the pot and place on a paper towel to drain. Set aside. 4. Season the chicken cubes with salt and pepper. 5. Set your Instant Pot to Sauté and melt the coconut oil. 6. Add the chicken cubes and brown for 3 to 4 minutes until golden brown. 7. Stir in the broth and ranch dressing. 8. Secure the lid. Select the Manual mode and set the cooking time for 20 minutes at High Pressure. 9. Once cooking is complete, do a quick pressure release. Carefully open the lid. 10. Stir in the Cheddar and cream cheese. Crumble the cooked bacon and scatter on top. Serve immediately.

Per Serving:
calories: 467 | fat: 25.8g | protein: 46.2g | carbs: 1.3g | net carbs: 1.2g | fiber: 0.1g

Smoky Whole Chicken

Prep time: 20 minutes | Cook time: 21 minutes | Serves 6

2 tablespoons extra-virgin olive oil
1 tablespoon kosher salt
1½ teaspoons smoked paprika
1 teaspoon freshly ground black pepper
½ teaspoon herbes de Provence
¼ teaspoon cayenne pepper
1 (3½-pound) whole chicken, rinsed and patted dry, giblets removed
1 large lemon, halved
6 garlic cloves, peeled and crushed with the flat side of a knife
1 large onion, cut into 8 wedges, divided
1 cup Chicken Bone Broth, low-sodium store-bought chicken broth, or water
2 large carrots, each cut into 4 pieces
2 celery stalks, each cut into 4 pieces

1. In a small bowl, combine the olive oil, salt, paprika, pepper, herbes de Provence, and cayenne. 2. Place the chicken on a cutting board and rub the olive oil mixture under the skin and all over the outside. Stuff the cavity with the lemon halves, garlic cloves, and 3 to 4 wedges of onion. 3. Pour the broth into the electric pressure cooker. Add the remaining onion wedges, carrots, and celery. Insert a wire rack or trivet on top of the vegetables. 4. Place the chicken, breast-side up, on the rack. 5. Close and lock the lid of the pressure cooker. Set the valve to sealing. 6. Cook on high pressure for 21 minutes. 7. When the cooking is complete, hit Cancel and allow the pressure to release naturally for 15 minutes, then quick release any remaining pressure. 8. Once the pin drops, unlock and remove the lid. 9. Carefully remove the chicken to a clean cutting board. Remove the skin and cut the chicken into pieces or shred/chop the meat, and serve.

Per Serving:
calorie: 362 | fat: 9g | protein: 60g | carbs: 8g | sugars: 3g | fiber: 2g | sodium: 611mg

Chicken and Mixed Greens Salad

Prep time: 5 minutes | Cook time: 20 minutes | Serves 4

Chicken:
2 tablespoons avocado oil
1 pound (454 g) chicken breast, cubed
½ cup filtered water
½ teaspoon ground turmeric
½ teaspoon dried parsley
½ teaspoon dried basil
½ teaspoon kosher salt
½ teaspoon freshly ground black pepper
Salad:
1 avocado, mashed
1 cup chopped arugula
1 cup chopped Swiss chard
1 cup chopped kale
½ cup chopped spinach
2 tablespoons pine nuts, toasted

1. Combine all the chicken ingredients in the Instant Pot. 2. Secure the lid. Select the Manual mode and set the cooking time for 20 minutes at High Pressure. 3. Meanwhile, toss all the salad ingredients in a large salad bowl. 4. Once cooking is complete, do a quick pressure release. Carefully open the lid. 5. Remove the chicken to the salad bowl and serve.

Per Serving:
calories: 378 | fat: 23.3g | protein: 35.3g | carbs: 7.6g | net carbs: 3.5g | fiber: 4.1g

Chicken Thighs with Feta

Prep time: 7 minutes | Cook time: 15 minutes | Serves 2

4 lemon slices
2 chicken thighs
1 tablespoon Greek seasoning
4 ounces (113 g) feta, crumbled
1 teaspoon butter
½ cup water

1. Rub the chicken thighs with Greek seasoning. 2. Then spread the chicken with butter. 3. Pour water in the instant pot and place the trivet. 4. Place the chicken on the foil and top with the lemon slices. Top it with feta. 5. Wrap the chicken in the foil and transfer on the trivet. 6. Cook on the Sauté mode for 10 minutes. Then make a quick pressure release for 5 minutes. 7. Discard the foil from the chicken thighs and serve!

Per Serving:
calories: 341 | fat: 24g | protein: 27g | carbs: 6g | net carbs: 6g | fiber: 0g

Chicken Alfredo with Bacon

Prep time: 10 minutes | Cook time: 27 minutes | Serves 4

2 (6-ounce / 170-g) boneless, skinless chicken breasts, butterflied
½ teaspoon garlic powder
¼ teaspoon dried parsley
¼ teaspoon dried thyme
¼ teaspoon salt
⅛ teaspoon pepper
2 tablespoons coconut oil
1 cup water
1 stick butter
2 cloves garlic, finely minced
¼ cup heavy cream
½ cup grated Parmesan cheese
¼ cup cooked crumbled bacon

1. Sprinkle the chicken breasts with the garlic powder, parsley, thyme, salt, and pepper. 2. Set your Instant Pot to Sauté and melt the coconut oil. 3. Add the chicken and sear for 3 to 5 minutes until golden brown on both sides. 4. Remove the chicken with tongs and set aside. 5. Pour the water into the Instant Pot and insert the trivet. Place the chicken on the trivet. 6. Secure the lid. Select the Manual mode and set the cooking time for 20 minutes at High Pressure. 7. Once cooking is complete, do a quick pressure release. Carefully open the lid. 8. Remove the chicken from the pot to a platter and set aside. 9. Pour the water out of the Instant Pot, reserving ½ cup; set aside. 10. Set your Instant Pot to Sauté again and melt the butter. 11. Add the garlic, heavy cream, cheese, and reserved water to the Instant Pot. Cook for 3 to 4 minutes until the sauce starts to thicken, stirring frequently. 12. Stir in the crumbled bacon and pour the mixture over the chicken. Serve immediately.

Per Serving:
calories: 526| fat: 42g | protein: 28g | carbs: 3g | net carbs: 3g | fiber: 0g

Pesto Chicken

Prep time: 5 minutes | Cook time: 25 minutes | Serves 2

2 (6-ounce / 170-g) boneless, skinless chicken breasts, butterflied
½ teaspoon salt
¼ teaspoon pepper
¼ teaspoon dried parsley
¼ teaspoon garlic powder
2 tablespoons coconut oil
1 cup water
¼ cup whole-milk ricotta cheese
¼ cup pesto
¼ cup shredded whole-milk Mozzarella cheese
Chopped parsley, for garnish (optional)

1. Sprinkle the chicken breasts with salt, pepper, parsley, and garlic powder. 2. Set your Instant Pot to Sauté and melt the coconut oil. 3. Add the chicken and brown for 3 to 5 minutes. Remove the chicken from the pot to a 7-cup glass bowl. 4. Pour the water into the Instant Pot and use a wooden spoon or rubber spatula to make sure no seasoning is stuck to bottom of pot. 5. Scatter the ricotta cheese on top of the chicken. Pour the pesto over chicken, and sprinkle the Mozzarella cheese over chicken. Cover with aluminum foil. Add the trivet to the Instant Pot and place the bowl on the trivet. 6. Secure the lid. Select the Manual mode and set the cooking time for 20 minutes at High Pressure. 7. Once cooking is complete, do a natural pressure release for 10 minutes, then release any remaining pressure. Carefully open the lid. 8. Serve the chicken garnished with the chopped parsley, if desired.

Per Serving:
calories: 519 | fat: 31.9g | protein: 46.4g | carbs: 4.2g | net carbs: 3.5g | fiber: 0.7g

Bruschetta and Cheese Stuffed Chicken

Prep time: 10 minutes | Cook time: 10 minutes | Serves 4

6 ounces (170 g) diced Roma tomatoes
2 tablespoons avocado oil
1 tablespoon thinly sliced fresh basil, plus more for garnish
1½ teaspoons balsamic vinegar
Pinch of salt
Pinch of black pepper
4 boneless, skinless chicken breasts (about 2 pounds / 907 g)
12 ounces (340 g) goat cheese, divided
2 teaspoons Italian seasoning, divided
1 cup water

1. Prepare the bruschetta by mixing the tomatoes, avocado oil, basil, vinegar, salt, and pepper in a small bowl. Let it marinate until the chicken is done. 2. Pat the chicken dry with a paper towel. Butterfly the breast open but do not cut all the way through. Stuff each breast with 3 ounces (85 g) of the goat cheese. Use toothpicks to close the edges. 3. Sprinkle ½ teaspoon of the Italian seasoning on top of each breast. 4. Pour the water into the pot. Place the trivet inside. Lay a piece of aluminum foil on top of the trivet and place the chicken breasts on top. It is okay if they overlap. 5. Close the lid and seal the vent. Cook on High Pressure for 10 minutes. Quick release the steam. 6. Remove the toothpicks and top each breast with one-fourth of the bruschetta.

Per Serving:
calories: 581 | fat: 34g | protein: 64g | carbs: 5g | net carbs: 4g | fiber: 1g

Mexican Chicken with Red Salsa

Prep time: 10 minutes | Cook time: 20 minutes | Serves 8

2 pounds (907 g) boneless, skinless chicken thighs, cut into bite-size pieces
1½ tablespoons ground cumin
1½ tablespoons chili powder
1 tablespoon salt
2 tablespoons vegetable oil
1 (14½-ounce / 411-g) can diced tomatoes, undrained
1 (5-ounce / 142-g) can sugar-free tomato paste
1 small onion, chopped
3 garlic cloves, minced
2 ounces (57 g) pickled jalapeños from a can, with juice
½ cup sour cream

1. Preheat the Instant Pot by selecting Sauté and adjusting to high heat. 2. In a medium bowl, coat the chicken with the cumin, chili powder, and salt. 3. Put the oil in the inner cooking pot. When it is shimmering, add the coated chicken pieces. (This step lets the spices bloom a bit to get their full flavor.) Cook the chicken for 4 to 5 minutes. 4. Add the tomatoes, tomato paste, onion, garlic, and jalapeños. 5. Lock the lid into place. Select Manual and adjust the pressure to High. Cook for 15 minutes. When the cooking is complete, let the pressure release naturally for 10 minutes, then quick-release any remaining pressure. Unlock and remove the lid. 6. Use two forks to shred the chicken. Serve topped with the sour cream. This dish is good with mashed cauliflower, steamed vegetables, or a salad.

Per Serving:
calories: 329 | fat: 24g | protein: 21g | carbs: 8g | net carbs: 6g | fiber: 2g

Parmesan-Crusted Chicken

Prep time: 15 minutes | Cook time: 13 minutes | Serves 2

1 tomato, sliced
8 ounces (227 g) chicken fillets
2 ounces (57 g) Parmesan, sliced
1 teaspoon butter
4 tablespoons water, for sprinkling
1 cup water, for cooking

1. Pour water and insert the steamer rack in the instant pot. 2. Then grease the baking mold with butter. 3. Slice the chicken fillets into halves and put them in the mold. 4. Sprinkle the chicken with water and top with tomato and Parmesan. 5. Cover the baking mold with foil and place it on the rack. 6. Close and seal the lid. 7. Cook the meal in Manual mode for 13 minutes. Then allow the natural pressure release for 10 minutes.

Per Serving:
calories: 329 | fat: 16g | protein: 42g | carbs: 2g | net carbs: 2g | fiber: 0g

Shredded Chicken

Prep time: 5 minutes | Cook time: 14 minutes | Serves 4

½ teaspoon salt
½ teaspoon pepper
½ teaspoon dried oregano
½ teaspoon dried basil
½ teaspoon garlic powder
2 (6-ounce / 170-g) boneless, skinless chicken breasts
1 tablespoon coconut oil
1 cup water

1. In a small bowl, combine the salt, pepper, oregano, basil, and garlic powder. Rub this mix over both sides of the chicken. 2. Set your Instant Pot to Sauté and heat the coconut oil until sizzling. 3. Add the chicken and sear for 3 to 4 minutes until golden on both sides. 4. Remove the chicken and set aside. 5. Pour the water into the Instant Pot and use a wooden spoon or rubber spatula to make sure no seasoning is stuck to bottom of pot. 6. Add the trivet to the Instant Pot and place the chicken on top. 7. Secure the lid. Select the Manual mode and set the cooking time for 10 minutes at High Pressure. 8. Once cooking is complete, do a natural pressure release for 5 minutes, then release any remaining pressure. Carefully open the lid. 9. Remove the chicken and shred, then serve.

Per Serving:
calories: 135 | fat: 5g | protein: 20g | carbs: 0g | net carbs: 0g | fiber: 0g

Cider Chicken with Pecans

Prep time: 10 minutes | Cook time: 15 minutes | Serves 2

6 ounces (170 g) chicken fillet, cubed
2 pecans, chopped
1 teaspoon coconut aminos
½ bell pepper, chopped
1 tablespoon coconut oil
¼ cup apple cider vinegar
¼ cup chicken broth

1. Melt coconut oil on Sauté mode and add chicken cubes. 2. Add bell pepper, and pecans. 3. Sauté the ingredients for 10 minutes and add apple cider vinegar, chicken broth, and coconut aminos. 4. Sauté the chicken for 5 minutes more.

Per Serving:
calories: 341 | fat: 23g | protein: 27g | carbs: 5g | net carbs: 3g | fiber: 2g

Chicken with Spiced Sesame Sauce

Prep time: 20 minutes | Cook time: 8 minutes | Serves 5

2 tablespoons tahini (sesame sauce)
¼ cup water
1 tablespoon low-sodium soy sauce
¼ cup chopped onion
1 teaspoon red wine vinegar
2 teaspoons minced garlic
1 teaspoon shredded ginger root (Microplane works best)
2 pounds chicken breast, chopped into 8 portions

1. Place first seven ingredients in bottom of the inner pot of the Instant Pot. 2. Add coarsely chopped chicken on top. 3. Secure the lid and make sure vent is at sealing. Set for 8 minutes using Manual setting. When cook time is up, let the pressure release naturally for 10 minutes, then perform a quick release. 4. Remove ingredients and shred chicken with fork. Combine with other ingredients in pot for a tasty sandwich filling or sauce.

Per Serving:
calorie: 215 | fat: 7g | protein: 35g | carbs: 2g | sugars: 0g | fiber: 0g | sodium: 178mg

Lemony Chicken with Fingerling Potatoes and Olives

Prep time: 20 minutes | Cook time: 21 minutes | Serves 4

4 (5- to 7-ounce / 142- to 198-g) bone-in chicken thighs, trimmed
½ teaspoon table salt
¼ teaspoon pepper
2 teaspoons extra-virgin olive oil, plus extra for drizzling
4 garlic cloves, peeled and smashed
½ cup chicken broth
1 small lemon, sliced thin
1½ pounds (680 g) fingerling potatoes, unpeeled
¼ cup pitted brine-cured green or black olives, halved
2 tablespoons coarsely chopped fresh parsley

1. Pat chicken dry with paper towels and sprinkle with salt and pepper. Using highest sauté function, heat oil in Instant Pot for 5 minutes (or until just smoking). Place chicken skin side down in pot and cook until well browned on first side, about 5 minutes; transfer to plate. 2. Add garlic to fat left in pot and cook, using highest sauté function, until golden and fragrant, about 2 minutes. Stir in broth and lemon, scraping up any browned bits. Return chicken skin side up to pot and add any accumulated juices. Arrange potatoes on top. Lock lid in place and close pressure release valve. Select high pressure cook function and cook for 9 minutes. 3. Turn off Instant Pot and quick-release pressure. Carefully remove lid, allowing steam to escape away from you. Transfer chicken to serving dish and discard skin, if desired. Stir olives and parsley into potatoes and season with salt and pepper to taste. Serve chicken with potatoes.

Per Serving:
calories: 280 | fat: 7g | protein: 20g | carbs: 33g | fiber: 4g | sodium: 580mg

Cheesy Stuffed Cabbage

Prep time: 30 minutes | Cook time: 18 minutes | Serves 6 to 8

1–2 heads savoy cabbage
1 pound ground turkey
1 egg
1 cup reduced-fat shredded cheddar cheese
2 tablespoons evaporated skim milk
¼ cup reduced-fat shredded Parmesan cheese
¼ cup reduced-fat shredded mozzarella cheese
¼ cup finely diced onion
¼ cup finely diced bell pepper
¼ cup finely diced mushrooms
1 teaspoon salt
½ teaspoon black pepper
1 teaspoon garlic powder
6 basil leaves, fresh and cut chiffonade
1 tablespoon fresh parsley, chopped
1 quart of your favorite pasta sauce

1. Remove the core from the cabbages. 2. Boil pot of water and place 1 head at a time into the water for approximately 10 minutes. 3. Allow cabbage to cool slightly. Once cooled, remove the leaves carefully and set aside. You'll need about 15 or 16. 4. Mix together the meat and all remaining ingredients except the pasta sauce. 5. One leaf at a time, put a heaping tablespoon of meat mixture in the center. 6. Tuck the sides in and then roll tightly. 7. Add ½ cup sauce to the bottom of the inner pot of the Instant Pot. 8. Place the rolls, fold-side down, into the pot and layer them, putting a touch of sauce between each layer and finally on top. (You may want to cook the rolls in two batches.) 9. Lock lid and make sure vent is at sealing. Set timer on 18 minutes on Manual at high pressure, then manually release the pressure when cook time is over.

Per Serving:
calories: 199| fat: 8g | protein: 2mg | carbs: 14g | sugars: 7g | fiber: 3g | sodium: 678mg

Orange Chicken Thighs with Bell Peppers

Prep time: 15 to 20 minutes | Cook time: 7 minutes | Serves 4 to 6

6 boneless skinless chicken thighs, cut into bite-sized pieces
2 packets crystallized True Orange flavoring
½ teaspoon True Orange Orange Ginger seasoning
½ teaspoon coconut aminos
¼ teaspoon Worcestershire sauce
Olive oil or cooking spray
2 cups bell pepper strips, any color combination (I used red)
1 onion, chopped
1 tablespoon green onion, chopped fine
3 cloves garlic, minced or chopped
½ teaspoon pink salt
½ teaspoon black pepper
1 teaspoon garlic powder
1 teaspoon ground ginger
¼–½ teaspoon red pepper flakes
2 tablespoons tomato paste
½ cup chicken bone broth or water
1 tablespoon brown sugar substitute (I use Sukrin Gold)
½ cup Seville orange spread (I use Crofter's brand)

1. Combine the chicken with the 2 packets of crystallized orange flavor, the orange ginger seasoning, the coconut aminos, and the Worcestershire sauce. Set aside. 2. Turn the Instant Pot to Sauté and add a touch of olive oil or cooking spray to the inner pot. Add in the orange ginger marinated chicken thighs. 3. Sauté until lightly browned. Add in the peppers, onion, green onion, garlic, and seasonings. Mix well. 4. Add the remaining ingredients; mix to combine. 5. Lock the lid, set the vent to sealing, set to 7 minutes. 6. Let the pressure release naturally for 2 minutes, then manually release the rest when cook time is up.

Per Serving:
calories: 120| fat: 2g | protein: 12g | carbs: 8g | sugars: 10g | fiber: 1.6g | sodium: 315mg

Chicken Meatballs with Green Cabbage

Prep time: 15 minutes | Cook time: 4 minutes | Serves 4

1 pound (454 g) ground chicken
¼ cup heavy (whipping) cream
2 teaspoons salt, divided
½ teaspoon ground caraway seeds
1½ teaspoons freshly ground black pepper, divided
¼ teaspoon ground allspice
4 to 6 cups thickly chopped green cabbage
½ cup coconut milk
2 tablespoons unsalted butter

1. To make the meatballs, put the chicken in a bowl. Add the cream, 1 teaspoon of salt, the caraway, ½ teaspoon of pepper, and the allspice. Mix thoroughly. Refrigerate the mixture for 30 minutes. Once the mixture has cooled, it is easier to form the meatballs. 2. Using a small scoop, form the chicken mixture into small-to medium-size meatballs. Place half the meatballs in the inner cooking pot of your Instant Pot and cover them with half the cabbage. Place the remaining meatballs on top of the cabbage, then cover them with the rest of the cabbage. 3. Pour in the milk, place pats of the butter here and there, and sprinkle with the remaining 1 teaspoon of salt and 1 teaspoon of pepper. 4. Lock the lid into place. Select Manual and adjust the pressure to High. Cook for 4 minutes. When the cooking is complete, quick-release the pressure. Unlock the lid. Serve the meatballs on top of the cabbage.

Per Serving:
calories: 338 | fat: 23g | protein: 23g | carbs: 7g | net carbs: 4g | fiber: 3g

Parmesan Carbonara Chicken

Prep time: 15 minutes | Cook time: 25 minutes | Serves 5

1 pound (454 g) chicken, skinless, boneless, chopped
1 cup heavy cream
1 cup chopped spinach
2 ounces (57 g) Parmesan, grated
1 teaspoon ground black pepper
1 tablespoon coconut oil
2 ounces (57 g) bacon, chopped

1. Put the coconut oil and chopped chicken in the instant pot. 2. Sauté the chicken for 10 minutes. Stir it from time to time. 3. Then add ground black pepper, and spinach. Stir the mixture well and sauté for 5 minutes more. 4. Then add heavy cream and Parmesan. Close and seal the lid. 5. Cook the meal on Manual mode (High Pressure) for 10 minutes. Allow the natural pressure release for 10 minutes.

Per Serving:
calories: 343 | fat: 22g | protein: 35g | carbs: 2g | net carbs: 2g | fiber: 0g

Chicken Escabèche

Prep time: 5 minutes | Cook time: 15 minutes | Serves 4

1 cup filtered water
1 pound (454 g) chicken, mixed pieces
3 garlic cloves, smashed
2 bay leaves
1 onion, chopped
½ cup red wine vinegar
½ teaspoon coriander
½ teaspoon ground cumin
½ teaspoon mint, finely chopped
½ teaspoon kosher salt
½ teaspoon freshly ground black pepper

1. Pour the water into the Instant Pot and insert the trivet. 2. Thoroughly combine the chicken, garlic, bay leaves, onion, vinegar, coriander, cumin, mint, salt, and black pepper in a large bowl. 3. Put the bowl on the trivet and cover loosely with aluminum foil. 4. Secure the lid. Select the Manual mode and set the cooking time for 15 minutes at High Pressure. 5. Once cooking is complete, do a natural pressure release for 10 minutes, then release any remaining pressure. Carefully open the lid. 6. Remove the dish from the Instant Pot and cool for 5 to 10 minutes before serving.

Per Serving:
calories: 196 | fat: 3.7g | protein: 33.5g | carbs: 4.0g | net carbs: 3.3g | fiber: 0.7g

Simple Chicken Masala

Prep time: 10 minutes | Cook time: 17 minutes | Serves 3

12 ounces (340 g) chicken fillet
1 tablespoon masala spices
1 tablespoon avocado oil
3 tablespoons organic almond milk

1. Heat up avocado oil in the instant pot on Sauté mode for 2 minutes. 2. Meanwhile, chop the chicken fillet roughly and mix it up with masala spices. 3. Add almond milk and transfer the chicken in the instant pot. 4. Cook the chicken bites on Sauté mode for 15 minutes. Stir the meal occasionally.

Per Serving:
calories: 211 | fat: 9g | protein: 25g | carbs: 6g | net carbs: 6g | fiber: 0g

Stuffed Chicken with Spinach and Feta

Prep time: 10 minutes | Cook time: 25 minutes | Serves 4

½ cup frozen spinach
⅓ cup crumbled feta cheese
1¼ teaspoons salt, divided
4 (6-ounce / 170-g) boneless, skinless chicken breasts, butterflied
¼ teaspoon pepper
¼ teaspoon dried oregano
¼ teaspoon dried parsley
¼ teaspoon garlic powder
2 tablespoons coconut oil
1 cup water

1. Combine the spinach, feta cheese, and ¼ teaspoon of salt in a medium bowl. Divide the mixture evenly and spoon onto the chicken breasts. 2. Close the chicken breasts and secure with toothpicks or butcher's string. Sprinkle the chicken with the remaining 1 teaspoon of salt, pepper, oregano, parsley, and garlic powder. 3. Set your Instant Pot to Sauté and heat the coconut oil. 4. Sear each chicken breast until golden brown, about 4 to 5 minutes per side. 5. Remove the chicken breasts and set aside. 6. Pour the water into the Instant Pot and scrape the bottom to remove any chicken or seasoning that is stuck on. Add the trivet to the Instant Pot and place the chicken on the trivet. 7. Secure the lid. Select the Manual mode and set the cooking time for 15 minutes at High Pressure. 8. Once cooking is complete, do a natural pressure release for 15 minutes, then release any remaining pressure. Carefully open the lid. Serve warm.

Per Serving:
calories: 303 | fat: 12.1g | protein: 40.9g | carbs: 1.3g | net carbs: 0.6g | fiber: 0.7g

Tomato Chicken Legs

Prep time: 10 minutes | Cook time: 35 minutes | Serves 2

2 chicken legs
2 tomatoes, chopped
1 cup chicken stock
1 teaspoon peppercorns

1. Put all ingredients in the instant pot. 2. Close and seal the lid. Set Manual mode (High Pressure). 3. Cook the chicken legs for 35 minutes. 4. Make a quick pressure release. 5. Transfer the cooked chicken legs in the serving bowls and add 1 ladle of the chicken stock.

Per Serving:
calories: 294 | fat: 16g | protein: 31g | carbs: 6g | net carbs: 4g | fiber: 2g

Chicken in Wine

Prep time: 10 minutes | Cook time: 12 minutes | Serves 6

2 pounds chicken breasts, trimmed of skin and fat
10¾-ounce can 98% fat-free, reduced-sodium cream of mushroom soup
10¾-ounce can French onion soup
1 cup dry white wine or chicken broth

1. Place the chicken into the Instant Pot. 2. Combine soups and wine. Pour over chicken. 3. Secure the lid and make sure vent is set to sealing. Cook on Manual mode for 12 minutes. 4. When cook time is up, let the pressure release naturally for 5 minutes and then release the rest manually.

Per Serving:
calories: 225 | fat: 5g | protein: 35g | carbs: 7g | sugars: 3g | fiber: 1g | sodium: 645mg

Cajun Chicken

Prep time: 15 minutes | Cook time: 25 minutes | Serves 4

1 teaspoon Cajun seasoning
¼ cup apple cider vinegar
1 pound (454 g) chicken fillet
1 tablespoon sesame oil
¼ cup water

1. Put all ingredients in the instant pot. Close and seal the lid. 2. Cook the chicken fillets on Manual mode (High Pressure) for 25 minutes. 3. Allow the natural pressure release for 10 minutes.

Per Serving:
calories: 249 | fat: 12g | protein: 33g | carbs: 0g | net carbs: 0g | fiber: 0g

Chicken Reuben Bake

Prep time: 10 minutes | Cook time: 6 to 8 hours | Serves 6

4 boneless, skinless chicken-breast halves
¼ cup water
1-pound bag sauerkraut, drained and rinsed
4–5 (1 ounce each) slices Swiss cheese
¾ cup fat-free Thousand Island salad dressing
2 tablespoons chopped fresh parsley

1. Place chicken and water in inner pot of the Instant Pot along with ¼ cup water. Layer sauerkraut over chicken. Add cheese. Top with salad dressing. Sprinkle with parsley. 2. Secure the lid and cook on the Slow Cook setting on low 6–8 hours.

Per Serving:
calories: 217 | fat: 5g | protein: 28g | carbs: 13g | sugars: 6g | fiber: 2g | sodium: 693mg

Chicken Curry with Eggplant

Prep time: 15 minutes | Cook time: 12 minutes | Serves 4

1 eggplant, chopped
¼ cup chopped fresh cilantro
1 teaspoon curry powder
1 cup coconut cream
1 teaspoon coconut oil
1 pound (454 g) chicken breast, skinless, boneless, cubed

1. Put the coconut oil and chicken breast in the instant pot. 2. Sauté the ingredients on Sauté mode for 5 minutes. 3. Then stir well and add cilantro, eggplant, coconut cream, and curry powder. 4. Close and seal the lid. 5. Cook the meal on Manual mode (High Pressure) for 7 minutes. 6. Make a quick pressure release and transfer the cooked chicken in the serving bowls.

Per Serving:
calories: 308 | fat: 19g | protein: 27g | carbs: 10g | net carbs: 4g | fiber: 6g

Mushroom Chicken Alfredo

Prep time: 15 minutes | Cook time: 10 minutes | Serves 4

½ cup sliced cremini mushrooms
¼ cup chopped leek
1 tablespoon sesame oil
1 teaspoon chili flakes
1 cup heavy cream
1 pound (454 g) chicken fillet, chopped
1 teaspoon Italian seasoning
1 tablespoon cream cheese

1. Brush the instant pot boil with sesame oil from inside. 2. Put the chicken in the instant pot in one layer. 3. Then top it with mushrooms and leek. 4. Sprinkle the ingredients with chili flakes, heavy cream, Italian seasoning, and cream cheese. 5. Close and seal the lid. 6. Cook the meal on Manual mode (High Pressure) for 10 minutes. 7. When the time is finished, allow the natural pressure release for 10 minutes.

Per Serving:
calories: 367 | fat: 24g | protein: 34g | carbs: 2g | net carbs: 2g | fiber: 0g

Bacon-Wrapped Chicken Tenders

Prep time: 15 minutes | Cook time: 15 minutes | Serves 2

4 ounces (113 g) chicken fillet
2 bacon slices
½ teaspoon ground paprika
¼ teaspoon salt
1 teaspoon olive oil
1 cup water, for cooking

1. Cut the chicken fillet on 2 tenders and sprinkle them with salt, ground paprika, and olive oil. 2. Wrap the chicken tenders in the bacon and transfer in the steamer rack, 3. Pour water and insert the steamer rack with the chicken tenders in the instant pot. 4. Close and seal the lid and cook the meal on Manual mode (High Pressure) for 15 minutes. 5. When the time is finished, allow the natural pressure release for 10 minutes.

Per Serving:
calories: 232 | fat: 14g | protein: 23g | carbs: 1g | net carbs: 1g | fiber: 0g

Sesame Chicken with Broccoli

Prep time: 15 minutes | Cook time: 12 minutes | Serves 2

½ teaspoon five spices
½ teaspoon sesame seeds
½ cup chopped broccoli
6 ounces (170 g) chicken fillet, sliced
½ cup chicken broth
1 teaspoon coconut aminos
1 tablespoon avocado oil

1. In the mixing bowl, mix up avocado oil, coconut aminos, and sesame seeds. 2. Add five spices. 3. After this, mix up sliced chicken fillet and coconut aminos mixture. 4. Put the chicken in the instant pot. Add chicken broth and broccoli. 5. Close and seal the lid. 6. Cook the meal on Manual mode (High Pressure) for 12 minutes. Make a quick pressure release.

Per Serving:
calories: 195 | fat: 8g | protein: 27g | carbs: 3g | net carbs: 2g | fiber: 1g

Cheese Stuffed Chicken

Prep time: 15 minutes | Cook time: 20 minutes | Serves 4

12 ounces (340 g) chicken fillet
4 ounces (113 g) provolone cheese, sliced
1 tablespoon cream cheese
½ teaspoon dried cilantro
½ teaspoon smoked paprika
1 cup water, for cooking

1. Beat the chicken fillet well and rub it with dried cilantro and smoked paprika. 2. Then spread it with cream cheese and top with Provolone cheese. 3. Roll the chicken fillet into the roll and wrap in the foil. 4. Pour water and insert the rack in the instant pot. 5. Place the chicken roll on the rack. Close and seal the lid. 6. Cook it on Manual mode (High Pressure) for 20 minutes. 7. Make a quick pressure release and slice the chicken roll into the servings.

Per Serving:
calories: 271 | fat: 15g | protein: 32g | carbs: 1g | net carbs: 1g | fiber: 0g

Spicy Chicken with Bacon and Peppers

Prep time: 5 minutes | Cook time: 13 minutes | Serves 6

2 slices bacon, chopped
1½ pounds (680 g) ground chicken
2 garlic cloves, minced
½ cup green onions, chopped
1 green bell pepper, seeded and chopped
1 red bell pepper, seeded and chopped
1 serrano pepper, chopped
1 tomato, chopped
1 cup water
⅓ cup chicken broth
1 teaspoon paprika
1 teaspoon onion powder
¼ teaspoon ground allspice
2 bay leaves
Sea salt and ground black pepper, to taste

1. Press the Sauté button to heat your Instant Pot. 2. Add the bacon and cook for about 3 minutes until crisp. Reserve the bacon in a bowl. 3. Add the ground chicken to the bacon grease of the pot and brown for 2 to 3 minutes, crumbling it with a spatula. Reserve it in the bowl of bacon. 4. Add the garlic, green onions, and peppers and sauté for 3 minutes until tender. Add the remaining ingredients to the Instant Pot, along with the cooked bacon and chicken. Stir to mix well. 5. Lock the lid. Select the Poultry mode and set the cooking time for 5 minutes at High Pressure. 6. When the timer beeps, perform a natural pressure release for 10 minutes, then release any remaining pressure. Carefully remove the lid. Serve warm.

Per Serving:

calories: 236 | fat: 13.8g | protein: 24.9g | carbs: 3.0g | net carbs: 2.0g | fiber: 1.0g

Unstuffed Peppers with Ground Turkey and Quinoa

Prep time: 0 minutes | Cook time: 35 minutes | Serves 8

2 tablespoons extra-virgin olive oil
1 yellow onion, diced
2 celery stalks, diced
2 garlic cloves, chopped
2 pounds 93 percent lean ground turkey
2 teaspoons Cajun seasoning blend (plus 1 teaspoon fine sea salt if using a salt-free blend)
½ teaspoon freshly ground black pepper
¼ teaspoon cayenne pepper
1 cup quinoa, rinsed
1 cup low-sodium chicken broth
One 14½-ounce can fire-roasted diced tomatoes and their liquid
3 red, orange, and/or yellow bell peppers, seeded and cut into 1-inch squares
1 green onion, white and green parts, thinly sliced
1½ tablespoons chopped fresh flat-leaf parsley
Hot sauce (such as Crystal or Frank's RedHot) for serving

1. Select the Sauté setting on the Instant Pot and heat the oil for 2 minutes. Add the onion, celery, and garlic and sauté for about 4 minutes, until the onion begins to soften. Add the turkey, Cajun seasoning, black pepper, and cayenne and sauté, using a wooden spoon or spatula to break up the meat as it cooks, for about 6 minutes, until cooked through and no streaks of pink remain. 2. Sprinkle the quinoa over the turkey in an even layer. Pour the broth and the diced tomatoes and their liquid over the quinoa, spreading the tomatoes on top. Sprinkle the bell peppers over the top in an even layer. 3. Secure the lid and set the Pressure Release to Sealing. Press the Cancel button to reset the cooking program, then select the Pressure Cook or Manual setting and set the cooking time for 8 minutes at high pressure. (The pot will take about 15 minutes to come up to pressure before the cooking program begins.) 4. When the cooking program ends, let the pressure release naturally for at least 15 minutes, then move the Pressure Release to Venting to release any remaining steam. Open the pot and sprinkle the green onion and parsley over the top in an even layer. 5. Spoon the unstuffed peppers into bowls, making sure to dig down to the bottom of the pot so each person gets an equal amount of peppers, quinoa, and meat. Serve hot, with hot sauce on the side.

Per Serving:

calories: 320 | fat: 14g | protein: 27g | carbs: 23g | sugars: 3g | fiber: 3g | sodium: 739mg

Pulled BBQ Chicken and Texas-Style Cabbage Slaw

Prep time: 5 minutes | Cook time: 20 minutes | Serves 6

Chicken
1 cup water
¼ teaspoon fine sea salt
3 garlic cloves, peeled
2 bay leaves
2 pounds boneless, skinless chicken thighs (see Note)
Cabbage Slaw
½ head red or green cabbage, thinly sliced
1 red bell pepper, seeded and thinly sliced
2 jalapeño chiles, seeded and cut into narrow strips
2 carrots, julienned
1 large Fuji or Gala apple, julienned
½ cup chopped fresh cilantro
3 tablespoons fresh lime juice
3 tablespoons extra-virgin olive oil
½ teaspoon ground cumin
¼ teaspoon fine sea salt
¾ cup low-sugar or unsweetened barbecue sauce
Cornbread, for serving

1. To make the chicken: Combine the water, salt, garlic, bay leaves, and chicken thighs in the Instant Pot, arranging the chicken in a single layer. 2. Secure the lid and set the Pressure Release to Sealing. Select the Poultry, Pressure Cook, or Manual setting and set the cooking time for 10 minutes at high pressure. (The pot will take about 10 minutes to come up to pressure before the cooking program begins.) 3. To make the slaw: While the chicken is cooking, in a large bowl, combine the cabbage, bell pepper, jalapeños, carrots, apple, cilantro, lime juice, oil, cumin, and salt and toss together until the vegetables and apples are evenly coated. 4. When the cooking program ends, perform a quick pressure release by moving the Pressure Release to Venting, or let the pressure release naturally. Open the pot and, using tongs, transfer the chicken to a cutting board. Using two forks, shred the chicken into bite-size pieces. Wearing heat-resistant mitts, lift out the inner pot and discard the cooking liquid. Return the inner pot to the housing. 5. Return the chicken to the pot and stir in the barbecue sauce. You can serve it right away or heat it for a minute or two on the Sauté setting, then return the pot to its Keep Warm setting until ready to serve. 6. Divide the chicken and slaw evenly among six plates. Serve with wedges of cornbread on the side.

Per Serving:

calories: 320 | fat: 14g | protein: 32g | carbs: 18g | sugars: 7g | fiber: 4g | sodium: 386mg

Thanksgiving Turkey

Prep time: 5 minutes | Cook time: 60 minutes | Serves 8

1 turkey breast (7 pounds / 3.2 kg), giblets removed
4 tablespoons butter, softened
2 teaspoons ground sage
2 teaspoons garlic powder
2 teaspoons salt
2 teaspoons black pepper
½ onion, quartered
1 rib celery, cut into 3 or 4 pieces
1 cup chicken broth
2 or 3 bay leaves
1 teaspoon xanthan gum

1. Pat the turkey dry with a paper towel. 2. In a small bowl, combine the butter with the sage, garlic powder, salt, and pepper. Rub the butter mixture all over the top of the bird. Place the onion and celery inside the cavity. 3. Place the trivet in the pot. Add the broth and bay leaves to the pot. 4. Place the turkey on the trivet. If you need to remove the trivet to make the turkey fit, you can. The turkey will be near the top of the pot, which is fine. 5. Close the lid and seal the vent. Cook on High Pressure for 35 minutes. It is normal if it takes your pot a longer time to come to pressure. 6. Let the steam naturally release for 20 minutes before Manually releasing. Press Cancel. 7. Heat the broiler. 8. Carefully remove the turkey to a sheet pan. Place under the broiler for 5 to 10 minutes to crisp up the skin. 9. While the skin is crisping, use the juices to make a gravy. Pour the juices through a mesh sieve, reserving 2 cups of broth. Return the reserved broth to the pot. Turn the pot to Sauté mode. When the broth starts to boil, add the xanthan gum and whisk until the desired consistency is reached. Add more xanthan gum if you like a thicker gravy. 10. Remove the turkey from the broiler and place on a platter. Carve as desired and serve with the gravy.

Per Serving:
calories: 380 | fat: 18g | protein: 47g | carbs: 3g | net carbs: 1g | fiber: 2g

Mexican Turkey Tenderloin

Prep time: 5 minutes | Cook time: 8 minutes | Serves 6

1 cup Low-Sodium Salsa or bottled salsa
1 teaspoon chili powder
½ teaspoon ground cumin
¼ teaspoon dried oregano
1½ pounds unseasoned turkey tenderloin or boneless turkey breast, cut into 6 pieces
Freshly ground black pepper
½ cup shredded Monterey Jack cheese or Mexican cheese blend

1. In a small bowl or measuring cup, combine the salsa, chili powder, cumin, and oregano. Pour half of the mixture into the electric pressure cooker. 2. Nestle the turkey into the sauce. Grind some pepper onto each piece of turkey. Pour the remaining salsa mixture on top. 3. Close and lock the lid of the pressure cooker. Set the valve to sealing. 4. Cook on high pressure for 8 minutes. 5. When the cooking is complete, hit Cancel. Allow the pressure to release naturally for 10 minutes, then quick release any remaining pressure. 6. Once the pin drops, unlock and remove the lid. 7. Sprinkle the cheese on top, and put the lid back on for a few minutes to let the cheese melt. 8. Serve immediately.

Per Serving:
calorie: 156 | fat: 4g | protein: 28g | carbs: 4g | sugars: 2g | fiber: 1g | sodium: 525mg

BLT Chicken Salad

Prep time: 15 minutes | Cook time: 17 minutes | Serves 4

4 slices bacon
2 (6-ounce / 170-g) chicken breasts
1 teaspoon salt
½ teaspoon garlic powder
¼ teaspoon dried parsley
¼ teaspoon pepper
¼ teaspoon dried thyme
1 cup water
2 cups chopped romaine lettuce
Sauce:
⅓ cup mayonnaise
1 ounce (28 g) chopped pecans
½ cup diced Roma tomatoes
½ avocado, diced
1 tablespoon lemon juice

1. Press the Sauté button to heat your Instant Pot. 2. Add the bacon and cook for about 7 minutes, flipping occasionally, until crisp. Remove and place on a paper towel to drain. When cool enough to handle, crumble the bacon and set aside. 3. Sprinkle the chicken with salt, garlic powder, parsley, pepper, and thyme. 4. Pour the water into the Instant Pot. Use a wooden spoon to ensure nothing is stuck to the bottom of the pot. Add the trivet to the pot and place the chicken on top of the trivet. 5. Secure the lid. Select the Manual mode and set the cooking time for 10 minutes at High Pressure. 6. Meanwhile, whisk together all the ingredients for the sauce in a large salad bowl. 7. Once cooking is complete, do a quick pressure release. Carefully open the lid. 8. Remove the chicken and let sit for 10 minutes. Cut the chicken into cubes and transfer to the salad bowl, along with the cooked bacon. Gently stir until the chicken is thoroughly coated. Mix in the lettuce right before serving.

Per Serving:
calories: 431 | fat: 32.6g | protein: 24.3g | carbs: 5.1g | net carbs: 2.4g | fiber: 2.7g

Chicken Fajitas with Bell Peppers

Prep time: 10 minutes | Cook time: 5 minutes | Serves 4

1½ pounds (680 g) boneless, skinless chicken breasts
¼ cup avocado oil
2 tablespoons water
1 tablespoon Mexican hot sauce
2 cloves garlic, minced
1 teaspoon lime juice
1 teaspoon ground cumin
1 teaspoon salt
1 teaspoon erythritol
¼ teaspoon chili powder
¼ teaspoon smoked paprika
5 ounces (142 g) sliced yellow bell pepper strips
5 ounces (142 g) sliced red bell pepper strips
5 ounces (142 g) sliced green bell pepper strips

1. Slice the chicken into very thin strips lengthwise. Cut each strip in half again. Imagine the thickness of restaurant fajitas when cutting. 2. In a measuring cup, whisk together the avocado oil, water, hot sauce, garlic, lime juice, cumin, salt, erythritol, chili powder, and paprika to form a marinade. Add to the pot, along with the chicken and peppers. 3. Close the lid and seal the vent. Cook on High Pressure for 5 minutes. Quick release the steam.

Per Serving:
calories: 319 | fat: 18g | protein: 34g | carbs: 6g | net carbs: 4g | fiber: 2g

Chicken Tacos with Fried Cheese Shells

Prep time: 5 minutes | Cook time: 25 minutes | Serves 6

Chicken:
4 (6-ounce / 170-g) boneless, skinless chicken breasts
1 cup chicken broth
1 teaspoon salt
¼ teaspoon pepper
1 tablespoon chili powder
2 teaspoons garlic powder
2 teaspoons cumin
Cheese Shells:
1½ cups shredded whole-milk Mozzarella cheese

1. Combine all ingredients for the chicken in the Instant Pot. 2. Secure the lid. Select the Manual mode and set the cooking time for 20 minutes at High Pressure. 3. Once cooking is complete, do a quick pressure release. Carefully open the lid. 4. Shred the chicken and serve in bowls or cheese shells. 5. Make the cheese shells: Heat a nonstick skillet over medium heat. 6. Sprinkle ¼ cup of Mozzarella cheese in the skillet and fry until golden. Flip and turn off the heat. Allow the cheese to get brown. Fill with chicken and fold. The cheese will harden as it cools. Repeat with the remaining cheese and filling. 7. Serve warm.

Per Serving:

calories: 233 | fat: 8.2g | protein: 32.4g | carbs: 2.4g | net carbs: 1.7g | fiber: 1.7g

Chicken and Kale Sandwiches

Prep time: 10 minutes | Cook time: 10 minutes | Serves 2

4 ounces (113 g) kale leaves
8 ounces (227 g) chicken fillet
1 tablespoon butter
1 ounce (28 g) lemon
¼ cup water

1. Dice the chicken fillet. 2. Squeeze the lemon juice over the poultry. 3. Transfer the poultry into the instant pot; add water and butter. 4. Close the lid and cook the chicken on the Poultry mode for 10 minutes. 5. When the chicken is cooked, place it on the kale leaves to make the medium sandwiches.

Per Serving:

calories: 298 | fat: 14g | protein: 35g | carbs: 7g | net carbs: 6g | fiber: 1g

Speedy Chicken Cacciatore

Prep time: 5 minutes | Cook time: 30 minutes | Serves 6

2 pounds boneless, skinless chicken thighs
1½ teaspoons fine sea salt
½ teaspoon freshly ground black pepper
2 tablespoons extra-virgin olive oil
3 garlic cloves, chopped
2 large red bell peppers, seeded and cut into ¼ by 2-inch strips
2 large yellow onions, sliced
½ cup dry red wine
1½ teaspoons Italian seasoning
½ teaspoon red pepper flakes (optional)
One 14½-ounce can diced tomatoes and their liquid
2 tablespoons tomato paste
Cooked brown rice or whole-grain pasta for serving

1. Season the chicken thighs on both sides with 1 teaspoon of the salt and the black pepper. 2. Select the Sauté setting on the Instant Pot and heat the oil and garlic for 2 minutes, until the garlic is bubbling but not browned. Add the bell peppers, onions, and remaining ½ teaspoon salt and sauté for 3 minutes, until the onions begin to soften. Stir in the wine, Italian seasoning, and pepper flakes (if using). Using tongs, add the chicken to the pot, turning each piece to coat it in the wine and spices and nestling them in a single layer in the liquid. Pour the tomatoes and their liquid on top of the chicken and dollop the tomato paste on top. Do not stir them in. 3. Secure the lid and set the Pressure Release to Sealing. Press the Cancel button to reset the cooking program, then select the Poultry, Pressure Cook, or Manual setting and set the cooking time for 12 minutes at high pressure. (The pot will take about 15 minutes to come up to pressure before the cooking program begins.) 4. When the cooking program ends, perform a quick pressure release by moving the Pressure Release to Venting, or let the pressure release naturally. Open the pot and, using tongs, transfer the chicken and vegetables to a serving dish. 5. Spoon some of the sauce over the chicken and serve hot, with the rice on the side.

Per Serving:

calories: 297 | fat: 11g | protein: 32g | carbs: 16g | sugars: 3g | fiber: 3g | sodium: 772mg

Indian Chicken Breast

Prep time: 5 minutes | Cook time: 4 minutes | Serves 2

¼ teaspoon cumin seeds
½ teaspoon turmeric
1 teaspoon ground paprika
¾ teaspoon chili paste
½ teaspoon ground coriander
½ cup coconut milk
14 ounces (397 g) chicken breast, skinless, boneless
1 tablespoon coconut oil

1. Blend together the cumin seeds, turmeric, ground paprika, chili paste, coriander, coconut milk, and coconut oil. 2. When the mixture is smooth, pour it in the instant pot bowl. 3. Chop the chicken breast roughly and transfer it in the spice mixture. Stir gently with the help of the spatula. 4. Lock the lid and seal it. 5. Set the Manual mode for 4 minutes (High Pressure). 6. After this, make quick-release pressure. Enjoy!

Per Serving:

calories: 435 | fat: 17g | protein: 44g | carbs: 5g | net carbs: 3g | fiber: 2g

Rubbed Whole Chicken

Prep time: 20 minutes | Cook time: 25 minutes | Serves 4

1½ pound (680 g) whole chicken
1 tablespoon poultry seasoning
2 tablespoons avocado oil
2 cups water

1. Pour water in the instant pot. 2. Then rub the chicken with poultry seasoning and avocado oil. 3. Put the chicken in the instant pot. Close and seal the lid. 4. Cook the meal in Manual mode for 25 minutes. When the time is finished, allow the natural pressure release for 10 minutes.

Per Serving:

calories: 335 | fat: 14g | protein: 49g | carbs: 1g | net carbs: 1g | fiber: 0g

Chicken Carnitas

Prep time: 5 minutes | Cook time: 15 minutes | Serves 8

3 pounds (1.4 kg) whole chicken, cut into pieces
⅓ cup vegetable broth
3 cloves garlic, pressed
1 tablespoon avocado oil
1 guajillo chili, minced
Sea salt, to taste
½ teaspoon paprika
⅓ teaspoon cayenne pepper
½ teaspoon ground bay leaf
⅓ teaspoon black pepper
2 tablespoons chopped fresh coriander, for garnish
1 cup crème fraiche, for serving

1. Combine all the ingredients except the coriander and crème fraiche in the Instant Pot. 2. Lock the lid. Select the Poultry mode and set the cooking time for 15 minutes at High Pressure. 3. When the timer beeps, perform a quick pressure release. Carefully remove the lid. 4. Shred the chicken with two forks and discard the bones. Garnish with the coriander and serve with a dollop of crème fraiche.

Per Serving:
calories: 298 | fat: 15.9g | protein: 35.6g | carbs: 2.4g | net carbs: 2.1g | fiber: 0.3g

Poblano Chicken

Prep time: 10 minutes | Cook time: 29 minutes | Serves 4

2 Poblano peppers, sliced
16 ounces (454 g) chicken fillet
½ teaspoon salt
½ cup coconut cream
1 tablespoon butter
½ teaspoon chili powder

1. Heat up the butter on Sauté mode for 3 minutes. 2. Add Poblano and cook them for 3 minutes. 3. Meanwhile, cut the chicken fillet into the strips and sprinkle with salt and chili powder. 4. Add the chicken strips to the instant pot. 5. Then add coconut cream and close the lid. Cook the meal on Sauté mode for 20 minutes.

Per Serving:
calories: 320 | fat: 18g | protein: 34g | carbs: 4g | net carbs: 3g | fiber: 1g

Chicken Enchilada Bowl

Prep time: 10 minutes | Cook time: 35 minutes | Serves 4

2 (6-ounce / 170-g) boneless, skinless chicken breasts
2 teaspoons chili powder
½ teaspoon garlic powder
½ teaspoon salt
¼ teaspoon pepper
2 tablespoons coconut oil
¾ cup red enchilada sauce
¼ cup chicken broth
1 (4-ounce / 113-g) can green chilies
¼ cup diced onion
2 cups cooked cauliflower rice
1 avocado, diced
½ cup sour cream
1 cup shredded Cheddar cheese

1. Sprinkle the chili powder, garlic powder, salt, and pepper on chicken breasts. 2. Set your Instant Pot to Sauté and melt the coconut oil. Add the chicken breasts and sear each side for about 5 minutes until golden brown. 3. Pour the enchilada sauce and broth over the chicken. Using a wooden spoon or rubber spatula, scrape the bottom of pot to make sure nothing is sticking. Stir in the chilies and onion. 4. Secure the lid. Select the Manual mode and set the cooking time for 25 minutes at High Pressure. 5. Once cooking is complete, do a quick pressure release. Carefully open the lid. 6. Remove the chicken and shred with two forks. Serve the chicken over the cauliflower rice and place the avocado, sour cream, and Cheddar cheese on top.

Per Serving:
calories: 434 | fat: 26.1g | protein: 29.3g | carbs: 11.8g | net carbs: 7.0g | fiber: 4.8g

Thai Coconut Chicken

Prep time: 10 minutes | Cook time: 15 minutes | Serves 4

1 tablespoon coconut oil
1 pound (454 g) chicken, cubed
2 cloves garlic, minced
1 shallot, peeled and chopped
1 teaspoon Thai chili, minced
1 teaspoon fresh ginger root, julienned
⅓ teaspoon cumin powder
1 tomato, peeled and chopped
1 cup vegetable broth
⅓ cup unsweetened coconut milk
2 tablespoons coconut aminos
1 teaspoon Thai curry paste
Salt and freshly ground black pepper, to taste

1. Set your Instant Pot to Sauté and heat the coconut oil. 2. Brown the chicken cubes for 2 to 3 minutes, stirring frequently. Reserve the chicken in a bowl. 3. Add the garlic and shallot and sauté for 2 minutes until tender. Add a splash of vegetable broth to the pot, if needed. 4. Stir in the Thai chili, ginger, and cumin powder and cook for another 1 minute or until fragrant. 5. Add the cooked chicken, tomato, vegetable broth, milk, coconut aminos, and curry paste to the Instant Pot and stir well. 6. Lock the lid. Select the Manual mode and set the cooking time for 10 minutes at High Pressure. 7. When the timer beeps, perform a quick pressure release. Carefully remove the lid. Season with salt and pepper to taste and serve.

Per Serving:
calories: 196 | fat: 7.7g | protein: 25.9g | carbs: 4.5g | net carbs: 2.9g | fiber: 1.6g

Creamy Nutmeg Chicken

Prep time: 20 minutes | Cook time: 10 minutes | Serves 6

1 tablespoon canola oil
6 boneless chicken breast halves, skin and visible fat removed
¼ cup chopped onion
¼ cup minced parsley
2 (10¾-ounce) cans 98% fat-free, reduced-sodium cream of mushroom soup
½ cup fat-free sour cream
½ cup fat-free milk
1 tablespoon ground nutmeg
¼ teaspoon sage
¼ teaspoon dried thyme
¼ teaspoon crushed rosemary

1. Press the Sauté button on the Instant Pot and then add the canola oil. Place the chicken in the oil and brown chicken on both sides. Remove the chicken to a plate. 2. Sauté the onion and parsley in the remaining oil in the Instant Pot until the onions are tender. Press Cancel on the Instant Pot, then place the chicken back inside. 3. Mix together the remaining ingredients in a bowl then pour over the chicken. 4. Secure the lid and set the vent to sealing. Set on Manual mode for 10 minutes. 5. When cooking time is up, let the pressure release naturally.

Per Serving:
calories: 264 | fat: 8g | protein: 31g | carbs: 15g | sugars: 5g | fiber: 1g | sodium: 495mg

Chicken and Scallions Stuffed Peppers

Prep time: 5 minutes | Cook time: 20 minutes | Serves 5

1 tablespoon butter, at room temperature
½ cup scallions, chopped
1 pound (454 g) ground chicken
½ teaspoon sea salt
½ teaspoon chili powder
⅓ teaspoon paprika
⅓ teaspoon ground cumin
¼ teaspoon shallot powder
6 ounces (170 g) goat cheese, crumbled
1½ cups water
5 bell peppers, tops, membrane, and seeds removed
½ cup sour cream

1. Set your Instant Pot to Sauté and melt the butter. 2. Add the scallions and chicken and sauté for 2 to 3 minutes. 3. Stir in the sea salt, chili powder, paprika, cumin, and shallot powder. Add the crumbled goat cheese, stir, and reserve the mixture in a bowl. 4. Clean your Instant Pot. Pour the water into the Instant Pot and insert the trivet. 5. Stuff the bell peppers with enough of the chicken mixture, and don't pack the peppers too tightly. Put the peppers on the trivet. 6. Lock the lid. Select the Poultry mode and set the cooking time for 15 minutes at High Pressure. 7. When the timer beeps, perform a natural pressure release for 10 minutes, then release any remaining pressure. Carefully remove the lid. 8. Remove from the Instant Pot and serve with the sour cream.

Per Serving:
calories: 338 | fat: 19.8g | protein: 30.3g | carbs: 8.6g | net carbs: 7.4g | fiber: 1.2g

Tuscan Chicken Drumsticks

Prep time: 15 minutes | Cook time: 12 minutes | Serves 4

4 chicken drumsticks
1 cup chopped spinach
1 teaspoon minced garlic
1 teaspoon ground paprika
1 cup heavy cream
1 teaspoon cayenne pepper
1 ounce (28 g) sun-dried tomatoes, chopped

1. Put all ingredients in the instant pot. 2. Close and seal the lid. 3. Cook the meal on Manual mode (High Pressure) for 12 minutes. 4. Then allow the natural pressure release for 10 minutes. 5. Serve the chicken with hot sauce from the instant pot.

Per Serving:
calories: 188 | fat: 14g | protein: 14g | carbs: 2g | net carbs: 1g | fiber: 1g

Herbed Whole Turkey Breast

Prep time: 10 minutes | Cook time:30 minutes | Serves 12

3 tablespoons extra-virgin olive oil
1½ tablespoons herbes de Provence or poultry seasoning
2 teaspoons minced garlic
1 teaspoon lemon zest (from 1 small lemon)
1 tablespoon kosher salt
1½ teaspoons freshly ground black pepper
1 (6-pound) bone-in, skin-on whole turkey breast, rinsed and patted dry

1. In a small bowl, whisk together the olive oil, herbes de Provence, garlic, lemon zest, salt, and pepper. 2. Rub the outside of the turkey and under the skin with the olive oil mixture. 3. Pour 1 cup of water into the electric pressure cooker and insert a wire rack or trivet. 4. Place the turkey on the rack, skin-side up. 5. Close and lock the lid of the pressure cooker. Set the valve to sealing. 6. Cook on high pressure for 30 minutes. 7. When the cooking is complete, hit Cancel. Allow the pressure to release naturally for 20 minutes, then quick release any remaining pressure. 8. Once the pin drops, unlock and remove the lid. 9. Carefully transfer the turkey to a cutting board. Remove the skin, slice, and serve.

Per Serving:
calorie: 389 | fat: 19g | protein: 50g | carbs: 1g | sugars: 0g | fiber: 0g | sodium: 582mg

African Chicken Peanut Stew

Prep time: 10 minutes | Cook time: 10 minutes | Serves 6

1 cup chopped onion
2 tablespoons minced garlic
1 tablespoon minced fresh ginger
1 teaspoon salt
½ teaspoon ground cumin
½ teaspoon ground coriander
½ teaspoon freshly ground black pepper
½ teaspoon ground cinnamon
⅛ teaspoon ground cloves
1 tablespoon sugar-free tomato paste
1 pound (454 g) boneless, skinless chicken breasts or thighs, cut into large chunks
3 to 4 cups chopped Swiss chard
1 cup cubed raw pumpkin
½ cup water
1 cup chunky peanut butter

1. In the inner cooking pot of the Instant Pot, stir together the onion, garlic, ginger, salt, cumin, coriander, pepper, cinnamon, cloves, and tomato paste. Add the chicken, chard, pumpkin, and water. 2. Lock the lid into place. Select Manual and adjust the pressure to High. Cook for 10 minutes. When the cooking is complete, let the pressure release naturally. Unlock the lid. 3. Mix in the peanut butter a little at a time. Taste with each addition, as your reward for cooking. The final sauce should be thick enough to coat the back of a spoon in a thin layer. 4. Serve over mashed cauliflower, cooked zucchini noodles, steamed vegetables, or with a side salad.

Per Serving:
calories: 411 | fat: 27g | protein: 31g | carbs: 15g | net carbs: 10g | fiber: 5g

Chicken in Mushroom Gravy

Prep time: 10 minutes | Cook time: 10 minutes | Serves 6

6 (5 ounces each) boneless, skinless chicken-breast halves
Salt and pepper to taste
¼ cup dry white wine or low-sodium chicken broth
10¾-ounce can 98% fat-free, reduced-sodium cream of mushroom soup
4 ounces sliced mushrooms

1. Place chicken in the inner pot of the Instant Pot. Season with salt and pepper. 2. Combine wine and soup in a bowl, then pour over the chicken. Top with the mushrooms. 3. Secure the lid and make sure the vent is set to sealing. Set on Manual mode for 10 minutes. 4. When cooking time is up, let the pressure release naturally.

Per Serving:
calories: 204 | fat: 4g | protein: 34g | carbs: 6g | sugars: 1g | fiber: 1g | sodium: 320mg

Broccoli Chicken Divan

Prep time: 15 minutes | Cook time: 10 minutes | Serves 4

1 cup chopped broccoli
2 tablespoons cream cheese
½ cup heavy cream
1 tablespoon curry powder
¼ cup chicken broth
½ cup grated Cheddar cheese
6 ounces (170 g) chicken fillet, cooked and chopped

1. Mix up broccoli and curry powder and put the mixture in the instant pot. 2. Add heavy cream and cream cheese. 3. Then add chicken and mix up the ingredients. 4. Then add chicken broth and heavy cream. 5. Top the mixture with Cheddar cheese. Close and seal the lid. 6. Cook the meal on Manual mode (High Pressure) for 10 minutes. Allow the natural pressure release for 5 minutes, open the lid and cool the meal for 10 minutes.

Per Serving:
calories: 222 | fat: 15g | protein: 18g | carbs: 3g | net carbs: 2g | fiber: 1g

Pizza in a Pot

Prep time: 25 minutes | Cook time: 15 minutes | Serves 8

1 pound bulk lean sweet Italian turkey sausage, browned and drained
28-ounce can crushed tomatoes
15½-ounce can chili beans
2¼-ounce can sliced black olives, drained
1 medium onion, chopped
1 small green bell pepper, chopped
2 garlic cloves, minced
¼ cup grated Parmesan cheese
1 tablespoon quick-cooking tapioca
1 tablespoon dried basil
1 bay leaf

1. Set the Instant Pot to Sauté, then add the turkey sausage. Sauté until browned. 2. Add the remaining ingredients into the Instant Pot and stir. 3. Secure the lid and make sure the vent is set to sealing. Cook on Manual for 15 minutes. 4. When cook time is up, let the pressure release naturally for 5 minutes then perform a quick release. Discard bay leaf.

Per Serving:
calorie: 251 | fat: 10g | protein: 18g | carbs: 23g | sugars: 8g | fiber: 3g | sodium: 936mg

Marjoram Chicken Wings with Cream Cheese

Prep time: 7 minutes | Cook time: 10 minutes | Serves 2

1 teaspoon marjoram
1 teaspoon cream cheese
½ green pepper
½ teaspoon salt
½ teaspoon ground black pepper
14 ounces (397 g) chicken wings
¾ cup water
1 teaspoon coconut oil

1. Rub the chicken wings with the marjoram, salt, and ground black pepper. 2. Blend the green pepper until you get a purée. 3. Rub the chicken wings in the green pepper purée. 4. Then toss the coconut oil in the instant pot bowl and preheat it on the Sauté mode. 5. Add the chicken wings and cook them for 3 minutes from each side or until light brown. 6. Then add cream cheese and water. 7. Cook the meal on Manual mode for 4 minutes at High Pressure. 8. When the time is over, make a quick pressure release. 9. Let the cooked chicken wings chill for 1 to 2 minutes and serve them!

Per Serving:
calories: 411 | fat: 18g | protein: 58g | carbs: 2g | net carbs: 1g | fiber: 1g

Authentic Chicken Shawarma

Prep time: 15 minutes | Cook time: 17 minutes | Serves 4

1 pound (454 g) chicken fillet
½ teaspoon ground coriander
½ teaspoon smoked paprika
½ teaspoon dried thyme
1 tablespoon tahini sauce
1 teaspoon lemon juice
1 teaspoon heavy cream
1 cup water, for cooking

1. Rub the chicken fillet with ground coriander, smoked paprika, thyme, and wrap in the foil. 2. Then pour water and insert the steamer rack in the instant pot. 3. Place the wrapped chicken in the steamer; close and seal the lid. 4. Cook the chicken on Manual mode (High Pressure) for 17 minutes. Make a quick pressure release. 5. Make the sauce: Mix up heavy cream, lemon juice, and tahini paste. 6. Slice the chicken and sprinkle it with sauce.

Per Serving:
calories: 234 | fat: 10g | protein: 33g | carbs: 1g | net carbs: 1g | fiber: 0g

Chicken Casablanca

Prep time: 20 minutes | Cook time: 12 minutes | Serves 8

2 large onions, sliced
1 teaspoon ground ginger
3 garlic cloves, minced
2 tablespoons canola oil, divided
3 pounds skinless chicken pieces
3 large carrots, diced
2 large potatoes, unpeeled, diced
½ teaspoon ground cumin
½ teaspoon salt
½ teaspoon pepper
¼ teaspoon cinnamon
2 tablespoons raisins
14½-ounce can chopped tomatoes
3 small zucchini, sliced
15-ounce can garbanzo beans, drained
2 tablespoons chopped parsley

1. Using the Sauté function of the Instant Pot, cook the onions, ginger, and garlic in 1 tablespoon of the oil for 5 minutes, stirring constantly. Remove onions, ginger, and garlic from pot and set aside. 2. Brown the chicken pieces with the remaining oil, then add the cooked onions, ginger and garlic back in as well as all of the remaining ingredients, except the parsley. 3. Secure the lid and make sure vent is in the sealing position. Cook on Manual mode for 12 minutes. 4. When cook time is up, let the pressure release naturally for 5 minutes and then release the rest of the pressure manually.

Per Serving:
calories: 395 | fat: 10g | protein: 36g | carbs: 40g | sugars: 10g | fiber: 8g | sodium: 390mg

Thai Yellow Curry with Chicken Meatballs

Prep time: 5 minutes | Cook time: 30 minutes | Serves 4

1 pound 95 percent lean ground chicken
⅓ cup gluten-free panko (Japanese bread crumbs)
1 egg white
1 tablespoon coconut oil
1 yellow onion, cut into 1-inch pieces
One 14-ounce can light coconut milk
3 tablespoons yellow curry paste
¾ cup water
8 ounces carrots, halved lengthwise, then cut crosswise into 1-inch lengths (or quartered if very large)
8 ounces zucchini, quartered lengthwise, then cut crosswise into 1-inch lengths (or cut into halves, then thirds if large)
8 ounces cremini mushrooms, quartered
Fresh Thai basil leaves for serving (optional)
Fresno or jalapeño chile, thinly sliced, for serving (optional)
1 lime, cut into wedges
Cooked cauliflower "rice" for serving

1. In a medium bowl, combine the chicken, panko, and egg white and mix until evenly combined. Set aside. 2. Select the Sauté setting on the Instant Pot and heat the oil for 2 minutes. Add the onion and sauté for 5 minutes, until it begins to soften and brown. Add ½ cup of the coconut milk and the curry paste and sauté for 1 minute more, until bubbling and fragrant. Press the Cancel button to turn off the pot, then stir in the water. 3. Using a 1½-tablespoon cookie scoop, shape and drop meatballs into the pot in a single layer. 4. Secure the lid and set the Pressure Release to Sealing. Select the Pressure Cook or Manual setting and set the cooking time for 5 minutes at high pressure. (The pot will take about 5 minutes to come up to pressure before the cooking program begins.) 5. When the cooking program ends, perform a quick pressure release by moving the Pressure Release to Venting, or let the pressure release naturally. Open the pot and stir in the carrots, zucchini, mushrooms, and remaining 1¼ cups coconut milk. 6. Press the Cancel button to reset the cooking program, then select the Sauté setting. Bring the curry to a simmer (this will take about 2 minutes), then let cook, uncovered, for about 8 minutes, until the carrots are fork-tender. Press the Cancel button to turn off the pot. 7. Ladle the curry into bowls. Serve piping hot, topped with basil leaves and chile slices, if desired, and the lime wedges and cauliflower "rice" on the side.

Per Serving:
calories: 349 | fat: 15g | protein: 30g | carbs: 34g | sugars: 8g | fiber: 5g | sodium: 529mg

Paprika Chicken Wings

Prep time: 10 minutes | Cook time: 13 minutes | Serves 4

1 pound (454 g) boneless chicken wings
1 teaspoon ground paprika
1 teaspoon avocado oil
¼ teaspoon minced garlic
¾ cup beef broth

1. Pour the avocado oil in the instant pot. 2. Rub the chicken wings with ground paprika and minced garlic and put them in the instant pot. 3. Cook the chicken on Sauté mode for 4 minutes from each side. 4. Then add beef broth and close the lid. 5. Sauté the meal for 5 minutes more.

Per Serving:
calories: 226 | fat: 9g | protein: 34g | carbs: 1g | net carbs: 1g | fiber: 0g

Lemon Garlic Chicken

Prep time: 20 minutes | Cook time: 30 minutes | Serves 6

2 pounds (907 g) skinless chicken thighs
1 tablespoon avocado oil
1 teaspoon minced garlic
½ teaspoon ground coriander
1 teaspoon lemon zest
1 teaspoon lemon juice
⅓ cup chicken broth
1 cup water

1. Pour water and insert the steamer rack in the instant pot. Pour water and chicken broth in the instant pot bowl. 2. Put the chicken thighs in the bowl and sprinkle them with avocado oil, minced garlic, ground coriander, lemon zest, and lemon juice. 3. Then shake the chicken thighs gently and transfer them on the steamer rack. 4. Close and seal the lid. 5. Cook the chicken for 15 minutes on Manual mode (High Pressure). Then make a quick pressure release and transfer the chicken thighs on the plate.

Per Serving:
calories: 294 | fat: 12g | protein: 44g | carbs: 0g | net carbs: 0g | fiber: 0g

Lemony Chicken Thighs

Prep time: 15 minutes | Cook time: 15 minutes | Serves 3 to 5

1 cup low-sodium chicken bone broth
5 frozen bone-in chicken thighs
1 small onion, diced
5–6 cloves garlic, diced
Juice of 1 lemon
2 tablespoons margarine, melted
½ teaspoon salt
¼ teaspoon black pepper
1 teaspoon True Lemon Lemon Pepper seasoning
1 teaspoon parsley flakes
¼ teaspoon oregano
Rind of 1 lemon

1. Add the chicken bone broth into the inner pot of the Instant Pot. 2. Add the chicken thighs. 3. Add the onion and garlic. 4. Pour the fresh lemon juice in with the melted margarine. 5. Add the seasonings. 6. Lock the lid, make sure the vent is at sealing, then press the Poultry button. Set to 15 minutes. 7. When cook time is up, let the pressure naturally release for 3–5 minutes, then manually release the rest. 8. You can place these under the broiler for 2–3 minutes to brown. 9. Plate up and pour some of the sauce over top with fresh grated lemon rind.

Per Serving:
calories: 329 | fat: 24g | protein: 26g | carbs: 3g | sugars: 1g | fiber: 0g | sodium: 407mg

Chapter 7 Stews and Soups

Beef and Spinach Stew

Prep time: 20 minutes | Cook time: 30 minutes | Serves 4

1 pound (454 g) beef sirloin, chopped
2 cups spinach, chopped
3 cups chicken broth
1 cup coconut milk
1 teaspoon allspices
1 teaspoon coconut aminos

1. Put all ingredients in the Instant Pot. Stir to mix well. 2. Close the lid. Set the Manual mode and set cooking time for 30 minutes on High Pressure. 3. When timer beeps, use a natural pressure release for 10 minutes, then release any remaining pressure. Open the lid. 4. Blend with an immersion blender until smooth. 5. Serve warm.

Per Serving:
calories: 383 | fat: 22g | protein: 40g | carbs: 5g | net carbs: 3g | fiber: 2g

Turkey and Pinto Chili

Prep time: 0 minutes | Cook time: 60 minutes | Serves 8

2 tablespoons cold-pressed avocado oil
4 garlic cloves, diced
1 large yellow onion, diced
4 jalapeño chiles, seeded and diced
2 carrots, diced
4 celery stalks, diced
2 teaspoons fine sea salt
2 pounds 93 percent lean ground turkey
Two 4-ounce cans fire-roasted diced green chiles
4 tablespoons chili powder
2 teaspoons ground cumin
2 teaspoons ground coriander
1 teaspoon dried oregano
1 teaspoon dried sage
1 cup low-sodium chicken broth
3 cups drained cooked pinto beans, or two 15-ounce cans pinto beans, drained and rinsed
Two 14½-ounce cans no-salt petite diced tomatoes and their liquid
¼ cup tomato paste

1. Select the Sauté setting on the Instant Pot and heat the oil and garlic for 3 minutes, until the garlic is bubbling but not browned. Add the onion, jalapeños, carrots, celery, and salt and sauté for 5 minutes, until the onion begins to soften. Add the turkey and sauté, using a wooden spoon or spatula to break up the meat as it cooks, for 6 minutes, until cooked through and no streaks of pink remain. Stir in the green chiles, chili powder, cumin, coriander, oregano, sage, and broth, using a wooden spoon or spatula to nudge any browned bits from the bottom of the pot. 2. Pour in the beans in a layer on top of the turkey. Pour in the tomatoes and their liquid and add the tomato paste in a dollop on top. Do not stir in the beans, tomatoes, or tomato paste. 3. Secure the lid and set the Pressure Release to Sealing. Press the Cancel button to reset the cooking program, then select the Pressure Cook or Manual setting and set the cooking time for 15 minutes at high pressure. (The pot will take about 15 minutes to come up to pressure before the cooking program begins.) 4. When the cooking program ends, let the pressure release naturally for at least 20 minutes, then move the Pressure Release to Venting to release any remaining steam. Open the pot and stir the chili to mix all of the ingredients. 5. Press the Cancel button to reset the cooking program, then select the Sauté setting and set the cooking time for 10 minutes. Allow the chili to reduce and thicken. Do not stir the chili while it is cooking, as this will cause it to sputter more. 6. When the cooking program ends, the pot will turn off. Wearing heat-resistant mitts, remove the inner pot from the housing. Wait for about 2 minutes to allow the chili to stop simmering, then give it a final stir. 7. Ladle the chili into bowls and serve hot.

Per Serving:
calories: 354 | fat: 14g | protein: 30g | carbs: 28g | sugars: 6g | fiber: 9g | sodium: 819mg

Sicilian Fish Stew

Prep time: 10 minutes | Cook time: 10 minutes | Serves 4 to 6

2 tablespoons extra-virgin olive oil
2 onions, chopped fine
1 teaspoon table salt
½ teaspoon pepper
1 teaspoon minced fresh thyme or ¼ teaspoon dried
Pinch red pepper flakes
4 garlic cloves, minced, divided
1 (28-ounce / 794-g) can whole peeled tomatoes, drained with juice reserved, chopped coarse
1 (8-ounce / 227-g) bottle clam juice
¼ cup dry white wine
¼ cup golden raisins
2 tablespoons capers, rinsed
1½ pounds (680 g) skinless swordfish steak, 1 to 1½ inches thick, cut into 1-inch pieces
¼ cup pine nuts, toasted
¼ cup minced fresh mint
1 teaspoon grated orange zest

1. Using highest sauté function, heat oil in Instant Pot until shimmering. Add onions, salt, and pepper and cook until onions are softened, about 5 minutes. Stir in thyme, pepper flakes, and three-quarters of garlic and cook until fragrant, about 30 seconds. Stir in tomatoes and reserved juice, clam juice, wine, raisins, and capers. Nestle swordfish into pot and spoon some cooking liquid over top. 2. Lock lid in place and close pressure release valve. Select high pressure cook function and cook for 1 minute. Turn off Instant Pot and quick-release pressure. Carefully remove lid, allowing steam to escape away from you. 3. Combine pine nuts, mint, orange zest, and remaining garlic in bowl. Season stew with salt and pepper to taste. Sprinkle individual portions with pine nut mixture before serving.

Per Serving:
calories: 320 | fat: 16g | protein: 25g | carbs: 16g | fiber: 3g | sodium: 920mg

Ground Turkey Stew

Prep time: 5 minutes | Cook time: 25 minutes | Serves 5

1 tablespoon olive oil
1 onion, chopped
1 pound ground turkey
½ teaspoon garlic powder
1 teaspoon chili powder
¾ teaspoon cumin
2 teaspoons coriander
1 teaspoon dried oregano
½ teaspoon salt
1 green pepper, chopped
1 red pepper, chopped
1 tomato, chopped
1½ cups reduced-sodium tomato sauce
1 tablespoon low-sodium soy sauce
1 cup water
2 handfuls cilantro, chopped
15-ounce can reduced-salt black beans

1. Press the Sauté function on the control panel of the Instant Pot. 2. Add the olive oil to the inner pot and let it get hot. Add onion and sauté for a few minutes, or until light golden. 3. Add ground turkey. Break the ground meat using a wooden spoon to avoid formation of lumps. Sauté for a few minutes, until the pink color has faded. 4. Add garlic powder, chili powder, cumin, coriander, dried oregano, and salt. Combine well. Add green pepper, red pepper, and chopped tomato. Combine well. 5. Add tomato sauce, soy sauce, and water; combine well. 6. Close and secure the lid. Click on the Cancel key to cancel the Sauté mode. Make sure the pressure release valve on the lid is in the sealing position. 7. Click on Manual function first and then select high pressure. Click the + button and set the time to 15 minutes. 8. You can either have the steam release naturally (it will take around 20 minutes) or, after 10 minutes, turn the pressure release valve on the lid to venting and release steam. Be careful as the steam is very hot. After the pressure has released completely, open the lid. 9. If the stew is watery, turn on the Sauté function and let it cook for a few more minutes with the lid off. 10. Add cilantro and can of black beans, combine well, and let cook for a few minutes.

Per Serving:

calories: 209 | fat: 3g | protein: 24g | carbs: 21g | sugars: 8g | fiber: 6g | sodium: 609mg

Cream of Mushroom Soup

Prep time: 10 minutes | Cook time: 10 minutes | Serves 4

1 pound (454 g) sliced button mushrooms
3 tablespoons butter
2 tablespoons diced onion
2 cloves garlic, minced
2 cups chicken broth
½ teaspoon salt
¼ teaspoon pepper
½ cup heavy cream
¼ teaspoon xanthan gum

1. Press the Sauté button and then press the Adjust button to set heat to Less. Add mushrooms, butter, and onion to pot. Sauté for 5 to 8 minutes or until onions and mushrooms begin to brown. Add garlic and sauté until fragrant. Press the Cancel button. 2. Add broth, salt, and pepper. Click lid closed. Press the Manual button and adjust time for 3 minutes. When timer beeps, quick-release the pressure. Stir in heavy cream and xanthan gum. Allow a few minutes to thicken and serve warm.

Per Serving:

calories: 220 | fat: 19g | protein: 5g | carbs: 6g | net carbs: 5g | fiber: 1g

Beef and Mushroom Stew

Prep time: 15 minutes | Cook time: 30 minutes | Serves 4

2 tablespoons coconut oil
1 pound (454 g) cubed chuck roast
1 cup sliced button mushrooms
½ medium onion, chopped
2 cups beef broth
½ cup chopped celery
1 tablespoon sugar-free tomato paste
1 teaspoon thyme
2 garlic cloves, minced
½ teaspoon xanthan gum

1. Press the Sauté button and add coconut oil to Instant Pot. Brown cubes of chuck roast until golden, working in batches if necessary. (If the pan is overcrowded, they will not brown properly.) Set aside after browning is completed. 2. Add mushrooms and onions to pot. Sauté until mushrooms begin to brown and onions are translucent. Press the Cancel button. 3. Add broth to Instant Pot. Use wooden spoon to scrape bits from bottom if necessary. Add celery, tomato paste, thyme, and garlic. Click lid closed. Press the Manual button and adjust time for 35 minutes. When timer beeps, allow a natural release. 4. When pressure valve drops, stir in xanthan gum and allow to thicken. Serve warm.

Per Serving:

calories: 354 | fat: 25g | protein: 24g | carbs: 4g | net carbs: 2g | fiber: 2g

Creamy Carrot Soup with Warm Spices

Prep time: 15 minutes | Cook time: 10 minutes | Serves 6 to 8

2 tablespoons extra-virgin olive oil
2 onions, chopped
1 teaspoon table salt
1 tablespoon grated fresh ginger
1 tablespoon ground coriander
1 tablespoon ground fennel
1 teaspoon ground cinnamon
4 cups vegetable or chicken broth
2 cups water
2 pounds (907 g) carrots, peeled and cut into 2-inch pieces
½ teaspoon baking soda
2 tablespoons pomegranate molasses
½ cup plain Greek yogurt
½ cup hazelnuts, toasted, skinned, and chopped
½ cup chopped fresh cilantro or mint

1. Using highest sauté function, heat oil in Instant Pot until shimmering. Add onions and salt and cook until onions are softened, about 5 minutes. Stir in ginger, coriander, fennel, and cinnamon and cook until fragrant, about 30 seconds. Stir in broth, water, carrots, and baking soda. 2. Lock lid in place and close pressure release valve. Select high pressure cook function and cook for 3 minutes. Turn off Instant Pot and quick-release pressure. Carefully remove lid, allowing steam to escape away from you. 3. Working in batches, process soup in blender until smooth, 1 to 2 minutes. Return processed soup to Instant Pot and bring to simmer using highest sauté function. Season with salt and pepper to taste. Drizzle individual portions with pomegranate molasses and top with yogurt, hazelnuts, and cilantro before serving.

Per Serving:

calories: 190 | fat: 11g | protein: 4g | carbs: 20g | fiber: 5g | sodium: 820mg

Bacon, Leek, and Cauliflower Soup

Prep time: 15 minutes | Cook time: 15 minutes | Serves 6

6 slices bacon
1 leek, remove the dark green end and roots, sliced in half lengthwise, rinsed, cut into ½-inch-thick slices crosswise
½ medium yellow onion, sliced
4 cloves garlic, minced
3 cups chicken broth
1 large head cauliflower, roughly chopped into florets
1 cup water
1 teaspoon kosher salt
1 teaspoon ground black pepper
⅔ cup shredded sharp Cheddar cheese, divided
½ cup heavy whipping cream

1. Set the Instant Pot to Sauté mode. When heated, place the bacon on the bottom of the pot and cook for 5 minutes or until crispy. 2. Transfer the bacon slices to a plate. Let stand until cool enough to handle, crumble it with forks. 3. Add the leek and onion to the bacon fat remaining in the pot. Sauté for 5 minutes or until fragrant and the onion begins to caramelize. Add the garlic and sauté for 30 seconds more or until fragrant. 4. Stir in the chicken broth, cauliflower florets, water, salt, pepper, and three-quarters of the crumbled bacon. 5. Secure the lid. Press the Manual button and set cooking time for 3 minutes on High Pressure. 6. When timer beeps, perform a quick pressure release. Open the lid. 7. Stir in ½ cup of the Cheddar and the cream. Use an immersion blender to purée the soup until smooth. 8. Ladle into bowls and garnish with the remaining Cheddar and crumbled bacon. Serve immediately.

Per Serving:
calories: 251 | fat: 18.9g | protein: 10.5g | carbs: 12.0g | net carbs: 8.6g | fiber: 3.4g

Favorite Chili

Prep time: 10 minutes | Cook time: 35 minutes | Serves 5

1 pound extra-lean ground beef
1 teaspoon salt
½ teaspoons black pepper
1 tablespoon olive oil
1 small onion, chopped
2 cloves garlic, minced
1 green pepper, chopped
2 tablespoons chili powder
½ teaspoons cumin
1 cup water
16-ounce can chili beans
15-ounce can low-sodium crushed tomatoes

1. Press Sauté button and adjust once to Sauté More function. Wait until indicator says "hot." 2. Season the ground beef with salt and black pepper. 3. Add the olive oil into the inner pot. Coat the whole bottom of the pot with the oil. 4. Add ground beef into the inner pot. The ground beef will start to release moisture. Allow the ground beef to brown and crisp slightly, stirring occasionally to break it up. Taste and adjust the seasoning with more salt and ground black pepper. 5. Add diced onion, minced garlic, chopped pepper, chili powder, and cumin. Sauté for about 5 minutes, until the spices start to release their fragrance. Stir frequently. 6. Add water and 1 can of chili beans, not drained. Mix well. Pour in 1 can of crushed tomatoes. 7. Close and secure lid, making sure vent is set to sealing, and pressure cook on Manual at high pressure for 10 minutes. 8. Let the pressure release naturally when cooking time is up. Open the lid carefully.

Per Serving:
calories: 213 | fat: 10g | protein: 18g | carbs: 11g | sugars: 4g | fiber: 4g | sodium: 385mg

Bacon Broccoli Soup

Prep time: 12 minutes | Cook time: 12 minutes | Serves 6

2 large heads broccoli
2 strips bacon, chopped
2 tablespoons unsalted butter
¼ cup diced onions
Cloves squeezed from 1 head roasted garlic, or 2 cloves garlic, minced
3 cups chicken broth or beef broth
6 ounces (170 g) extra-sharp Cheddar cheese, shredded (about 1½ cups)
2 ounces (57 g) cream cheese, softened
½ teaspoon fine sea salt
¼ teaspoon ground black pepper
Pinch of ground nutmeg

1. Cut the broccoli florets off the stems, leaving as much of the stems intact as possible. Reserve the florets for another recipe. Trim the bottom end of each stem so that it is flat. Using a spiral slicer, cut the stems into "noodles." 2. Place the bacon in the Instant Pot and press Sauté. Cook, stirring occasionally, for 4 minutes, or until crisp. Remove the bacon with a slotted spoon and set aside on a paper towel-lined plate to drain, leaving the drippings in the pot. 3. Add the butter and onions to the Instant Pot and cook for 4 minutes, or until the onions are soft. Add the garlic (and, if using raw garlic, sauté for another minute). Add the broth, Cheddar cheese, cream cheese, salt, pepper, and nutmeg and sauté until the cheeses are melted, about 3 minutes. Press Cancel to stop the Sauté. 4. Use a stick blender to purée the soup until smooth. Alternatively, you can pour the soup into a regular blender or food processor and purée until smooth, then return it to the Instant Pot. If using a regular blender, you may need to blend the soup in two batches; if you overfill the blender jar, the soup will not purée properly. 5. Add the broccoli noodles to the puréed soup in the Instant Pot. Seal the lid, press Manual, and set the timer for 1 minute. Once finished, let the pressure release naturally. 6. Remove the lid and stir well. Ladle the soup into bowls and sprinkle some of the bacon on top of each serving.

Per Serving:
calories: 258 | fat: 19g | protein: 13g | carbs: 9g | net carbs: 8g | fiber: 1g

Easy Southern Brunswick Stew

Prep time: 20 minutes | Cook time: 8 minutes | Serves 12

2 pounds pork butt, visible fat removed
17-ounce can white corn
1¼ cups ketchup
2 cups diced, cooked potatoes
10-ounce package frozen peas
2 10¾-ounce cans reduced-sodium tomato soup
Hot sauce to taste, optional

1. Place pork in the Instant Pot and secure the lid. 2. Press the Slow Cook setting and cook on low 6–8 hours. 3. When cook time is over, remove the meat from the bone and shred, removing and discarding all visible fat. 4. Combine all the meat and remaining ingredients (except the hot sauce) in the inner pot of the Instant Pot. 5. Secure the lid once more and cook in Slow Cook mode on low for 30 minutes more. Add hot sauce if you wish.

Per Serving:
calories: 213 | fat: 7g | protein: 13g | carbs: 27g | sugars: 9g | fiber: 3g | sodium: 584mg

Garlic Beef Soup

Prep time: 12 minutes | Cook time: 42 minutes | Serves 8

10 strips bacon, chopped
1 medium white onion, chopped
Cloves squeezed from 3 heads roasted garlic, or 6 cloves garlic, minced
1 to 2 jalapeño peppers, seeded and chopped (optional)
2 pounds (907 g) boneless beef chuck roast, cut into 4 equal-sized pieces
5 cups beef broth
1 cup chopped fresh cilantro, plus more for garnish
2 teaspoons fine sea salt
1 teaspoon ground black pepper
For Garnish:
1 avocado, peeled, pitted, and diced
2 radishes, very thinly sliced
2 tablespoons chopped fresh chives

1. Place the bacon in the Instant Pot and press Sauté. Cook, stirring occasionally, for 4 minutes, or until the bacon is crisp. Remove the bacon with a slotted spoon, leaving the drippings in the pot. Set the bacon on a paper towel-lined plate to drain. 2. Add the onion, garlic, and jalapeños, if using, to the Instant Pot and sauté for 3 minutes, or until the onion is soft. Press Cancel to stop the Sauté. 3. Add the beef, broth, cilantro, salt, and pepper. Stir to combine. 4. Seal the lid, press Manual, and set the timer for 35 minutes. Once finished, let the pressure release naturally. 5. Remove the lid and shred the beef with two forks. Taste the liquid and add more salt, if needed. 6. Ladle the soup into bowls. Garnish with the reserved bacon, avocado, radishes, chives, and more cilantro.

Per Serving:
calories: 456 | fat: 36g | protein: 25g | carbs: 6g | net carbs: 4g | fiber: 2g

Beef Meatball Minestrone

Prep time: 5 minutes | Cook time: 35 minutes | Serves 6

1 pound (454 g) ground beef
1 large egg
1½ tablespoons golden flaxseed meal
⅓ cup shredded Mozzarella cheese
¼ cup unsweetened tomato purée
1½ tablespoons Italian seasoning, divided
1½ teaspoons garlic powder, divided
1½ teaspoons sea salt, divided
1 tablespoon olive oil
2 garlic cloves, minced
½ medium yellow onion, minced
¼ cup pancetta, diced
1 cup sliced yellow squash
1 cup sliced zucchini
½ cup sliced turnips
4 cups beef broth
14 ounces (397 g) can diced tomatoes
½ teaspoon ground black pepper
3 tablespoons shredded Parmesan cheese

1. Preheat the oven to 400°F (205°C) and line a large baking sheet with aluminum foil. 2. In a large bowl, combine the ground beef, egg, flaxseed meal, Mozzarella, unsweetened tomato purée, ½ tablespoon of Italian seasoning, ½ teaspoon of garlic powder, and ½ teaspoon of sea salt. Mix the ingredients until well combined. 3. Make the meatballs by shaping 1 heaping tablespoon of the ground beef mixture into a meatball. Repeat with the remaining mixture and then transfer the meatballs to the prepared baking sheet. 4. Place the meatballs in the oven and bake for 15 minutes. When the baking time is complete, remove from the oven and set aside. 5. Select Sauté mode of the Instant Pot. Once the pot is hot, add the olive oil, garlic, onion, and pancetta. Sauté for 2 minutes or until the garlic becomes fragrant and the onions begin to soften. 6. Add the yellow squash, zucchini, and turnips to the pot. Sauté for 3 more minutes. 7. Add the beef broth, diced tomatoes, black pepper, and remaining garlic powder, sea salt, and Italian seasoning to the pot. Stir to combine and then add the meatballs. 8. Lock the lid. Select Manual mode and set cooking time for 15 minutes on High Pressure. 9. When cooking is complete, allow the pressure to release naturally for 10 minutes and then release the remaining pressure. 10. Open the lid and gently stir the soup. Ladle into serving bowls and top with Parmesan. Serve hot.

Per Serving:
calories: 373 | fat: 18.8g | protein: 34.7g | carbs: 15.0g | net carbs: 11.3g | fiber: 3.7g

Mushroom Pizza Soup

Prep time: 10 minutes | Cook time: 22 minutes | Serves 3

1 teaspoon coconut oil
¼ cup cremini mushrooms, sliced
5 ounces (142 g) Italian sausages, chopped
½ jalapeño pepper, sliced
½ teaspoon Italian seasoning
1 teaspoon unsweetened tomato purée
1 cup water
4 ounces (113 g) Mozzarella, shredded

1. Melt the coconut oil in the Instant Pot on Sauté mode. 2. Add the mushrooms and cook for 10 minutes. 3. Add the chopped sausages, sliced jalapeño, Italian seasoning, and unsweetened tomato purée. Pour in the water and stir to mix well. 4. Close the lid and select Manual mode. Set cooking time for 12 minutes on High Pressure. 5. When timer beeps, use a quick pressure release and open the lid. 6. Ladle the soup in the bowls. Top it with Mozzarella. Serve warm.

Per Serving:
calories: 289 | fat: 23.2g | protein: 17.7g | carbs: 2.5g | net carbs: 2.3g | fiber: 0.2g

Vegetarian Chili

Prep time: 25 minutes | Cook time: 10 minutes | Serves 6

2 teaspoons olive oil
3 garlic cloves, minced
2 onions, chopped
1 green bell pepper, chopped
1 cup textured vegetable protein (T.V.P.)
1-pound can beans of your choice, drained
1 jalapeño pepper, seeds removed, chopped
28-ounce can diced Italian tomatoes
1 bay leaf
1 tablespoon dried oregano
½ teaspoons salt
¼ teaspoons pepper

1. Set the Instant Pot to the Sauté function. As it's heating, add the olive oil, garlic, onions, and bell pepper. Stir constantly for about 5 minutes as it all cooks. Press Cancel. 2. Place all of the remaining ingredients into the inner pot of the Instant pot and stir. 3. Secure the lid and make sure vent is set to sealing. Cook on Manual mode for 10 minutes. 4. When cook time is up, let the steam release naturally for 5 minutes and then manually release the rest.

Per Serving:
calories: 242 | fat: 2g | protein: 17g | carbs: 36g | sugars: 9g | fiber: 12g | sodium: 489mg

Green Chile Corn Chowder

Prep time: 20 minutes | Cook time: 7 to 8 hours | Serves 8

16-ounce can cream-style corn
3 potatoes, peeled and diced
2 tablespoons chopped fresh chives
4-ounce can diced green chilies, drained
2-ounce jar chopped pimentos, drained
½ cup chopped cooked ham
2 10½-ounce cans 100% fat-free lower-sodium chicken broth
Pepper to taste
Tabasco sauce to taste
1 cup fat-free milk

1. Combine all ingredients, except milk, in the inner pot of the Instant Pot. 2. Secure the lid and cook using the Slow Cook function on low 7–8 hours or until potatoes are tender. 3. When cook time is up, remove the lid and stir in the milk. Cover and let simmer another 20 minutes.

Per Serving:
calories: 124 | fat: 2g | protein: 6g | carbs: 21g | sugars: 7g | fiber: 2g | sodium: 563mg

Pork Chili

Prep time: 15 minutes | Cook time: 4 hour to 8 minutes | Serves 5

1 pound boneless pork ribs
2 14½-ounce cans fire-roasted diced tomatoes
4¼-ounce cans diced green chiles, drained
½ cup chopped onion
1 clove garlic, minced
1 tablespoon chili powder

1. Layer the ingredients into the Instant Pot inner pot in the order given. 2. Secure the lid. Cook on the high Slow Cook function for 4 hours or on low 6–8 hours, or until pork is tender but not dry. 3. Cut up or shred meat. Stir into the chili and serve.

Per Serving:
calories: 180 | fat: 7g | protein: 18g | carbs: 12g | sugars: 6g | fiber: 3g | sodium: 495mg

Lamb and Broccoli Soup

Prep time: 10 minutes | Cook time: 25 minutes | Serves 4

7 ounces (198 g) lamb fillet, chopped
1 tablespoon avocado oil
½ cup broccoli, roughly chopped
¼ daikon, chopped
2 bell peppers, chopped
¼ teaspoon ground cumin
5 cups beef broth

1. Sauté the lamb fillet with avocado oil in the Instant Pot for 5 minutes. 2. Add the broccoli, daikon, bell peppers, ground cumin, and beef broth. 3. Close the lid. Select Manual mode and set cooking time for 20 minutes on High Pressure. 4. When timer beeps, use a natural pressure release for 10 minutes, then release any remaining pressure. Open the lid. 5. Serve warm.

Per Serving:
calories: 169 | fat: 6.0g | protein: 21.0g | carbs: 6.8g | net carbs: 5.5g | fiber: 1.3g

Cauliflower Soup

Prep time: 10 minutes | Cook time: 6 minutes | Serves 4

2 cups chopped cauliflower
2 tablespoons fresh cilantro
1 cup coconut cream
2 cups beef broth
3 ounces (85 g) Provolone cheese, chopped

1. Put cauliflower, cilantro, coconut cream, beef broth, and cheese in the Instant Pot. Stir to mix well. 2. Select Manual mode and set cooking time for 6 minutes on High Pressure. 3. When timer beeps, allow a natural pressure release for 4 minutes, then release any remaining pressure. Open the lid. 4. Blend the soup and ladle in bowls to serve.

Per Serving:
calories: 244 | fat: 21g | protein: 10g | carbs: 7g | net carbs: 4g | fiber: 3g

Provençal Chicken Soup

Prep time: 20 minutes | Cook time: 30 minutes | Serves 6 to 8

1 tablespoon extra-virgin olive oil
2 fennel bulbs, 2 tablespoons fronds minced, stalks discarded, bulbs halved, cored, and cut into ½-inch pieces
1 onion, chopped
1¾ teaspoons table salt
2 tablespoons tomato paste
4 garlic cloves, minced
1 tablespoon minced fresh thyme or 1 teaspoon dried
2 anchovy fillets, minced
7 cups water, divided
1 (14½-ounce / 411-g) can diced tomatoes, drained
2 carrots, peeled, halved lengthwise, and sliced ½ inch thick
2 (12-ounce / 340-g) bone-in split chicken breasts, trimmed
4 (5- to 7-ounce / 142- to 198-g) bone-in chicken thighs, trimmed
½ cup pitted brine-cured green olives, chopped
1 teaspoon grated orange zest

1. Using highest sauté function, heat oil in Instant Pot until shimmering. Add fennel pieces, onion, and salt and cook until vegetables are softened, about 5 minutes. Stir in tomato paste, garlic, thyme, and anchovies and cook until fragrant, about 30 seconds. Stir in 5 cups water, scraping up any browned bits, then stir in tomatoes and carrots. Nestle chicken breasts and thighs in pot. 2. Lock lid in place and close pressure release valve. Select high pressure cook function and cook for 20 minutes. Turn off Instant Pot and quick-release pressure. Carefully remove lid, allowing steam to escape away from you. 3. Transfer chicken to cutting board, let cool slightly, then shred into bite-size pieces using 2 forks; discard skin and bones. 4. Using wide, shallow spoon, skim excess fat from surface of soup. Stir chicken and any accumulated juices, olives, and remaining 2 cups water into soup and let sit until heated through, about 3 minutes. Stir in fennel fronds and orange zest, and season with salt and pepper to taste. Serve.

Per Serving:
calories: 170 | fat: 5g | protein: 19g | carbs: 11g | fiber: 3g | sodium: 870mg

Cauliflower Rice and Chicken Thigh Soup

Prep time: 15 minutes | Cook time: 13 minutes | Serves 5

2 cups cauliflower florets
1 pound (454 g) boneless, skinless chicken thighs
4½ cups chicken broth
½ yellow onion, chopped
2 garlic cloves, minced
1 tablespoon unflavored gelatin powder
2 teaspoons sea salt
½ teaspoon ground black pepper
½ cup sliced zucchini
⅓ cup sliced turnips
1 teaspoon dried parsley
3 celery stalks, chopped
1 teaspoon ground turmeric
½ teaspoon dried marjoram
1 teaspoon dried thyme
½ teaspoon dried oregano

1. Add the cauliflower florets to a food processor and pulse until a ricelike consistency is achieved. Set aside. 2. Add the chicken thighs, chicken broth, onions, garlic, gelatin powder, sea salt, and black pepper to the pot. Gently stir to combine. 3. Lock the lid. Select Manual mode and set cooking time for 10 minutes on High Pressure. 4. When cooking is complete, quick release the pressure and open the lid. 5. Transfer the chicken thighs to a cutting board. Chop the chicken into bite-sized pieces and then return the chopped chicken to the pot. 6. Add the cauliflower rice, zucchini, turnips, parsley, celery, turmeric, marjoram, thyme, and oregano to the pot. Stir to combine. 7. Lock the lid. Select Manual mode and set cooking time for 3 minutes on High Pressure. 8. When cooking is complete, quick release the pressure. 9. Open the lid. Ladle the soup into serving bowls. Serve hot.

Per Serving:
calories: 247 | fat: 10.4g | protein: 30.2g | carbs: 8.3g | net carbs: 6.1g | fiber: 2.2g

Pasta e Fagioli with Ground Beef

Prep time: 0 minutes | Cook time: 30 minutes | Serves 8

2 tablespoons extra-virgin olive oil
4 garlic cloves, minced
1 yellow onion, diced
2 large carrots, diced
4 celery stalks, diced
1½ pounds 95 percent extra-lean ground beef
4 cups low-sodium vegetable broth
2 teaspoons Italian seasoning
½ teaspoon freshly ground black pepper
1¼ cups chickpea-based elbow pasta or whole-wheat elbow pasta
1½ cups drained cooked kidney beans, or one 15-ounce can kidney beans, rinsed and drained
One 28-ounce can whole San Marzano tomatoes and their liquid
2 tablespoons chopped fresh flat-leaf parsley

1. Select the Sauté setting on the Instant Pot and heat the oil and garlic for 2 minutes, until the garlic is bubbling but not browned. Add the onion, carrots, and celery and sauté for 5 minutes, until the onion begins to soften. Add the beef and sauté, using a wooden spoon or spatula to break up the meat as it cooks, for 5 minutes; it's fine if some streaks of pink remain, the beef does not need to be cooked through. 2. Stir in the broth, Italian seasoning, pepper, and pasta, making sure all of the pasta is submerged in the liquid. Add the beans and stir to mix. Add the tomatoes and their liquid, crushing the tomatoes with your hands as you add them to the pot. Do not stir them in. 3. Secure the lid and set the Pressure Release to Sealing. Press the Cancel button to reset the cooking program, then select the Pressure Cook or Manual setting and set the cooking time for 2 minutes at low pressure. (The pot will take about 15 minutes to come up to pressure before the cooking program begins.) 4. When the cooking program ends, let the pressure release naturally for 10 minutes, then move the Pressure Release to Venting to release any remaining steam. Open the pot and stir the soup to mix all of the ingredients. 5. Ladle the soup into bowls, sprinkle with the parsley, and serve right away.

Per Serving:
calories: 278 | fat: 9g | protein: 26g | carbs: 25g | sugars: 4g | fiber: 6g | sodium: 624mg

Cabbage Roll Soup

Prep time: 10 minutes | Cook time: 8 minutes | Serves 4

½ pound (227 g) 84% lean ground pork
½ pound (227 g) 85% lean ground beef
½ medium onion, diced
½ medium head cabbage, thinly sliced
2 tablespoons sugar-free tomato paste
½ cup diced tomatoes
2 cups chicken broth
1 teaspoon salt
½ teaspoon thyme
½ teaspoon garlic powder
¼ teaspoon pepper

1. Press the Sauté button and add beef and pork to Instant Pot. Brown meat until no pink remains. Add onion and continue cooking until onions are fragrant and soft. Press the Cancel button. 2. Add remaining ingredients to Instant Pot. Press the Manual button and adjust time for 8 minutes. 3. When timer beeps, allow a 15-minute natural release and then quick-release the remaining pressure. Serve warm.

Per Serving:
calories: 304 | fat: 16g | protein: 24g | carbs: 12g | net carbs: 8g | fiber: 4g

Blue Cheese Mushroom Soup

Prep time: 15 minutes | Cook time: 20 minutes | Serves 4

2 cups chopped white mushrooms
3 tablespoons cream cheese
4 ounces (113 g) scallions, diced
4 cups chicken broth
1 teaspoon olive oil
½ teaspoon ground cumin
1 teaspoon salt
2 ounces (57 g) blue cheese, crumbled

1. Combine the mushrooms, cream cheese, scallions, chicken broth, olive oil, and ground cumin in the Instant Pot. 2. Seal the lid. Select Manual mode and set cooking time for 20 minutes on High Pressure. 3. When timer beeps, use a quick pressure release and open the lid. 4. Add the salt and blend the soup with an immersion blender. 5. Ladle the soup in the bowls and top with blue cheese. Serve warm.

Per Serving:
calories: 142 | fat: 9.4g | protein: 10.1g | carbs: 4.8g | net carbs: 3.7g | fiber: 1.1g

Tomato-Basil Parmesan Soup

Prep time: 5 minutes | Cook time: 12 minutes | Serves 12

2 tablespoons unsalted butter or coconut oil
½ cup finely diced onions
Cloves squeezed from 1 head roasted garlic , or 2 cloves garlic, minced
1 tablespoon dried basil leaves
1 teaspoon dried oregano leaves
1 (8-ounce / 227-g) package cream cheese, softened
4 cups chicken broth
2 (14½-ounce / 411-g) cans diced tomatoes
1 cup shredded Parmesan cheese, plus more for garnish
1 teaspoon fine sea salt
¼ teaspoon ground black pepper
Fresh basil leaves, for garnish

1. Place the butter in the Instant Pot and press Sauté. Once melted, add the onions, garlic, basil, and oregano and cook, stirring often, for 4 minutes, or until the onions are soft. Press Cancel to stop the Sauté. 2. Add the cream cheese and whisk to loosen. (If you don't use a whisk to loosen the cream cheese, you will end up with clumps in your soup.) Slowly whisk in the broth. Add the tomatoes, Parmesan, salt, and pepper and stir to combine. 3. Seal the lid, press Manual, and set the timer for 8 minutes. Once finished, turn the valve to venting for a quick release. 4. Remove the lid and purée the soup with a stick blender, or transfer the soup to a regular blender or food processor and process until smooth. If using a regular blender, you may need to blend the soup in two batches; if you overfill the blender jar, the soup will not purée properly. 5. Season with salt and pepper to taste, if desired. Ladle the soup into bowls and garnish with more Parmesan and basil leaves.

Per Serving:
calories: 146 | fat: 10g | protein: 8g | carbs: 4g | net carbs: 3g | fiber: 1g

Unstuffed Cabbage Soup

Prep time: 15 minutes | Cook time: 20 minutes | Serves 5

2 tablespoons coconut oil
1 pound ground sirloin or turkey
1 medium onion, diced
2 cloves garlic, minced
1 small head cabbage, chopped, cored, cut into roughly 2-inch pieces.
6-ounce can low-sodium tomato paste
32-ounce can low-sodium diced tomatoes, with liquid
2 cups low-sodium beef broth
1½ cups water
¾ cup brown rice
1–2 teaspoons salt
½ teaspoon black pepper
1 teaspoon oregano
1 teaspoon parsley

1. Melt coconut oil in the inner pot of the Instant Pot using Sauté function. Add ground meat. Stir frequently until meat loses color, about 2 minutes. 2. Add onion and garlic and continue to sauté for 2 more minutes, stirring frequently. 3. Add chopped cabbage. 4. On top of cabbage layer tomato paste, tomatoes with liquid, beef broth, water, rice, and spices. 5. Secure the lid and set vent to sealing. Using Manual setting, select 20 minutes. 6. When time is up, let the pressure release naturally for 10 minutes, then do a quick release.

Per Serving:
calories: 282 | fat: 6g | protein: 23g | carbs: 34g | sugars: 6g | fiber: 3g | sodium: 898mg

Broccoli and Red Feta Soup

Prep time: 10 minutes | Cook time: 25 minutes | Serves 4

1 cup broccoli, chopped
½ cup coconut cream
1 teaspoon unsweetened tomato purée
4 cups beef broth
1 teaspoon chili flakes
6 ounces (170 g) feta, crumbled

1. Put broccoli, coconut cream, tomato purée, and beef broth in the Instant Pot. Sprinkle with chili flakes and stir to mix well. 2. Close the lid and select Manual mode. Set cooking time for 8 minutes on High Pressure. 3. When timer beeps, make a quick pressure release and open the lid. 4. Add the feta cheese and stir the soup on Sauté mode for 5 minutes or until the cheese melt. 5. Serve immediately.

Per Serving:
calories: 229 | fat: 17.7g | protein: 12.3g | carbs: 6.1g | net carbs: 4.8g | fiber: 1.3g

Hearty Hamburger and Lentil Stew

Prep time: 0 minutes | Cook time: 55 minutes | Serves 8

2 tablespoons cold-pressed avocado oil
2 garlic cloves, chopped
1 large yellow onion, diced
2 carrots, diced
2 celery stalks, diced
2 pounds 95 percent lean ground beef
½ cup small green lentils
2 cups low-sodium roasted beef bone broth or vegetable broth
1 tablespoon Italian seasoning
1 tablespoon paprika
1½ teaspoons fine sea salt
1 extra-large russet potato, diced
1 cup frozen green peas
1 cup frozen corn
One 14½-ounce can no-salt petite diced tomatoes and their liquid
¼ cup tomato paste

1. Select the Sauté setting on the Instant Pot and heat the oil and garlic for 3 minutes, until the garlic is bubbling but not browned. Add the onion, carrots, and celery and sauté for 5 minutes, until the onion begins to soften. Add the beef and sauté, using a wooden spoon or spatula to break up the meat as it cooks, for 6 minutes, until cooked through and no streaks of pink remain. 2. Stir in the lentils, broth, Italian seasoning, paprika, and salt. Add the potato, peas, corn, and tomatoes and their liquid in layers on top of the lentils and beef, then add the tomato paste in a dollop on top. Do not stir in the vegetables and tomato paste. 3. Secure the lid and set the Pressure Release to Sealing. Press the Cancel button to reset the cooking program, then select the Pressure Cook or Manual setting and set the cooking time for 20 minutes at high pressure. (The pot will take about 20 minutes to come up to pressure before the cooking program begins.) 4. When the cooking program ends, let the pressure release naturally for at least 15 minutes, then move the Pressure Release to Venting to release any remaining steam. Open the pot and stir the stew to mix all of the ingredients. 5. Ladle the stew into bowls and serve hot.

Per Serving:
calories: 334 | fat: 8g | protein: 34g | carbs: 30g | sugars: 6g | fiber: 7g | sodium: 902mg

Vegetable and Chickpea Stew

Prep time: 25 minutes | Cook time: 30 minutes | Serves 6 to 8

¼ cup extra-virgin olive oil, plus extra for drizzling
2 red bell peppers, stemmed, seeded, and cut into 1-inch pieces
1 onion, chopped fine
½ teaspoon table salt
½ teaspoon pepper
1½ tablespoons baharat
4 garlic cloves, minced
1 tablespoon tomato paste
4 cups vegetable or chicken broth
1 (28-ounce / 794-g) can whole peeled tomatoes, drained with juice reserved, chopped
1 pound (454 g) Yukon Gold potatoes, peeled and cut into ½-inch pieces
2 zucchini, quartered lengthwise and sliced 1 inch thick
1 (15-ounce / 425-g) can chickpeas, rinsed
⅓ cup chopped fresh mint

1. Using highest sauté function, heat oil in Instant Pot until shimmering. Add bell pepper, onion, salt, and pepper and cook until vegetables are softened and lightly browned, 5 to 7 minutes. Stir in baharat, garlic, and tomato paste and cook until fragrant, about 1 minute. Stir in broth and tomatoes and reserved juice, scraping up any browned bits, then stir in potatoes. 2. Lock lid in place and close pressure release valve. Select high pressure cook function and cook for 9 minutes. Turn off Instant Pot and quick-release pressure. Carefully remove lid, allowing steam to escape away from you. 3. Stir zucchini and chickpeas into stew and cook, using highest sauté function, until zucchini is tender, 10 to 15 minutes. Turn off multicooker. Season with salt and pepper to taste. Drizzle individual portions with extra oil, and sprinkle with mint before serving.

Per Serving:
calories: 200 | fat: 8g | protein: 5g | carbs: 28g | fiber: 5g | sodium: 740mg

Chicken Brunswick Stew

Prep time: 0 minutes | Cook time: 30 minutes | Serves 6

2 tablespoons extra-virgin olive oil
2 garlic cloves, chopped
1 large yellow onion, diced
2 pounds boneless, skinless chicken (breasts, tenders, or thighs), cut into bite-size pieces
1 teaspoon dried thyme
1 teaspoon smoked paprika
1 teaspoon fine sea salt
½ teaspoon freshly ground black pepper
1 cup low-sodium chicken broth
1 tablespoon hot sauce (such as Tabasco or Crystal)
1 tablespoon raw apple cider vinegar
1½ cups frozen corn
1½ cups frozen baby lima beans
One 14½-ounce can fire-roasted diced tomatoes and their liquid
2 tablespoons tomato paste
Cornbread, for serving

1. Select the Sauté setting on the Instant Pot and heat the oil and garlic for 2 minutes, until the garlic is bubbling but not browned. Add the onion and sauté for 3 minutes, until it begins to soften. Add the chicken and sauté for 3 minutes more, until mostly opaque. The chicken does not have to be cooked through. Add the thyme, paprika, salt, and pepper and sauté for 1 minute more. 2. Stir in the broth, hot sauce, vinegar, corn, and lima beans. Add the diced tomatoes and their liquid in an even layer and dollop the tomato paste on top. Do not stir them in. 3. Secure the lid and set the Pressure Release to Sealing. Press the Cancel button to reset the cooking program, then select the Pressure Cook or Manual setting and set the cooking time for 5 minutes at high pressure. (The pot will take about 15 minutes to come up to pressure before the cooking program begins.) 4. When the cooking program ends, let the pressure release naturally for at least 10 minutes, then move the Pressure Release to Venting to release any remaining steam. Open the pot and stir the stew to mix all of the ingredients. 5. Ladle the stew into bowls and serve hot, with cornbread alongside.

Per Serving:
calories: 349 | fat: 7g | protein: 40g | carbs: 17g | sugars: 7g | fiber: 7g | sodium: 535mg

Chicken and Zoodles Soup

Prep time: 25 minutes | Cook time: 15 minutes | Serves 2

2 cups water
6 ounces (170 g) chicken fillet, chopped
1 teaspoon salt
2 ounces (57 g) zucchini, spiralized
1 tablespoon coconut aminos

1. Pour water in the Instant Pot. Add chopped chicken fillet and salt. Close the lid. 2. Select Manual mode and set cooking time for 15 minutes on High Pressure. 3. When cooking is complete, perform a natural pressure release for 10 minutes, then release any remaining pressure. Open the lid. 4. Fold in the zoodles and coconut aminos. 5. Leave the soup for 10 minutes to rest. Serve warm.

Per Serving:
calories: 175 | fat: 6.3g | protein: 24.8g | carbs: 4.5g | net carbs: 1.5g | fiber: 3.0g

Instantly Good Beef Stew

Prep time: 20 minutes | Cook time: 35 minutes | Serves 6

3 tablespoons olive oil,divided
2 pounds stewing beef, cubed
2 cloves garlic, minced
1 large onion, chopped
3 ribs celery, sliced
3 large potatoes, cubed
2–3 carrots, sliced
8 ounces no-salt-added tomato sauce
10 ounces low-sodium beef broth
2 teaspoons Worcestershire sauce
¼ teaspoon pepper
1 bay leaf

1. Set the Instant Pot to the Sauté function, then add in 1 tablespoon of the oil. Add in ⅓ of the beef cubes and brown and sear all sides. Repeat this process twice more with the remaining oil and beef cubes. Set the beef aside. 2. Place the garlic, onion, and celery into the pot and sauté for a few minutes. Press Cancel. 3. Add the beef back in as well as all of the remaining ingredients. 4. Secure the lid and make sure the vent is set to sealing. Choose Manual for 35 minutes. 5. When cook time is up, let the pressure release naturally for 15 minutes, then release any remaining pressure manually. 6. Remove the lid, remove the bay leaf, then serve.

Per Serving:
calories: 401 | fat: 20g | protein: 35g | carbs: 19g | sugars: 5g | fiber: 3g | sodium: 157mg

Cabbage and Pork Soup

Prep time: 10 minutes | Cook time: 12 minutes | Serves 3

1 teaspoon butter
½ cup shredded white cabbage
½ teaspoon ground coriander
½ teaspoon salt
½ teaspoon chili flakes
2 cups chicken broth
½ cup ground pork

1. Melt the butter in the Instant Pot on Sauté mode. 2. Add cabbage and sprinkle with ground coriander, salt, and chili flakes. 3. Fold in the chicken broth and ground pork. 4. Close the lid and select Manual mode. Set cooking time for 12 minutes on High Pressure. 5. When timer beeps, use a quick pressure release. Open the lid. 6. Ladle the soup and serve warm.

Per Serving:
calories: 350 | fat: 23.9g | protein: 30.2g | carbs: 1.3g | net carbs: 1.0g | fiber: 0.3g

Beef and Eggplant Tagine

Prep time: 15 minutes | Cook time: 25 minutes | Serves 6

1 pound (454 g) beef fillet, chopped
1 eggplant, chopped
6 ounces (170 g) scallions, chopped
4 cups beef broth
1 teaspoon ground allspices
1 teaspoon erythritol
1 teaspoon coconut oil

1. Put all ingredients in the Instant Pot. Stir to mix well. 2. Close the lid. Select Manual mode and set cooking time for 25 minutes on High Pressure. 3. When timer beeps, use a natural pressure release for 15 minutes, then release any remaining pressure. Open the lid. 4. Serve warm.

Per Serving:
calories: 158 | fat: 5.3g | protein: 21.1g | carbs: 8.2g | net carbs: 4.7g | fiber: 3.5g

Spanish-Style Turkey Meatball Soup

Prep time: 10 minutes | Cook time: 15 minutes | Serves 6 to 8

1 slice hearty white sandwich bread, torn into quarters
¼ cup whole milk
1 ounce (28 g) Manchego cheese, grated (½ cup), plus extra for serving
5 tablespoons minced fresh parsley, divided
½ teaspoon table salt
1 pound (454 g) ground turkey
1 tablespoon extra-virgin olive oil
1 onion, chopped
1 red bell pepper, stemmed, seeded, and cut into ¾-inch pieces
4 garlic cloves, minced
2 teaspoons smoked paprika
½ cup dry white wine
8 cups chicken broth
8 ounces (227 g) kale, stemmed and chopped

1. Using fork, mash bread and milk together into paste in large bowl. Stir in Manchego, 3 tablespoons parsley, and salt until combined. Add turkey and knead mixture with your hands until well combined. Pinch off and roll 2-teaspoon-size pieces of mixture into balls and arrange on large plate (you should have about 35 meatballs); set aside. 2. Using highest sauté function, heat oil in Instant Pot until shimmering. Add onion and bell pepper and cook until softened and lightly browned, 5 to 7 minutes. Stir in garlic and paprika and cook until fragrant, about 30 seconds. Stir in wine, scraping up any browned bits, and cook until almost completely evaporated, about 5 minutes. Stir in broth and kale, then gently submerge meatballs. 3. Lock lid in place and close pressure release valve. Select high pressure cook function and cook for 3 minutes. Turn off Instant Pot and quick-release pressure. Carefully remove lid, allowing steam to escape away from you. 4. Stir in remaining 2 tablespoons parsley and season with salt and pepper to taste. Serve, passing extra Manchego separately.

Per Serving:
calories: 170 | fat: 5g | protein: 21g | carbs: 9g | fiber: 2g | sodium: 750mg

Beef and Okra Stew

Prep time: 15 minutes | Cook time: 25 minutes | Serves 3

8 ounces (227 g) beef sirloin, chopped
¼ teaspoon cumin seeds
1 teaspoon dried basil
1 tablespoon avocado oil
¼ cup coconut cream
1 cup water
6 ounces (170 g) okra, chopped

1. Sprinkle the beef sirloin with cumin seeds and dried basil and put in the Instant Pot. 2. Add avocado oil and roast the meat on Sauté mode for 5 minutes. Flip occasionally. 3. Add coconut cream, water, and okra. 4. Close the lid and select Manual mode. Set cooking time for 25 minutes on High Pressure. 5. When timer beeps, use a natural pressure release for 10 minutes, the release any remaining pressure. Open the lid. 6. Serve warm.

Per Serving:
calories: 216 | fat: 10.2g | protein: 24.6g | carbs: 5.7g | net carbs: 3.2g | fiber: 2.5g

Butternut Squash Soup

Prep time: 30 minutes | Cook time: 15 minutes | Serves 4

2 tablespoons margarine
1 large onion, chopped
2 cloves garlic, minced
1 teaspoon thyme
½ teaspoon sage
Salt and pepper to taste
2 large butternut squash, peeled, seeded, and cubed (about 4 pounds)
4 cups low-sodium chicken stock

1. In the inner pot of the Instant Pot, melt the margarine using Sauté function. 2. Add onion and garlic and cook until soft, 3 to 5 minutes. 3. Add thyme and sage and cook another minute. Season with salt and pepper. 4. Stir in butternut squash and add chicken stock. 5. Secure the lid and make sure vent is at sealing. Using Manual setting, cook squash and seasonings 10 minutes, using high pressure. 6. When time is up, do a quick release of the pressure. 7. Puree the soup in a food processor or use immersion blender right in the inner pot. If soup is too thick, add more stock. Adjust salt and pepper as needed.

Per Serving:
calories: 279 | fat: 7g | protein: 6g | carbs: 56g | sugars: 10g | fiber: 9g | sodium: 144mg

Spicy Sausage and Chicken Stew

Prep time: 10 minutes | Cook time: 25 minutes | Serves 10

1 tablespoon coconut oil
2 pounds (907 g) bulk Italian sausage
2 boneless, skinless chicken thighs, cut into ½-inch pieces
½ cup chopped onions
1 (28-ounce / 794-g) can whole peeled tomatoes, drained
1 cup sugar-free tomato sauce
1 (4½-ounce / 128-g) can green chilies
3 tablespoons minced garlic
2 tablespoons smoked paprika
1 tablespoon ground cumin
1 tablespoon dried oregano leaves
2 teaspoons fine sea salt
1 teaspoon cayenne pepper
1 cup chicken broth
1 ounce (28 g) unsweetened baking chocolate, chopped
¼ cup lime juice
Chopped fresh cilantro leaves, for garnish
Red pepper flakes, for garnish

1. Place the coconut oil in the Instant Pot and press Sauté. Once melted, add the sausage, chicken, and onions and cook, stirring to break up the sausage, until the sausage is starting to cook through and the onions are soft, about 5 minutes. 2. Meanwhile, make the tomato purée: Place the tomatoes, tomato sauce, and chilies in a food processor and process until smooth. 3. Add the garlic, paprika, cumin, oregano, salt, and cayenne pepper to the Instant Pot and stir to combine. Then add the tomato purée, broth, and chocolate and stir well. Press Cancel to stop the Sauté. 4. Seal the lid, press Manual, and set the timer for 20 minutes. Once finished, let the pressure release naturally. 5. Just before serving, stir in the lime juice. Ladle the stew into bowls and garnish with cilantro and red pepper flakes.

Per Serving:
calories: 341 | fat: 23g | protein: 21g | carbs: 10g | net carbs: 8g | fiber: 2g

Savory Beef Stew with Mushrooms and Turnips

Prep time: 0 minutes | Cook time: 55 minutes | Serves 6

1½ pounds beef stew meat
¾ teaspoon fine sea salt
¾ teaspoon freshly ground black pepper
1 tablespoon cold-pressed avocado oil
3 garlic cloves, minced
1 yellow onion, diced
2 celery stalks, diced
8 ounces cremini mushrooms, quartered
1 cup low-sodium roasted beef bone broth
2 tablespoons Worcestershire sauce
1 tablespoon Dijon mustard
1 teaspoon dried rosemary, crumbled
1 bay leaf
3 tablespoons tomato paste
8 ounces carrots, cut into 1-inch-thick rounds
1 pound turnips, cut into 1-inch pieces
1 pound parsnips, halved lengthwise, then cut crosswise into 1-inch pieces

1. Sprinkle the beef all over with the salt and pepper. 2. Select the Sauté setting on the Instant Pot and heat the oil and garlic for 2 minutes, until the garlic is bubbling but not browned. Add the onion, celery, and mushrooms and sauté for 5 minutes, until the onion begins to soften and the mushrooms are giving up their liquid. Stir in the broth, Worcestershire sauce, mustard, rosemary, and bay leaf. Stir in the beef. Add the tomato paste in a dollop on top. Do not stir it in. 3. Secure the lid and set the Pressure Release to Sealing. Press the Cancel button to reset the cooking program, then select the Meat/Stew, Pressure Cook, or Manual setting and set the cooking time for 20 minutes at high pressure. (The pot will take about 10 minutes to come up to pressure before the cooking program begins.) 4. When the cooking program ends, perform a quick pressure release by moving the Pressure Release to Venting, or let the pressure release naturally. Open the pot, remove and discard the bay leaf, and stir in the tomato paste. Place the carrots, turnips, and parsnips on top of the meat. 5. Secure the lid and set the Pressure Release to Sealing. Press the Cancel button to reset the cooking program, then select the Pressure Cook or Manual setting and set the cooking time for 3 minutes at low pressure. (The pot will take about 15 minutes to come up to pressure before the cooking program begins.) 6. When the cooking program ends, perform a quick pressure release by moving the Pressure Release to Venting. Open the pot and stir to combine all of the ingredients. 7. Ladle the stew into bowls and serve hot.

Per Serving:
calories: 304 | fat: 8g | protein: 29g | carbs: 30g | sugars: 10g | fiber: 8g | sodium: 490mg

Beef, Mushroom, and Wild Rice Soup

Prep time: 0 minutes | Cook time: 55 minutes | Serves 6

2 tablespoons extra-virgin olive oil or unsalted butter
2 garlic cloves, minced
8 ounces shiitake mushrooms, stems removed and sliced
1 teaspoon fine sea salt
2 carrots, diced
2 celery stalks, diced
1 yellow onion, diced
1 teaspoon dried thyme
1½ pounds beef stew meat, larger pieces halved, or beef chuck, trimmed of fat and cut into ¾-inch pieces
4 cups low-sodium roasted beef bone broth
1 cup wild rice, rinsed
1 tablespoon Worcestershire sauce
2 tablespoons tomato paste

1. Select the Sauté setting on the Instant Pot and heat the oil and garlic for about 1 minute, until the garlic is bubbling but not browned. Add the mushrooms and salt and sauté for 5 minutes, until the mushrooms have wilted and given up some of their liquid. Add the carrots, celery, and onion and sauté for 4 minutes, until the onion begins to soften. Add the thyme and beef and sauté for 3 minutes more, until the beef is mostly opaque on the outside. Stir in the broth, rice, Worcestershire sauce, and tomato paste, using a wooden spoon to nudge any browned bits from the bottom of the pot. 2. Secure the lid and set the Pressure Release to Sealing. Press the Cancel button to reset the cooking program, then select the Pressure Cook or Manual setting and set the cooking time for 25 minutes at high pressure. (The pot will take about 15 minutes to come up to pressure before the cooking program begins.) 3. When the cooking program ends, let the pressure release naturally for at least 15 minutes, then move the Pressure Release to Venting to release any remaining steam. Open the pot. Ladle the soup into bowls and serve hot.

Per Serving:
calories: 316 | fat: 8g | protein: 29g | carbs: 32g | sugars: 6g | fiber: 8g | sodium: 783mg

Chicken Enchilada Soup

Prep time: 10 minutes | Cook time: 40 minutes | Serves 6

2 (6-ounce / 170-g) boneless, skinless chicken breasts
½ tablespoon chili powder
½ teaspoon salt
½ teaspoon garlic powder
¼ teaspoon pepper
½ cup red enchilada sauce
½ medium onion, diced
1 (4-ounce / 113-g) can green chilies
2 cups chicken broth
⅛ cup pickled jalapeños
4 ounces (113 g) cream cheese
1 cup uncooked cauliflower rice
1 avocado, diced
1 cup shredded mild Cheddar cheese
½ cup sour cream

1. Sprinkle seasoning over chicken breasts and set aside. Pour enchilada sauce into Instant Pot and place chicken on top. 2. Add onion, chilies, broth, and jalapeños to the pot, then place cream cheese on top of chicken breasts. Click lid closed. Adjust time for 25 minutes. When timer beeps, quick-release the pressure and shred chicken with forks. 3. Mix soup together and add cauliflower rice, with pot on Keep Warm setting. Replace lid and let pot sit for 15 minutes, still on Keep Warm. This will cook cauliflower rice. Serve with avocado, Cheddar, and sour cream.

Per Serving:
calories: 318 | fat: 19g | protein: 21g | carbs: 10g | net carbs: 7g | fiber: 3g

Beef Oxtail Soup with White Beans, Tomatoes, and Aleppo Pepper

Prep time: 20 minutes | Cook time: 1 hour 10 minutes | Serves 6 to 8

4 pounds (1.8 kg) oxtails, trimmed
1 teaspoon table salt
1 tablespoon extra-virgin olive oil
1 onion, chopped fine
2 carrots, peeled and chopped fine
¼ cup ground dried Aleppo pepper
6 garlic cloves, minced
2 tablespoons tomato paste
¾ teaspoon dried oregano
½ teaspoon ground cinnamon
½ teaspoon ground cumin
6 cups water
1 (28-ounce / 794-g) can diced tomatoes, drained
1 (15-ounce / 425-g) can navy beans, rinsed
1 tablespoon sherry vinegar
¼ cup chopped fresh parsley
½ preserved lemon, pulp and white pith removed, rind rinsed and minced (2 tablespoons)

1. Pat oxtails dry with paper towels and sprinkle with salt. Using highest sauté function, heat oil in Instant Pot for 5 minutes (or until just smoking). Brown half of oxtails, 4 to 6 minutes per side; transfer to plate. Set aside remaining uncooked oxtails. 2. Add onion and carrots to fat left in pot and cook, using highest sauté function, until softened, about 5 minutes. Stir in Aleppo pepper, garlic, tomato paste, oregano, cinnamon, and cumin and cook until fragrant, about 30 seconds. Stir in water, scraping up any browned bits, then stir in tomatoes. Nestle remaining uncooked oxtails into pot along with browned oxtails and add any accumulated juices. 3. Lock lid in place and close pressure release valve. Select high pressure cook function and cook for 45 minutes. Turn off Instant Pot and quick-release pressure. Carefully remove lid, allowing steam to escape away from you. 4. Transfer oxtails to cutting board, let cool slightly, then shred into bite-size pieces using 2 forks; discard bones and excess fat. Strain broth through fine-mesh strainer into large container; return solids to now-empty pot. Using wide, shallow spoon, skim excess fat from surface of liquid; return to pot. 5. Stir shredded oxtails and any accumulated juices and beans into pot. Using highest sauté function, cook until soup is heated through, about 5 minutes. Stir in vinegar and parsley and season with salt and pepper to taste. Serve, passing preserved lemon separately.

Per Serving:
calories: 380 | fat: 18g | protein: 38g | carbs: 17g | fiber: 5g | sodium: 890mg

Ham and Potato Chowder

Prep time: 25 minutes | Cook time: 8 hour s | Serves 5

5-ounce package scalloped potatoes
Sauce mix from potato package
1 cup extra-lean, reduced-sodium, cooked ham, cut into narrow strips
4 teaspoons sodium-free bouillon powder
4 cups water
1 cup chopped celery
⅓ cup chopped onions
Pepper to taste
2 cups fat-free half-and-half
⅓ cup flour

1. Combine potatoes, sauce mix, ham, bouillon powder, water, celery, onions, and pepper in the inner pot of the Instant Pot. 2. Secure the lid and cook using the Slow Cook function on low for 7 hours. 3. Combine half-and-half and flour. Remove the lid and gradually add to the inner pot, blending well. 4. Secure the lid once more and cook on the low Slow Cook function for up to 1 hour more, stirring occasionally until thickened.

Per Serving:
calories: 241 | fat: 3g | protein: 11g | carbs: 41g | sugars: 8g | fiber: 3g | sodium: 836mg

Italian Vegetable Soup

Prep time: 20 minutes | Cook time: 5 to 9 hours | Serves 6

3 small carrots, sliced
1 small onion, chopped
2 small potatoes, diced
2 tablespoons chopped parsley
1 garlic clove, minced
3 teaspoons sodium-free beef bouillon powder
1¼ teaspoons dried basil
¼ teaspoon pepper
16-ounce can red kidney beans, undrained
3 cups water
14½-ounce can stewed tomatoes, with juice
1 cup diced, extra-lean, lower-sodium cooked ham

1. In the inner pot of the Instant Pot, layer the carrots, onion, potatoes, parsley, garlic, beef bouillon, basil, pepper, and kidney beans. Do not stir. Add water. 2. Secure the lid and cook on the Low Slow Cook mode for 8–9 hours, or on high 4½–5½ hours, until vegetables are tender. 3. Remove the lid and stir in the tomatoes and ham. Secure the lid again and cook on high Slow Cook mode for 10–15 minutes more.

Per Serving:
calories: 156 | fat: 1g | protein: 9g | carbs: 29g | sugars: 8g | fiber: 5g | sodium: 614mg

Chicken and Asparagus Soup

Prep time: 7 minutes | Cook time: 11 minutes | Serves 8

1 tablespoon unsalted butter (or coconut oil for dairy-free)
¼ cup finely chopped onions
2 cloves garlic, minced
1 (14-ounce / 397-g) can full-fat coconut milk
1 (14-ounce / 397-g) can sugar-free tomato sauce
1 cup chicken broth
1 tablespoon red curry paste
Lime wedges, for garnish
1 teaspoon fine sea salt
½ teaspoon ground black pepper
2 pounds (907 g) boneless, skinless chicken breasts, cut into ½-inch chunks
2 cups asparagus, trimmed and cut into 2-inch pieces
Fresh cilantro leaves, for garnish

1. Place the butter in the Instant Pot and press Sauté. Once melted, add the onions and garlic and sauté for 4 minutes, or until the onions are soft. Press Cancel to stop the Sauté. 2. Add the coconut milk, tomato sauce, broth, curry paste, salt, and pepper and whisk to combine well. Stir in the chicken and asparagus. 3. Seal the lid, press Manual, and set the timer for 7 minutes. Once finished, turn the valve to venting for a quick release. 4. Remove the lid and stir well. Taste and adjust the seasoning to your liking. Ladle the soup into bowls and garnish with cilantro. Serve with lime wedges or a squirt of lime juice.

Per Serving:
calories: 235 | fat: 13g | protein: 24g | carbs: 8g | net carbs: 6g | fiber: 2g

Hot and Sour Soup

Prep time: 0 minutes | Cook time: 30 minutes | Serves 6

4 cups boiling water
1 ounce dried shiitake mushrooms
2 tablespoons cold-pressed avocado oil
3 garlic cloves, chopped
4 ounces cremini or button mushrooms, sliced
1 pound boneless pork loin, sirloin, or tip, thinly sliced against the grain into ¼-inch-thick, ½-inch-wide, 2-inch-long strips
1 teaspoon ground ginger
½ teaspoon ground white pepper
2 cups low-sodium chicken broth or vegetable broth
One 8-ounce can sliced bamboo shoots, drained and rinsed
2 tablespoons low-sodium soy sauce
1 tablespoon chile garlic sauce
1 teaspoon toasted sesame oil
2 teaspoons Lakanto Monkfruit Sweetener Classic
2 large eggs
¼ cup rice vinegar
2 tablespoons cornstarch
4 green onions, white and green parts, thinly sliced
¼ cup chopped fresh cilantro

1. In a large liquid measuring cup or heatproof bowl, pour the boiling water over the shiitake mushrooms. Cover and let soak for 30 minutes. Drain the mushrooms, reserving the soaking liquid. Remove and discard the stems and thinly slice the caps. 2. Select the Sauté setting on the Instant Pot and heat the avocado oil and garlic for 2 minutes, until the garlic is bubbling but not browned. Add the cremini and shiitake mushrooms and sauté for 3 minutes, until the mushrooms are beginning to wilt. Add the pork, ginger, and white pepper and sauté for about 5 minutes, until the pork is opaque and cooked through. 3. Pour the mushroom soaking liquid into the pot, being careful to leave behind any sediment at the bottom of the measuring cup or bowl. Using a wooden spoon, nudge any browned bits from the bottom of the pot. Stir in the broth, bamboo shoots, soy sauce, chile garlic sauce, sesame oil, and sweetener. 4. Secure the lid and set the Pressure Release to Sealing. Press the Cancel button to reset the cooking program, then select the Pressure Cook or Manual setting and set the cooking time for 5 minutes at high pressure. (The pot will take about 10 minutes to come up to pressure before the cooking program begins.) 5. While the soup is cooking, in a small bowl, beat the eggs until no streaks of yolk remain. 6. When the cooking program ends, let the pressure release naturally for at least 15 minutes, then move the Pressure Release to Venting to release any remaining steam. 7. In a small bowl, stir together the vinegar and cornstarch until the cornstarch dissolves. Open the pot and stir the vinegar mixture into the soup. Press the Cancel button to reset the cooking program, then select the Sauté setting. Bring the soup to a simmer and cook, stirring occasionally, for about 3 minutes, until slightly thickened. While stirring the soup constantly, pour in the beaten eggs in a thin stream. Press the Cancel button to turn off the pot and then stir in the green onions and cilantro. 8. Ladle the soup into bowls and serve hot.

Per Serving:
calories: 231 | fat: 13g | protein: 21g | carbs: 14g | sugars: 2g | fiber: 3g | sodium: 250mg

All-Purpose Chicken Broth

Prep time: 10 minutes | Cook time: 1 hour 25 minutes | Makes 3 quarts

3 pounds (1.4 kg) chicken wings
1 tablespoon vegetable oil
1 onion, chopped
3 garlic cloves, lightly crushed and peeled
12 cups water, divided
½ teaspoon table salt
3 bay leaves

1. Pat chicken wings dry with paper towels. Using highest sauté function, heat oil in Instant Pot for 5 minutes (or until just smoking). Brown half of chicken wings on all sides, about 10 minutes; transfer to bowl. Repeat with remaining chicken wings; transfer to bowl. 2. Add onion to fat left in pot and cook until softened and well browned, 8 to 10 minutes. Stir in garlic and cook until fragrant, about 30 seconds. Stir in 1 cup water, scraping up any browned bits. Stir in remaining 11 cups water, salt, bay leaves, and chicken and any accumulated juices. 3. Lock lid in place and close pressure release valve. Select high pressure cook function and cook for 1 hour. Turn off Instant Pot and let pressure release naturally for 15 minutes. Quick-release any remaining pressure, then carefully remove lid, allowing steam to escape away from you. 4. Strain broth through fine-mesh strainer into large container, pressing on solids to extract as much liquid as possible; discard solids. Using wide, shallow spoon, skim excess fat from surface of broth. (Broth can be refrigerated for up to 4 days or frozen for up to 2 months.)

Per Serving:
calories: 20 | fat: 0g | protein: 4g | carbs: 0g | fiber: 0g | sodium: 95mg

Green Garden Soup

Prep time: 20 minutes | Cook time: 29 minutes | Serves 5

1 tablespoon olive oil
1 garlic clove, diced
½ cup cauliflower florets
1 cup kale, chopped
2 tablespoons chives, chopped
1 teaspoon sea salt
6 cups beef broth

1. Heat the olive oil in the Instant Pot on Sauté mode for 2 minutes and add the garlic. Sauté for 2 minutes or until fragrant. 2. Add cauliflower, kale, chives, sea salt, and beef broth. 3. Close the lid. Select Manual mode and set cooking time for 5 minutes on High Pressure. 4. When timer beeps, use a quick pressure release and open the lid. 5. Ladle the soup into the bowls. Serve warm.

Per Serving:
calories: 80 | fat: 4.5g | protein: 6.5g | carbs: 2.3g | net carbs: 1.8g | fiber: 0.5g

Chicken and Vegetable Soup

Prep time: 5 minutes | Cook time: 2 minutes | Serves 4

1 pound (454 g) boneless, skinless chicken thighs, diced small
1 (10-ounce / 283-g) bag frozen vegetables
2 cups water
1 teaspoon poultry seasoning
1 tablespoon powdered chicken broth base
1 teaspoon salt
1 teaspoon freshly ground black pepper
1 cup heavy (whipping) cream

1. Put the chicken, vegetables, water, poultry seasoning, chicken broth base, salt, and pepper in the inner cooking pot of your Instant Pot. 2. Lock the lid into place. Select Manual and adjust the pressure to High. Cook for 2 minutes. When the cooking is complete, quick-release the pressure (you may want to do this in short bursts so the soup doesn't spurt out). Unlock the lid. 3. Add the cream, stir, and serve. Or, if you prefer, you can mash up the chicken with the back of a wooden spoon to break it into shreds before adding the cream.

Per Serving:
calories: 327 | fat: 19g | protein: 26g | carbs: 13g | net carbs: 10g | fiber: 3g

Curried Chicken Soup

Prep time: 10 minutes | Cook time: 10 minutes | Serves 6

1 pound (454 g) boneless, skinless chicken thighs
1½ cups unsweetened coconut milk
½ onion, finely diced
3 or 4 garlic cloves, crushed
1 (2-inch) piece ginger, finely chopped
1 cup sliced mushrooms, such as cremini and shiitake
4 ounces (113 g) baby spinach
1 teaspoon salt
½ teaspoon ground turmeric
½ teaspoon cayenne
1 teaspoon garam masala
¼ cup chopped fresh cilantro

1. In the inner cooking pot of your Instant Pot, add the chicken, coconut milk, onion, garlic, ginger, mushrooms, spinach, salt, turmeric, cayenne, garam masala, and cilantro. 2. Lock the lid into place. Select Manual and adjust the pressure to High. Cook for 10 minutes. When the cooking is complete, let the pressure release naturally. Unlock the lid. 3. Use tongs to transfer the chicken to a bowl. Shred the chicken, then stir it back into the soup. 4. Eat and rejoice.

Per Serving:
calories: 378 | fat: 26g | protein: 26g | carbs: 6g | net carbs: 2g | fiber: 4g

Summer Vegetable Soup

Prep time: 10 minutes | Cook time: 6 minutes | Serves 6

3 cups finely sliced leeks
6 cups chopped rainbow chard, stems and leaves separated
1 cup chopped celery
2 tablespoons minced garlic, divided
1 teaspoon dried oregano
1 teaspoon salt
2 teaspoons freshly ground black pepper
3 cups chicken broth, plus more as needed
2 cups sliced yellow summer squash, ½-inch slices
¼ cup chopped fresh parsley
¾ cup heavy (whipping) cream
4 to 6 tablespoons grated Parmesan cheese

1. Put the leeks, chard, celery, 1 tablespoon of garlic, oregano, salt, pepper, and broth into the inner cooking pot of the Instant Pot. 2. Lock the lid into place. Select Manual and adjust the pressure to High. Cook for 3 minutes. When the cooking is complete, quick-release the pressure. Unlock the lid. 3. Add more broth if needed. 4. Turn the pot to Sauté and adjust the heat to high. Add the yellow squash, parsley, and remaining 1 tablespoon of garlic. 5. Allow the soup to cook for 2 to 3 minutes, or until the squash is softened and cooked through. 6. Stir in the cream and ladle the soup into bowls. Sprinkle with the Parmesan cheese and serve.

Per Serving:
calories: 210 | fat: 14g | protein: 10g | carbs: 12g | net carbs: 8g | fiber: 4g

French Market Soup

Prep time: 20 minutes | Cook time: 1 hour | Serves 8

2 cups mixed dry beans, washed with stones removed
7 cups water
1 ham hock, all visible fat removed
1 teaspoon salt
¼ teaspoon pepper
16-ounce can low-sodium tomatoes
1 large onion, chopped
1 garlic clove, minced
1 chile, chopped, or 1 teaspoon chili powder
¼ cup lemon juice

1. Combine all ingredients in the inner pot of the Instant Pot. 2. Secure the lid and make sure vent is set to sealing. Using Manual, set the Instant Pot to cook for 60 minutes. 3. When cooking time is over, let the pressure release naturally. When the Instant Pot is ready, unlock the lid, then remove the bone and any hard or fatty pieces. Pull the meat off the bone and chop into small pieces. Add the ham back into the Instant Pot.

Per Serving:
calories: 191 | fat: 4g | protein: 12g | carbs: 29g | sugars: 5g | fiber: 7g | sodium: 488mg

Chicken Poblano Pepper Soup

Prep time: 10 minutes | Cook time: 20 minutes | Serves 8

1 cup diced onion
3 poblano peppers, chopped
5 garlic cloves
2 cups diced cauliflower
1½ pounds (680 g) chicken breast, cut into large chunks
¼ cup chopped fresh cilantro
1 teaspoon ground coriander
1 teaspoon ground cumin
1 to 2 teaspoons salt
2 cups water
2 ounces (57 g) cream cheese, cut into small chunks
1 cup sour cream

1. To the inner cooking pot of the Instant Pot, add the onion, poblanos, garlic, cauliflower, chicken, cilantro, coriander, cumin, salt, and water. 2. Lock the lid into place. Select Manual and adjust the pressure to High. Cook for 15 minutes. When the cooking is complete, let the pressure release naturally for 10 minutes, then quick-release any remaining pressure. Unlock the lid. 3. Remove the chicken with tongs and place in a bowl. 4. Tilting the pot, use an immersion blender to roughly purée the vegetable mixture. It should still be slightly chunky. 5. Turn the Instant Pot to Sauté and adjust to high heat. When the broth is hot and bubbling, add the cream cheese and stir until it melts. Use a whisk to blend in the cream cheese if needed. 6. Shred the chicken and stir it back into the pot. Once it is heated through, serve, topped with sour cream, and enjoy.

Per Serving:
calories: 202 | fat: 10g | protein: 20g | carbs: 8g | net carbs: 5g | fiber: 3g

Spiced Chicken Soup with Squash and Chickpeas

Prep time: 15 minutes | Cook time: 30 minutes | Serves 6 to 8

2 tablespoons extra-virgin olive oil
1 onion, chopped
1¾ teaspoons table salt
2 tablespoons tomato paste
4 garlic cloves, minced
1 tablespoon ground coriander
1½ teaspoons ground cumin
1 teaspoon ground cardamom
½ teaspoon ground allspice
¼ teaspoon cayenne pepper
7 cups water, divided
2 (12-ounce / 340-g) bone-in split chicken breasts, trimmed
4 (5- to 7-ounce / 142- to 198-g) bone-in chicken thighs, trimmed
1½ pounds (680 g) butternut squash, peeled, seeded, and cut into 1½-inch pieces (4 cups)
1 (15-ounce / 425-g) can chickpeas, rinsed
½ cup chopped fresh cilantro

1. Using highest sauté function, heat oil in Instant Pot until shimmering. Add onion and salt and cook until onion is softened, about 5 minutes. Stir in tomato paste, garlic, coriander, cumin, cardamom, allspice, and cayenne and cook until fragrant, about 30 seconds. Stir in 5 cups water, scraping up any browned bits. Nestle chicken breasts and thighs in pot, then arrange squash evenly around chicken. 2. Lock lid in place and close pressure release valve. Select high pressure cook function and cook for 20 minutes. Turn off Instant Pot and quick-release pressure. Carefully remove lid, allowing steam to escape away from you. 3. Transfer chicken to cutting board, let cool slightly, then shred into bite-size pieces using 2 forks; discard skin and bones. 4. Using wide, shallow spoon, skim excess fat from surface of soup, then break squash into bite-size pieces. Stir chicken and any accumulated juices, chickpeas, and remaining 2 cups water into soup and let sit until heated through, about 3 minutes. Stir in cilantro and season with salt and pepper to taste. Serve.

Per Serving:
calories: 190 | fat: 7g | protein: 20g | carbs: 16g | fiber: 4g | sodium: 700mg

French Onion Soup

Prep time: 10 minutes | Cook time: 20 minutes | Serves 10

½ cup light, soft tub margarine
8–10 large onions, sliced
3 14-ounce cans 98% fat-free, lower-sodium beef broth
2½ cups water
3 teaspoons sodium-free chicken bouillon powder
1½ teaspoons Worcestershire sauce
3 bay leaves
10 (1-ounce) slices French bread, toasted

1. Turn the Instant Pot to the Sauté function and add in the margarine and onions. Cook about 5 minutes, or until the onions are slightly soft. Press Cancel. 2. Add the beef broth, water, bouillon powder, Worcestershire sauce, and bay leaves and stir. 3. Secure the lid and make sure vent is set to sealing. Cook on Manual mode for 20 minutes. 4. Let the pressure release naturally for 15 minutes, then do a quick release. Open the lid and discard bay leaves. 5. Ladle into bowls. Top each with a slice of bread and some cheese if you desire.

Per Serving:
calories: 178 | fat: 4g | protein: 6g | carbs: 31g | sugars: 10g | fiber: 4g | sodium: 476mg

Broccoli Brie Soup

Prep time: 5 minutes | Cook time: 14 minutes | Serves 6

1 tablespoon coconut oil or unsalted butter
1 cup finely diced onions
1 head broccoli, cut into small florets
2½ cups chicken broth or vegetable broth
8 ounces (227 g) Brie cheese, cut off rind and cut into chunks
1 cup unsweetened almond milk or heavy cream, plus more for drizzling
Fine sea salt and ground black pepper, to taste
Extra-virgin olive oil, for drizzling
Coarse sea salt, for garnish

1. Place the coconut oil in the Instant Pot and press Sauté. Once hot, add the onions and sauté for 4 minutes, or until soft. Press Cancel to stop the Sauté. 2. Add the broccoli and broth. Seal the lid, press Manual, and set the timer for 10 minutes. Once finished, let the pressure release naturally. 3. Remove the lid and add the Brie and almond milk to the pot. Transfer the soup to a food processor or blender and process until smooth, or purée the soup right in the pot with a stick blender. 4. Season with salt and pepper to taste. Ladle the soup into bowls and drizzle with almond milk and olive oil. Garnish with coarse sea salt and freshly ground pepper.

Per Serving:
calories: 210 | fat: 16g | protein: 9g | carbs: 7g | net carbs: 6g | fiber: 1g

Creamy Sweet Potato Soup

Prep time: 15 minutes | Cook time: 10 minutes | Serves 6

2 tablespoons avocado oil
1 small onion, chopped
2 celery stalks, chopped
2 teaspoons minced garlic
1 teaspoon kosher salt
½ teaspoon freshly ground black pepper
1 teaspoon ground turmeric
½ teaspoon ground cinnamon
2 pounds sweet potatoes, peeled and cut into 1-inch cubes
3 cups Vegetable Broth or Chicken Bone Broth
Plain Greek yogurt, to garnish (optional)
Chopped fresh parsley, to garnish (optional)
Pumpkin seeds (pepitas), to garnish (optional)

1. Set the electric pressure cooker to the Sauté setting. When the pot is hot, pour in the avocado oil. 2. Sauté the onion and celery for 3 to 5 minutes or until the vegetables begin to soften. 3. Stir in the garlic, salt, pepper, turmeric, and cinnamon. Hit Cancel. 4. Stir in the sweet potatoes and broth. 5. Close and lock the lid of the pressure cooker. Set the valve to sealing. 6. Cook on high pressure for 10 minutes. 7. When the cooking is complete, hit Cancel and allow the pressure to release naturally. 8. Once the pin drops, unlock and remove the lid. 9. Use an immersion blender to purée the soup right in the pot. If you don't have an immersion blender, transfer the soup to a blender or food processor and purée. (Follow the instructions that came with your machine for blending hot foods.) 10. Spoon into bowls and serve topped with Greek yogurt, parsley, and/or pumpkin seeds (if using).

Per Serving:
calories: 175 | fat: 5.26g | protein: 4.69g | carbs: 28.87g | sugars: 3.99g | fiber: 3.5g | sodium: 706mg

Avocado and Serrano Chile Soup

Prep time: 10 minutes | Cook time: 7 minutes | Serves 4

2 avocados
1 small fresh tomatillo, quartered
2 cups chicken broth
2 tablespoons avocado oil
1 tablespoon butter
2 tablespoons finely minced onion
1 clove garlic, minced
½ Serrano chile, deseeded and ribs removed, minced, plus thin slices for garnish
¼ teaspoon sea salt
Pinch of ground white pepper
½ cup full-fat coconut milk
Fresh cilantro sprigs, for garnish

1. Scoop the avocado flesh into a food processor. Add the tomatillo and chicken broth and purée until smooth. Set aside. 2. Set the Instant Pot to Sauté mode and add the avocado oil and butter. When the butter melts, add the onion and garlic and sauté for a minute or until softened. Add the Serrano chile and sauté for 1 minute more. 3. Pour the puréed avocado mixture into the pot, add the salt and pepper, and stir to combine. 4. Secure the lid. Press the Manual button and set cooking time for 5 minutes on High Pressure. 5. When timer beeps, use a quick pressure release. Open the lid and stir in the coconut milk. 6. Serve hot topped with thin slices of Serrano chile, and cilantro sprigs.

Per Serving:
calories: 333 | fat: 32.1g | protein: 3.8g | carbs: 14.5g | net carbs: 6.6g | fiber: 7.9g

Buffalo Chicken Soup

Prep time: 7 minutes | Cook time: 10 minutes | Serves 2

1 ounce (28 g) celery stalk, chopped
4 tablespoons coconut milk
¾ teaspoon salt
¼ teaspoon white pepper
1 cup water
2 ounces (57 g) Mozzarella, shredded
6 ounces (170 g) cooked chicken, shredded
2 tablespoons keto-friendly Buffalo sauce

1. Place the chopped celery stalk, coconut milk, salt, white pepper, water, and Mozzarella in the Instant Pot. Stir to mix well. 2. Set the Manual mode and set timer for 7 minutes on High Pressure. 3. When timer beeps, use a quick pressure release and open the lid. 4. Transfer the soup on the bowls. Stir in the chicken and Buffalo sauce. Serve warm.

Per Serving:
calories: 287 | fat: 15g | protein: 33g | carbs: 4g | net carbs: 3g | fiber: 1g

Southwestern Bean Soup with Corn Dumplings

Prep time: 50 minutes | Cook time: 4 to 12 hours | Serves 8

15½-ounce can red kidney beans, rinsed and drained
15½-ounce can black beans, pinto beans, or great northern beans, rinsed and drained
3 cups water
14½-ounce can Mexican-style stewed tomatoes
10-ounce package frozen whole-kernel corn, thawed
1 cup sliced carrots
1 cup chopped onions
4-ounce can chopped green chilies
3 teaspoons sodium-free instant bouillon powder (any flavor)
1–2 teaspoons chili powder
2 cloves garlic, minced
Sauce:
⅓ cup flour
¼ cup yellow cornmeal
1 teaspoon baking powder
Dash of pepper
1 egg white, beaten
2 tablespoons milk
1 tablespoon oil

1. Combine the 11 soup ingredients in inner pot of the Instant Pot. 2. Secure the lid and cook on the Low Slow Cook setting for 10–12 hours or high for 4–5 hours. 3. Make dumplings by mixing together flour, cornmeal, baking powder, and pepper. 4. Combine egg white, milk, and oil. Add to flour mixture. Stir with fork until just combined. 5. At the end of the soup's cooking time, turn the Instant Pot to Slow Cook function high if you don't already have it there. Remove the lid and drop dumpling mixture by rounded teaspoonfuls to make 8 mounds atop the soup. 6. Secure the lid once more and cook for an additional 30 minutes.

Per Serving:
calories: 197 | fat: 1g | protein: 9g | carbs: 39g | sugars: 6g | fiber: 8g | sodium: 367mg

Chapter 8 Vegetables and Sides

Braised Radishes with Sugar Snap Peas and Dukkah

Prep time: 20 minutes | Cook time: 5 minutes | Serves 4

¼ cup extra-virgin olive oil, divided
1 shallot, sliced thin
3 garlic cloves, sliced thin
1½ pounds (680 g) radishes, 2 cups greens reserved, radishes trimmed and halved if small or quartered if large
½ cup water
½ teaspoon table salt
8 ounces (227 g) sugar snap peas, strings removed, sliced thin on bias
8 ounces (227 g) cremini mushrooms, trimmed and sliced thin
2 teaspoons grated lemon zest plus 1 teaspoon juice
1 cup plain Greek yogurt
½ cup fresh cilantro leaves
3 tablespoons dukkah

1. Using highest sauté function, heat 2 tablespoons oil in Instant Pot until shimmering. Add shallot and cook until softened, about 2 minutes. Stir in garlic and cook until fragrant, about 30 seconds. Stir in radishes, water, and salt. Lock lid in place and close pressure release valve. Select high pressure cook function and cook for 1 minute. 2. Turn off Instant Pot and quick-release pressure. Carefully remove lid, allowing steam to escape away from you. Stir in snap peas, cover, and let sit until heated through, about 3 minutes. Add radish greens, mushrooms, lemon zest and juice, and remaining 2 tablespoons oil and gently toss to combine. Season with salt and pepper to taste. 3. Spread ¼ cup yogurt over bottom of 4 individual serving plates. Using slotted spoon, arrange vegetable mixture on top and sprinkle with cilantro and dukkah. Serve.

Per Serving:
calories: 310 | fat: 23g | protein: 10g | carbs: 17g | fiber: 5g | sodium: 320mg

Spaghetti Squash

Prep time: 5 minutes | Cook time: 7 minutes | Serves 4

1 spaghetti squash (about 2 pounds)

1. Cut the spaghetti squash in half crosswise and use a large spoon to remove the seeds. 2. Pour 1 cup of water into the electric pressure cooker and insert a wire rack or trivet. 3. Place the squash halves on the rack, cut-side up. 4. Close and lock the lid of the pressure cooker. Set the valve to sealing. 5. Cook on high pressure for 7 minutes. 6. When the cooking is complete, hit Cancel and quick release the pressure. 7. Once the pin drops, unlock and remove the lid. 8. With tongs, remove the squash from the pot and transfer it to a plate. When it is cool enough to handle, scrape the squash with the tines of a fork to remove the strands. Discard the skin.

Per Serving:
calories: 121 | fat: 2.4g | protein: 2.4g | carbs: 28g | sugars: 11.2g | fiber: 6g | sodium: 68mg

Steamed Tomato with Halloumi Cheese

Prep time: 5 minutes | Cook time: 3 minutes | Serves 4

8 tomatoes, sliced
1 cup water
½ cup crumbled Halloumi cheese
2 tablespoons extra-virgin olive oil
2 tablespoons snipped fresh basil
2 garlic cloves, smashed

1. Pour the water into the Instant Pot and put the trivet in the pot. Place the tomatoes in the trivet. 2. Lock the lid. Select the Manual mode and set the cooking time for 3 minutes on High Pressure. When the timer goes off, perform a quick pressure release. Carefully open the lid. 3. Toss the tomatoes with the remaining ingredients and serve.

Per Serving:
calories: 141 | fat: 10.8g | protein: 4.5g | carbs: 8.1g | net carbs: 5.9g | fiber: 2.2g

Cauliflower Mac and Cheese

Prep time: 6 minutes | Cook time: 3 minutes | Serves 6

1 cup water
1 large cauliflower, chopped into bite-size florets
1 cup heavy whipping cream
½ cup sour cream
1 cup shredded Gruyère or Mozzarella cheese
2½ cups shredded sharp Cheddar cheese
1 teaspoon ground mustard
1 teaspoon ground turmeric
Sea salt, to taste
Pinch of cayenne pepper (optional)

1. Pour the water into the Instant Pot. Place a metal steaming basket inside. Put the cauliflower florets in the basket. Secure the lid and set the steam release valve to Sealing. Press the Manual button and set the cook time to 3 minutes. When the Instant Pot beeps, carefully switch the steam release valve to Venting to quick-release the pressure. When fully released, open the lid. 2. Meanwhile, prepare the cheese sauce. In a large skillet, gently bring the cream to a simmer over medium to medium-low heat. Whisk in the sour cream until smooth, then gradually whisk in the Gruyère and 2 cups of the Cheddar until melted. Stir in the ground mustard and turmeric. Taste and adjust the salt. 3. Remove the cauliflower from the pot and toss it in the cheese sauce to coat. Serve warm, topped with the remaining Cheddar and a sprinkling of cayenne (if using).

Per Serving:
calories: 371 | fat: 31g | protein: 18g | carbs: 8g | net carbs: 5g | fiber: 3g

Best Brown Rice

Prep time: 5 minutes | Cook time: 22 minutes | Serves 6 to 12

2 cups brown rice
2½ cups water

1. Rinse brown rice in a fine-mesh strainer. 2. Add rice and water to the inner pot of the Instant Pot. 3. Secure the lid and make sure vent is on sealing. 4. Use Manual setting and select 22 minutes cooking time on high pressure. 5. When cooking time is done, let the pressure release naturally for 10 minutes, then press Cancel and manually release any remaining pressure.

Per Serving:

calorie: 114 | fat: 1g | protein: 2g | carbs: 23g | sugars: 0g | fiber: 1g | sodium: 3mg

Cauliflower Rice Curry

Prep time: 5 minutes | Cook time: 2 minutes | Serves 4

1 (9-ounce / 255-g) head cauliflower, chopped
½ teaspoon garlic powder
½ teaspoon freshly ground black pepper
½ teaspoon ground turmeric
½ teaspoon curry powder
½ teaspoon kosher salt
½ teaspoon fresh paprika
¼ small onion, thinly sliced

1. Pour 1 cup of filtered water into the inner pot of the Instant Pot, then insert the trivet. In a well-greased, Instant Pot-friendly dish, add the cauliflower. Sprinkle the garlic powder, black pepper, turmeric, curry powder, salt, paprika, and onion over top. 2. Place the dish onto the trivet, and cover loosely with aluminum foil. Close the lid, set the pressure release to Sealing and select Manual. Set the Instant Pot to 2 minutes on High Pressure, and let cook. 3. Once cooked, perform a quick release. 4. Open the Instant Pot, and remove the dish. Serve, and enjoy!

Per Serving:

calories: 24 | fat: 0g | protein: 2g | carbs: 5g | net carbs: 3g | fiber: 2g

Lemon Garlic Asparagus

Prep time: 6 minutes | Cook time: 5 minutes | Serves 4

1 large bunch asparagus, woody ends cut off (medium-thick spears if possible)
1 cup water
2 tablespoons salted butter
2 large cloves garlic, minced
2 teaspoons fresh lemon juice (from ½ lemon)
¾ cup finely shredded Parmesan cheese (optional)
Salt, to taste

1. Cut the asparagus spears on a diagonal into 3 equal pieces, or trim the whole spears to fit your Instant Pot. 2. Pour the water into the Instant Pot. Place a metal steaming basket inside. Place the asparagus in the basket. Secure the lid and set the steam release valve to Sealing. Press the Manual button and set the cook time to 1 minute for tender (for softer, increase to 2 minutes; for crisp, decrease to 0). While it cooks, prepare a bowl with ice water. 3. When the Instant Pot beeps, carefully switch the steam release valve to Venting to quick-release the pressure. When fully released, open the lid and use tongs to transfer the asparagus to the ice bath. Let it sit for a minute, then drain and place the asparagus on a clean kitchen towel and pat dry. 4. Carefully remove the pot insert. Remove the steaming basket, drain the water, and wipe the pot insert dry. 5. Return the pot insert to the Instant Pot and press the Sauté button. Put the butter in the pot. When it has melted and starts to foam, add the garlic and sauté, stirring, for 1 minute. 6. Return the asparagus to the pot and stir well to coat it with the garlic-butter mixture. Add the lemon juice. Sauté until it reaches the desired doneness, about 1 minute more. 7. Transfer the asparagus to a serving bowl and stir in the Parmesan. Taste the asparagus and add salt to taste. Serve warm.

Per Serving:

calories: 70 | fat: 11g | protein: 10g | carbs: 4g | net carbs: 3g | fiber: 1g

Lemon Broccoli

Prep time: 5 minutes | Cook time: 4 minutes | Serves 4

2 cups broccoli florets
1 tablespoon ground paprika
1 tablespoon lemon juice
1 teaspoon grated lemon zest
1 teaspoon olive oil
½ teaspoon chili powder
1 cup water

1. Pour the water in the Instant Pot and insert the trivet. 2. In the Instant Pot pan, stir together the remaining ingredients. 3. Place the pan on the trivet. 4. Set the lid in place. Select the Manual mode and set the cooking time for 4 minutes on High Pressure. When the timer goes off, do a quick pressure release. Carefully open the lid. 5. Serve immediately.

Per Serving:

calories: 34 | fat: 1.7g | protein: 1.5g | carbs: 4.2g | net carbs: 2.4g | fiber: 1.8g

Vegetable Curry

Prep time: 25 minutes | Cook time: 3 minutes | Serves 10

16-ounce package baby carrots
3 medium potatoes, unpeeled, cubed
1 pound fresh or frozen green beans, cut in 2-inch pieces
1 medium green pepper, chopped
1 medium onion, chopped
1–2 cloves garlic, minced
15-ounce can garbanzo beans, drained
28-ounce can crushed tomatoes
3 teaspoons curry powder
1½ teaspoons chicken bouillon granules
1¾ cups boiling water
3 tablespoons minute tapioca

1. Combine carrots, potatoes, green beans, pepper, onion, garlic, garbanzo beans, crushed tomatoes, and curry powder in the Instant Pot. 2. Dissolve bouillon in boiling water, then stir in tapioca. Pour over the contents of the Instant Pot and stir. 3. Secure the lid and make sure vent is set to sealing. Press Manual and set for 3 minutes. 4. When cook time is up, manually release the pressure.

Per Serving:

calories: 166 | fat: 1g | protein: 6g | carbs: 35g | sugars: 10g | fiber: 8g | sodium: 436mg

Parmesan Zoodles

Prep time: 5 minutes | Cook time: 5 minutes | Serves 2

1 large zucchini, trimmed and spiralized
1 tablespoon butter
1 garlic clove, diced
½ teaspoon chili flakes
3 ounces (85 g) Parmesan cheese, grated

1. Set the Instant Pot on the Sauté mode and melt the butter. Add the garlic and chili flakes to the pot. Sauté for 2 minutes, or until fragrant. 2. Stir in the zucchini spirals and sauté for 2 minutes, or until tender. 3. Add the grated Parmesan cheese to the pot and stir well. Continue to cook it for 1 minute, or until the cheese melts. 4. Transfer to a plate and serve immediately

Per Serving:
calories: 217 | fat: 15.3g | protein: 15.7g | carbs: 7.4g | net carbs: 5.7g | fiber: 1.7g

Almond Butter Zucchini Noodles

Prep time: 10 minutes | Cook time: 4 minutes | Serves 4

2 tablespoons coconut oil
1 yellow onion, chopped
2 zucchini, julienned
1 cup shredded Chinese cabbage
2 garlic cloves, minced
2 tablespoons almond butter
Sea salt and freshly ground black pepper, to taste
1 teaspoon cayenne pepper

1. Press the Sauté button to heat up your Instant Pot. Heat the coconut oil and sweat the onion for 2 minutes. 2. Add the other ingredients. 3. Secure the lid. Choose Manual mode and High Pressure; cook for 2 minutes. Once cooking is complete, use a quick pressure release; carefully remove the lid. Bon appétit!

Per Serving:
calories: 145 | fat: 15g | protein: 1g | carbs: 4g | net carbs: 2g | fiber: 2g

Lemony Asparagus with Gremolata

Prep time: 15 minutes | Cook time: 2 minutes | Serves 2 to 4

Gremolata:
1 cup finely chopped fresh Italian flat-leaf parsley leaves
3 garlic cloves, peeled and grated
Zest of 2 small lemons
Asparagus:
1½ pounds (680 g) asparagus, trimmed
1 cup water
Lemony Vinaigrette:
1½ tablespoons fresh lemon juice
1 teaspoon Swerve
1 teaspoon Dijon mustard
2 tablespoons extra-virgin olive oil
Kosher salt and freshly ground black pepper, to taste
Garnish:
3 tablespoons slivered almonds

1. In a small bowl, stir together all the ingredients for the gremolata. 2. Pour the water into the Instant Pot. Arrange the asparagus in a steamer basket. Lower the steamer basket into the pot. 3. Lock the lid. Select the Steam mode and set the cooking time for 2 minutes on Low Pressure. 4. Meanwhile, prepare the lemony vinaigrette: In a bowl, combine the lemon juice, swerve and mustard and whisk to combine. Slowly drizzle in the olive oil and continue to whisk. Season generously with salt and pepper. 5. When the timer goes off, perform a quick pressure release. Carefully open the lid. Remove the steamer basket from the Instant Pot. 6. Transfer the asparagus to a serving platter. Drizzle with the vinaigrette and sprinkle with the gremolata. Serve the asparagus topped with the slivered almonds.

Per Serving:
calories: 132 | fat: 9.3g | protein: 2.9g | carbs: 12.7g | net carbs: 7.8g | fiber: 4.9g

Lemon Cabbage and Tempeh

Prep time: 8 minutes | Cook time: 10 minutes | Serves 3

2 tablespoons sesame oil
½ cup chopped scallions
2 cups shredded cabbage
6 ounces (170 g) tempeh, cubed
1 tablespoon coconut aminos
1 cup vegetable stock
2 garlic cloves, minced
1 tablespoon lemon juice
Salt and pepper, to taste
¼ teaspoon paprika
¼ cup roughly chopped fresh cilantro

1. Press the Sauté button to heat up your Instant Pot. Heat the sesame oil and sauté the scallions until tender and fragrant. 2. Then, add the cabbage, tempeh, coconut aminos, vegetable stock, garlic, lemon juice, salt, pepper, and paprika. 3. Secure the lid. Choose Manual mode and Low Pressure; cook for 3 minutes. Once cooking is complete, use a quick pressure release; carefully remove the lid. 4. Press the Sauté button to thicken the sauce if desired. Divide between serving bowls, garnish with fresh cilantro, and serve warm. Bon appétit!

Per Serving:
calories: 172 | fat: 12g | protein: 10g | carbs: 9g | net carbs: 7g | fiber: 2g

Moroccan Zucchini

Prep time: 10 minutes | Cook time: 6 minutes | Serves 4

2 tablespoons avocado oil
½ medium onion, diced
1 clove garlic, minced
¼ teaspoon cayenne pepper
¼ teaspoon ground coriander
¼ teaspoon ground cumin
¼ teaspoon ground ginger
Pinch of ground cinnamon
1 Roma (plum) tomato, diced
2 medium zucchini, cut into 1-inch pieces
½ tablespoon fresh lemon juice
¼ cup bone broth or vegetable stock

1. Set the Instant Pot to Sauté. When hot, add the oil. Add the onion and sauté, stirring frequently, until translucent, about 2 minutes. Add the garlic, cayenne, coriander, cumin, ginger, and cinnamon and cook until fragrant, about 1 minute. Stir in the tomato and zucchini and cook 2 minutes longer. 2. Press Cancel. Add the lemon juice and broth. Secure the lid and set the steam release valve to Sealing. Press the Manual button, adjust the pressure to Low, and set the cook time to 1 minute. 3. When the Instant Pot beeps, carefully switch the steam release valve to Venting to quick-release the pressure. When fully released, open the lid. Stir and serve warm.

Per Serving:
calories: 92 | fat: 7g | protein: 2g | carbs: 4g | net carbs: 3g | fiber: 1g

Buttery Whole Cauliflower

Prep time: 5 minutes | Cook time: 8 minutes | Serves 4

1 large cauliflower, rinsed and patted dry
1 cup water
4 tablespoons melted butter
2 cloves garlic, minced
Pinch of sea salt
Pinch of fresh ground black pepper
1 tablespoon chopped fresh flat leaf parsley, for garnish

1. Pour the water into the Instant Pot and put the trivet in the pot. Place the cauliflower on the trivet. 2. Lock the lid. Select the Manual mode and set the cooking time for 3 minutes at High Pressure. 3. Preheat the oven to 550ºF (288ºC). Line a baking sheet with parchment paper. 4. In a small bowl, whisk together the butter, garlic, sea salt and black pepper. Set aside. 5. When the timer beeps, use a quick pressure release. Carefully open the lid. 6. Transfer the cauliflower to the lined baking sheet. Dab and dry the surface with a clean kitchen towel. Brush the cauliflower with the garlic butter. 7. Place the baking sheet with the cauliflower in the preheated oven and roast for 5 minutes, or until the cauliflower is golden brown. Drizzle with any remaining garlic butter and sprinkle with the chopped parsley. Serve immediately.

Per Serving:
calories: 141 | fat: 12g | protein: 3g | carbs: 8g | net carbs: 4g | fiber: 4g

Zucchini and Daikon Fritters

Prep time: 10 minutes | Cook time: 8 minutes | Serves 4

2 large zucchinis, grated
1 daikon, diced
1 egg, beaten
1 teaspoon ground flax meal
1 teaspoon salt
1 tablespoon coconut oil

1. In the mixing bowl, combine all the ingredients, except for the coconut oil. Form the zucchini mixture into fritters. 2. Press the Sauté button on the Instant Pot and melt the coconut oil. 3. Place the zucchini fritters in the hot oil and cook for 4 minutes on each side, or until golden brown. 4. Transfer to a plate and serve.

Per Serving:
calories: 77 | fat: 5.0g | protein: 3.7g | carbs: 6.2g | net carbs: 4.2g | fiber: 2.0g

Satarash with Eggs

Prep time: 10 minutes | Cook time: 5 minutes | Serves 4

2 tablespoons olive oil
1 white onion, chopped
2 cloves garlic
2 ripe tomatoes, puréed
1 green bell pepper, deseeded and sliced
1 red bell pepper, deseeded and sliced
1 teaspoon paprika
½ teaspoon dried oregano
½ teaspoon turmeric
Kosher salt and ground black pepper, to taste
1 cup water
4 large eggs, lightly whisked

1. Press the Sauté button on the Instant Pot and heat the olive oil. Add the onion and garlic to the pot and sauté for 2 minutes, or until fragrant. Stir in the remaining ingredients, except for the eggs. 2. Lock the lid. Select the Manual mode and set the cooking time for 3 minutes on High Pressure. When the timer goes off, perform a quick pressure release. Carefully open the lid. 3. Fold in the eggs and stir to combine. Lock the lid and let it sit in the residual heat for 5 minutes. Serve warm.

Per Serving:
calories: 169 | fat: 11.9g | protein: 7.8g | carbs: 8.9g | net carbs: 6.8g | fiber: 2.1g

Parmesan Cauliflower Mash

Prep time: 7 minutes | Cook time: 5 minutes | Serves 4

1 head cauliflower, cored and cut into large florets
½ teaspoon kosher salt
½ teaspoon garlic pepper
2 tablespoons plain Greek yogurt
¾ cup freshly grated Parmesan cheese
1 tablespoon unsalted butter or ghee (optional)
Chopped fresh chives

1. Pour 1 cup of water into the electric pressure cooker and insert a steamer basket or wire rack. 2. Place the cauliflower in the basket. 3. Close and lock the lid of the pressure cooker. Set the valve to sealing. 4. Cook on high pressure for 5 minutes. 5. When the cooking is complete, hit Cancel and quick release the pressure. 6. Once the pin drops, unlock and remove the lid. 7. Remove the cauliflower from the pot and pour out the water. Return the cauliflower to the pot and add the salt, garlic pepper, yogurt, and cheese. Use an immersion blender or potato masher to purée or mash the cauliflower in the pot. 8. Spoon into a serving bowl, and garnish with butter (if using) and chives.

Per Serving:
calories: 141 | fat: 6g | protein: 12g | carbs: 12g | sugars: 9g | fiber: 4g | sodium: 592mg

Italian Wild Mushrooms

Prep time: 30 minutes | Cook time: 3 minutes | Serves 10

2 tablespoons canola oil
2 large onions, chopped
4 garlic cloves, minced
3 large red bell peppers, chopped
3 large green bell peppers, chopped
12-ounce package oyster mushrooms, cleaned and chopped
3 fresh bay leaves
10 fresh basil leaves, chopped
1 teaspoon salt
1½ teaspoons pepper
28-ounce can Italian plum tomatoes, crushed or chopped

1. Press Sauté on the Instant Pot and add in the oil. Once the oil is heated, add the onions, garlic, peppers, and mushroom to the oil. Sauté just until mushrooms begin to turn brown. 2. Add remaining ingredients. Stir well. 3. Secure the lid and make sure vent is set to sealing. Press Manual and set time for 3 minutes. 4. When cook time is up, release the pressure manually. Discard bay leaves.

Per Serving:
calories: 82 | fat: 3g | protein: 3g | carbs: 13g | sugars: 8g | fiber: 4g | sodium: 356mg

Sesame Zoodles with Scallions

Prep time: 10 minutes | Cook time: 3 minutes | Serves 6

2 large zucchinis, trimmed and spiralized
¼ cup chicken broth
1 tablespoon chopped scallions
1 tablespoon coconut aminos
1 teaspoon sesame oil
1 teaspoon sesame seeds
¼ teaspoon chili flakes

1. Set the Instant Pot on the Sauté mode. Add the zucchini spirals to the pot and pour in the chicken broth. Sauté for 3 minutes and transfer to the serving bowls. 2. Sprinkle with the scallions, coconut aminos, sesame oil, sesame seeds and chili flakes. Gently stir the zoodles. 3. Serve immediately.

Per Serving:
calories: 28 | fat: 2g | protein: 2g | carbs: 0g | net carbs: 0g | fiber: 0g

Braised Cabbage with Ginger

Prep time: 10 minutes | Cook time: 8 minutes | Serves 6

1 tablespoon avocado oil
1 tablespoon butter or ghee (or more avocado oil)
½ medium onion, diced
1 medium bell pepper (any color), diced
1 teaspoon sea salt
½ teaspoon ground black pepper
1 clove garlic, minced
1-inch piece fresh ginger, grated
1 pound (454 g) green or red cabbage, cored and leaves chopped
½ cup bone broth or vegetable broth

1. Set the Instant Pot to Sauté and heat the oil and butter together. When the butter has stopped foaming, add the onion, bell pepper, salt, and black pepper. Sauté, stirring frequently, until just softened, about 3 minutes. Add the garlic and ginger and cook 1 minute longer. Add the cabbage and stir to combine. Pour in the broth. 2. Secure the lid and set the steam release valve to Sealing. Press the Manual button and set the cook time to 2 minutes. 3. When the Instant Pot beeps, carefully switch the steam release valve to Venting to quick-release the pressure. When fully released, open the lid. Stir the cabbage and transfer it to a serving dish. Serve warm.

Per Serving:
calories: 73 | fat: 5g | protein: 2g | carbs: 7g | net carbs: 5g | fiber: 2g

Individual Asparagus and Goat Cheese Frittatas

Prep time: 15 minutes | Cook time: 15 minutes | Serves 4

1 tablespoon extra-virgin olive oil
8 ounces (227 g) asparagus, trimmed and sliced ¼ inch thick
1 red bell pepper, stemmed, seeded, and chopped
2 shallots, minced
2 ounces (57 g) goat cheese, crumbled (½ cup)
1 tablespoon minced fresh tarragon
1 teaspoon grated lemon zest
8 large eggs
½ teaspoon table salt

1. Using highest sauté function, heat oil in Instant Pot until shimmering. Add asparagus, bell pepper, and shallots; cook until softened, about 5 minutes. Turn off Instant Pot and transfer vegetables to bowl. Stir in goat cheese, tarragon, and lemon zest. 2. Arrange trivet included with Instant Pot in base of now-empty insert and add 1 cup water. Spray four 6-ounce ramekins with vegetable oil spray. Beat eggs, ¼ cup water, and salt in large bowl until thoroughly combined. Divide vegetable mixture between prepared ramekins, then pour egg mixture over top (you may have some left over). Set ramekins on trivet. Lock lid in place and close pressure release valve. Select high pressure cook function and cook for 10 minutes. 3. Turn off Instant Pot and quick-release pressure. Carefully remove lid, allowing steam to escape away from you. Using tongs, transfer ramekins to wire rack and let cool slightly. Run paring knife around inside edge of ramekins to loosen frittatas, then invert onto individual serving plates. Serve.

Per Serving:
calories: 240 | fat: 16g | protein: 17g | carbs: 6g | fiber: 2g | sodium: 500mg

Potatoes with Parsley

Prep time: 10 minutes | Cook time: 5 minutes | Serves 4

3 tablespoons margarine, divided
2 pounds medium red potatoes (about 2 ounces each), halved lengthwise
1 clove garlic, minced
½ teaspoon salt
½ cup low-sodium chicken broth
2 tablespoons chopped fresh parsley

1. Place 1 tablespoon margarine in the inner pot of the Instant Pot and select Sauté. 2. After margarine is melted, add potatoes, garlic, and salt, stirring well. 3. Sauté 4 minutes, stirring frequently. 4. Add chicken broth and stir well. 5. Seal lid, make sure vent is on sealing, then select Manual for 5 minutes on high pressure. 6. When cooking time is up, manually release the pressure. 7. Strain potatoes, toss with remaining 2 tablespoons margarine and chopped parsley, and serve immediately.

Per Serving:
calories: 237 | fat: 9g | protein: 5g | carbs: 37g | sugars: 3g | fiber: 4g | sodium: 389mg

Vegetable Medley

Prep time: 20 minutes | Cook time: 2 minutes | Serves 8

2 medium parsnips
4 medium carrots
1 turnip, about 4½ inches diameter
1 cup water
1 teaspoon salt
3 tablespoons sugar
2 tablespoons canola or olive oil
½ teaspoon salt

1. Clean and peel vegetables. Cut in 1-inch pieces. 2. Place the cup of water and 1 teaspoon salt into the Instant Pot's inner pot with the vegetables. 3. Secure the lid and make sure vent is set to sealing. Press Manual and set for 2 minutes. 4. When cook time is up, release the pressure manually and press Cancel. Drain the water from the inner pot. 5. Press Sauté and stir in sugar, oil, and salt. Cook until sugar is dissolved. Serve.

Per Serving:
calories: 63 | fat: 2g | protein: 1g | carbs: 12g | sugars: 6g | fiber: 2g | sodium: 327mg

Corn on the Cob

Prep time: 5 minutes | Cook time: 12 to 15 minutes | Serves 4

2 large ears fresh corn
Olive oil for misting
Salt, to taste (optional)

1. Shuck corn, remove silks, and wash. 2. Cut or break each ear in half crosswise. 3. Spray corn with olive oil. 4. Air fry at 390°F (199°C) for 12 to 15 minutes or until browned as much as you like. 5. Serve plain or with coarsely ground salt.

Per Serving:
calories: 67 | fat: 1g | protein: 2g | carbs: 14g | fiber: 2g | sodium: 156mg

Sauerkraut and Mushroom Casserole

Prep time: 6 minutes | Cook time: 15 minutes | Serves 6

1 tablespoon olive oil
1 celery rib, diced
½ cup chopped leeks
2 pounds (907 g) canned sauerkraut, drained
6 ounces (170 g) brown mushrooms, sliced
1 teaspoon caraway seeds
1 teaspoon brown mustard
1 bay leaf
1 cup dry white wine

1. Press the Sauté button to heat up your Instant Pot. Now, heat the oil and cook celery and leeks until softened. 2. Add the sauerkraut and mushrooms and cook for 2 minutes more. 3. Add the remaining ingredients and stir to combine well. 4. Secure the lid. Choose Manual mode and High Pressure; cook for 10 minutes. Once cooking is complete, use a natural pressure release; carefully remove the lid. Bon appétit!

Per Serving:
calories: 90 | fat: 3g | protein: 2g | carbs: 8g | net carbs: 3g | fiber: 5g

Asparagus and Mushroom Soup

Prep time: 10 minutes | Cook time: 7 minutes | Serves 4

2 tablespoons coconut oil
½ cup chopped shallots
2 cloves garlic, minced
1 pound (454 g) asparagus, washed, trimmed, and chopped
4 ounces (113 g) button mushrooms, sliced
4 cups vegetable broth
2 tablespoons balsamic vinegar
Himalayan salt, to taste
¼ teaspoon ground black pepper
¼ teaspoon paprika
¼ cup vegan sour cream

1. Press the Sauté button to heat up your Instant Pot. Heat the oil and cook the shallots and garlic for 2 to 3 minutes. 2. Add the remaining ingredients, except for sour cream, to the Instant Pot. 3. Secure the lid. Choose Manual mode and High Pressure; cook for 4 minutes. Once cooking is complete, use a quick pressure release; carefully remove the lid. 4. Spoon into four soup bowls; add a dollop of sour cream to each serving and serve immediately. Bon appétit!

Per Serving:
calories: 171 | fat: 12g | protein: 10g | carbs: 9g | net carbs: 6g | fiber: 3g

Stir Fried Asparagus and Kale

Prep time: 5 minutes | Cook time: 3 minutes | Serves 4

8 ounces (227 g) asparagus, chopped
2 cups chopped kale
2 bell peppers, chopped
1 tablespoon avocado oil
1 teaspoon apple cider vinegar
½ teaspoon minced ginger
½ cup water

1. Pour the water into the Instant Pot. 2. In the Instant Pot pan, stir together the remaining ingredients. 3. Insert the trivet and place the pan on it. 4. Set the lid in place. Select the Manual mode and set the cooking time for 3 minutes on High Pressure. When the timer goes off, perform a quick pressure release. Carefully open the lid. 5. Serve immediately.

Per Serving:
calories: 56 | fat: 4g | protein: 2g | carbs: 4g | net carbs: 2g | fiber: 2g

Parmesan-Topped Acorn Squash

Prep time: 10 minutes | Cook time: 20 minutes | Serves 4

1 acorn squash (about 1 pound)
1 tablespoon extra-virgin olive oil
1 teaspoon dried sage leaves, crumbled
¼ teaspoon freshly grated nutmeg
⅛ teaspoon kosher salt
⅛ teaspoon freshly ground black pepper
2 tablespoons freshly grated Parmesan cheese

1. Cut the acorn squash in half lengthwise and remove the seeds. Cut each half in half for a total of 4 wedges. Snap off the stem if it's easy to do. 2. In a small bowl, combine the olive oil, sage, nutmeg, salt, and pepper. Brush the cut sides of the squash with the olive oil mixture. 3. Pour 1 cup of water into the electric pressure cooker and insert a wire rack or trivet. 4. Place the squash on the trivet in a single layer, skin-side down. 5. Close and lock the lid of the pressure cooker. Set the valve to sealing. 6. Cook on high pressure for 20 minutes. 7. When the cooking is complete, hit Cancel and quick release the pressure. 8. Once the pin drops, unlock and remove the lid. 9. Carefully remove the squash from the pot, sprinkle with the Parmesan, and serve.

Caramelized Onions

Prep time: 10 minutes | Cook time: 35 minutes | Serves 8

4 tablespoons margarine
6 large Vidalia or other sweet onions, sliced into thin half rings
10-ounce can chicken, or vegetable, broth

1. Press Sauté on the Instant Pot. Add in the margarine and let melt. 2. Once the margarine is melted, stir in the onions and sauté for about 5 minutes. Pour in the broth and then press Cancel. 3. Secure the lid and make sure vent is set to sealing. Press Manual and set time for 20 minutes. 4. When cook time is up, release the pressure manually. Remove the lid and press Sauté. Stir the onion mixture for about 10 more minutes, allowing extra liquid to cook off.

Per Serving:
calorie: 123 | fat: 6g | protein: 2g | carbs: 15g | sugars: 10g | fiber: 3g | sodium: 325mg

Thyme Cabbage

Prep time: 10 minutes | Cook time: 5 minutes | Serves 4

1 pound (454 g) white cabbage
2 tablespoons butter
1 teaspoon dried thyme
½ teaspoon salt
1 cup water

1. Cut the white cabbage on medium size petals and sprinkle with the butter, dried thyme and salt. Place the cabbage petals in the Instant Pot pan. 2. Pour the water and insert the trivet in the Instant Pot. Put the pan on the trivet. 3. Set the lid in place. Select the Manual mode and set the cooking time for 5 minutes on High Pressure. When the timer goes off, do a quick pressure release. Carefully open the lid. 4. Serve immediately.

Per Serving:
calories: 81 | fat: 6.0g | protein: 1.6g | carbs: 6.6g | net carbs: 3.8g | fiber: 2.8g

Perfect Sweet Potatoes

Prep time: 5 minutes | Cook time: 15 minutes | Serves 4 to 6

4–6 medium sweet potatoes
1 cup of water

1. Scrub skin of sweet potatoes with a brush until clean. Pour water into inner pot of the Instant Pot. Place steamer basket in the bottom of the inner pot. Place sweet potatoes on top of steamer basket. 2. Secure the lid and turn valve to seal. 3. Select the Manual mode and set to pressure cook on high for 15 minutes. 4. Allow pressure to release naturally (about 10 minutes). 5. Once the pressure valve lowers, remove lid and serve immediately.

Per Serving:
calories: 112 | fat: 0g | protein: 2g | carbs: 26g | sugars: 5g | fiber: 4g | sodium: 72mg

Indian Okra

Prep time: 8 minutes | Cook time: 7 minutes | Serves 6

1 pound (454 g) young okra
4 tablespoons ghee or avocado oil
½ teaspoon cumin seeds
¼ teaspoon ground turmeric
Pinch of ground cinnamon
½ medium onion, diced
2 cloves garlic, minced
2 teaspoons minced fresh ginger
1 serrano chile, seeded and ribs removed, minced
1 small tomato, diced
½ teaspoon sea salt
¼ teaspoon cayenne pepper (optional)
1 cup vegetable stock or filtered water

1. Rinse and thoroughly dry the okra. Slice it on a diagonal into slices ½ to ¾ inch thick, discarding the stems. 2. Set the Instant Pot to Sauté. Once hot, add the ghee and heat until melted. Stir in the cumin seeds, turmeric, and cinnamon and cook until they are fragrant, about 1 minute. This may cause the cumin seeds to jump and pop. Add the onion and cook, stirring frequently, until soft and translucent, about 3 minutes. Add the garlic, ginger, and serrano chile and sauté for an additional minute. Press Cancel. 3. Stir in the tomato, okra, salt, cayenne (if using), and stock. Secure the lid and set the steam release valve to Sealing. Press the Manual button and set the cook time to 2 minutes. 4. When the Instant Pot beeps, carefully switch the steam release valve to Venting to quick-release the pressure. When fully released, open the lid. Stir gently and allow the okra to rest on the Keep Warm setting for a few minutes before serving.

Per Serving:
calories: 114 | fat: 9g | protein: 2g | carbs: 9g | net carbs: 6g | fiber: 3g

Vinegary Broccoli with Cheese

Prep time: 5 minutes | Cook time: 5 minutes | Serves 4

1 pound (454 g) broccoli, cut into florets
1 cup water
2 garlic cloves, minced
1 cup crumbled Cottage cheese
2 tablespoons balsamic vinegar
1 teaspoon cumin seeds
1 teaspoon mustard seeds
Salt and pepper, to taste

1. Pour the water into the Instant Pot and put the steamer basket in the pot. Place the broccoli in the steamer basket. 2. Close and secure the lid. Select the Manual setting and set the cooking time for 5 minutes at High Pressure. Once the timer goes off, do a quick pressure release. Carefully open the lid. 3. Stir in the remaining ingredients. 4. Serve immediately.

Per Serving:
calories: 105 | fat: 3.0g | protein: 9.5g | carbs: 11.9g | net carbs: 8.7g | fiber: 3.2g

Lemony Brussels Sprouts with Poppy Seeds

Prep time: 10 minutes | Cook time: 2 minutes | Serves 4

1 pound (454 g) Brussels sprouts
2 tablespoons avocado oil, divided
1 cup vegetable broth or chicken bone broth
1 tablespoon minced garlic
½ teaspoon kosher salt
Freshly ground black pepper, to taste
½ medium lemon
½ tablespoon poppy seeds

1. Trim the Brussels sprouts by cutting off the stem ends and removing any loose outer leaves. Cut each in half lengthwise (through the stem). 2. Set the electric pressure cooker to the Sauté/More setting. When the pot is hot, pour in 1 tablespoon of the avocado oil. 3. Add half of the Brussels sprouts to the pot, cut-side down, and let them brown for 3 to 5 minutes without disturbing. Transfer to a bowl and add the remaining tablespoon of avocado oil and the remaining Brussels sprouts to the pot. Hit Cancel and return all of the Brussels sprouts to the pot. 4. Add the broth, garlic, salt, and a few grinds of pepper. Stir to distribute the seasonings. 5. Close and lock the lid of the pressure cooker. Set the valve to sealing. 6. Cook on high pressure for 2 minutes. 7. While the Brussels sprouts are cooking, zest the lemon, then cut it into quarters. 8. When the cooking is complete, hit Cancel and quick release the pressure. 9. Once the pin drops, unlock and remove the lid. 10. Using a slotted spoon, transfer the Brussels sprouts to a serving bowl. Toss with the lemon zest, a squeeze of lemon juice, and the poppy seeds. Serve immediately.

Per Serving:
calories: 125 | fat: 8g | protein: 4g | carbs: 13g | sugars: 3g | fiber: 5g | sodium: 504mg

Beet and Watercress Salad with Orange and Dill

Prep time: 20 minutes | Cook time: 8 minutes | Serves 4

2 pounds (907 g) beets, scrubbed, trimmed, and cut into ¾-inch pieces
½ cup water
1 teaspoon caraway seeds
½ teaspoon table salt
1 cup plain Greek yogurt
1 small garlic clove, minced to paste
5 ounces (142 g) watercress, torn into bite-size pieces
1 tablespoon extra-virgin olive oil, divided, plus extra for drizzling
1 tablespoon white wine vinegar, divided
1 teaspoon grated orange zest plus 2 tablespoons juice
¼ cup hazelnuts, toasted, skinned, and chopped
¼ cup coarsely chopped fresh dill
Coarse sea salt

1. Combine beets, water, caraway seeds, and table salt in Instant Pot. Lock lid in place and close pressure release valve. Select high pressure cook function and cook for 8 minutes. Turn off Instant Pot and quick-release pressure. Carefully remove lid, allowing steam to escape away from you. 2. Using slotted spoon, transfer beets to plate; set aside to cool slightly. Combine yogurt, garlic, and 3 tablespoons beet cooking liquid in bowl; discard remaining cooking liquid. In large bowl toss watercress with 2 teaspoons oil and 1 teaspoon vinegar. Season with table salt and pepper to taste. 3. Spread yogurt mixture over surface of serving dish. Arrange watercress on top of yogurt mixture, leaving 1-inch border of yogurt mixture. Add beets to now-empty large bowl and toss with orange zest and juice, remaining 2 teaspoons vinegar, and remaining 1 teaspoon oil. Season with table salt and pepper to taste. Arrange beets on top of watercress mixture. Drizzle with extra oil and sprinkle with hazelnuts, dill, and sea salt. Serve.

Per Serving:
calories: 240 | fat: 15g | protein: 9g | carbs: 19g | fiber: 5g | sodium: 440mg

Mushroom Stroganoff with Vodka

Prep time: 8 minutes | Cook time: 8 minutes | Serves 4

2 tablespoons olive oil
½ teaspoon crushed caraway seeds
½ cup chopped onion
2 garlic cloves, smashed
¼ cup vodka
¾ pound (340 g) button mushrooms, chopped
1 celery stalk, chopped
1 ripe tomato, puréed
1 teaspoon mustard seeds
Sea salt and freshly ground pepper, to taste
2 cups vegetable broth

1. Press the Sauté button to heat up your Instant Pot. Now, heat the oil and sauté caraway seeds until fragrant, about 40 seconds. 2. Then, add the onion and garlic, and continue sautéing for 1 to 2 minutes more, stirring frequently. 3. After that, add the remaining ingredients and stir to combine. 4. Secure the lid. Choose Manual mode and High Pressure; cook for 5 minutes. Once cooking is complete, use a quick pressure release; carefully remove the lid. 5. Ladle into individual bowls and serve warm. Bon appétit!

Per Serving:
calories: 128 | fat: 9g | protein: 6g | carbs: 7g | net carbs: 4g | fiber: 3g

Chanterelle Mushrooms with Cheddar Cheese

Prep time: 10 minutes | Cook time: 5 minutes | Serves 4

1 tablespoon olive oil
2 cloves garlic, minced
1 (1-inch) ginger root, grated
16 ounces (454 g) Chanterelle mushrooms, brushed clean and sliced
½ cup unsweetened tomato purée
½ cup water
2 tablespoons dry white wine
1 teaspoon dried basil
½ teaspoon dried thyme
½ teaspoon dried dill weed
⅓ teaspoon freshly ground black pepper
Kosher salt, to taste
1 cup shredded Cheddar cheese

1. Press the Sauté button on the Instant Pot and heat the olive oil. Add the garlic and grated ginger to the pot and sauté for 1 minute, or until fragrant. Stir in the remaining ingredients, except for the cheese. 2. Lock the lid. Select the Manual mode and set the cooking time for 5 minutes on Low Pressure. When the timer goes off, perform a quick pressure release. Carefully open the lid.. 3. Serve topped with the shredded cheese.

Per Serving:
calories: 206 | fat: 13.7g | protein: 9.3g | carbs: 12.3g | net carbs: 7.1g | fiber: 5.2g

Green Beans with Potatoes and Basil

Prep time: 20 minutes | Cook time: 10 minutes | Serves 4

2 tablespoons extra-virgin olive oil, plus extra for drizzling
1 onion, chopped fine
2 tablespoons minced fresh oregano or 2 teaspoons dried
2 tablespoons tomato paste
4 garlic cloves, minced
1 (14½-ounce / 411-g) can whole peeled tomatoes, drained with juice reserved, chopped
1 cup water
1 teaspoon table salt
¼ teaspoon pepper
1½ pounds (680 g) green beans, trimmed and cut into 2-inch lengths
1 pound (454 g) Yukon Gold potatoes, peeled and cut into 1-inch pieces
3 tablespoons chopped fresh basil or parsley
2 tablespoons toasted pine nuts
Shaved Parmesan cheese

1. Using highest sauté function, heat oil in Instant Pot until shimmering. Add onion and cook until softened, about 5 minutes. Stir in oregano, tomato paste, and garlic and cook until fragrant, about 30 seconds. Stir in tomatoes and their juice, water, salt, and pepper, then stir in green beans and potatoes. Lock lid in place and close pressure release valve. Select high pressure cook function and cook for 5 minutes. 2. Turn off Instant Pot and quick-release pressure. Carefully remove lid, allowing steam to escape away from you. Season with salt and pepper to taste. Sprinkle individual portions with basil, pine nuts, and Parmesan and drizzle with extra oil. Serve.

Per Serving:
calories: 280 | fat: 10g | protein: 7g | carbs: 42g | fiber: 8g | sodium: 880mg

Cauliflower Curry

Prep time: 10 minutes | Cook time: 3 minutes | Serves 6

1 pound (454 g) cauliflower, chopped
3 ounces (85 g) scallions, chopped
1 cup coconut milk
¼ cup crushed tomatoes
1 tablespoon coconut oil
1 teaspoon garam masala
1 teaspoon ground turmeric

1. Add all the ingredients to the Instant Pot and stir to combine. 2. Lock the lid. Select the Manual mode and set the cooking time for 3 minutes at High Pressure. When the timer goes off, use a natural pressure release for 5 minutes, then release any remaining pressure. Carefully open the lid. 3. Stir the cooked dish well before serving.

Per Serving:
calories: 142 | fat: 12.2g | protein: 3.1g | carbs: 8.2g | net carbs: 4.7g | fiber: 3.5g

Chapter 9 Desserts

Cocoa Cookies

Prep time: 15 minutes | Cook time: 25 minutes | Serves 4

½ cup coconut flour
3 tablespoons cream cheese
1 teaspoon cocoa powder
1 tablespoon erythritol
¼ teaspoon baking powder
1 teaspoon apple cider vinegar
1 tablespoon butter
1 cup water, for cooking

1. Make the dough: Mix up coconut flour, cream cheese, cocoa powder, erythritol, baking powder, apple cider vinegar, and butter. Knead the dough, 2. Then transfer the dough in the baking pan and flatten it in the shape of a cookie. 3. Pour water and insert the steamer rack in the instant pot. 4. Put the pan with a cookie in the instant pot. Close and seal the lid. 5. Cook the cookie on Manual (High Pressure) for 25 minutes. Make a quick pressure release. Cool the cookie well.

Per Serving:
calories: 113 | fat: 7g | protein: 2g | carbs: 14g | net carbs: 8g | fiber: 6g

Chocolate Chip Banana Cake

Prep time: 15 minutes | Cook time: 25 minutes | Serves 8

Nonstick cooking spray
3 ripe bananas
½ cup buttermilk
3 tablespoons honey
1 teaspoon vanilla extract
2 large eggs, lightly beaten
3 tablespoons extra-virgin olive oil
1½ cups whole wheat pastry flour
⅛ teaspoon ground nutmeg
1 teaspoon ground cinnamon
¼ teaspoon salt
1 teaspoon baking soda
⅓ cup dark chocolate chips

1. Spray a 7-inch Bundt pan with nonstick cooking spray. 2. In a large bowl, mash the bananas. Add the buttermilk, honey, vanilla, eggs, and olive oil, and mix well. 3. In a medium bowl, whisk together the flour, nutmeg, cinnamon, salt, and baking soda. 4. Add the flour mixture to the banana mixture and mix well. Stir in the chocolate chips. Pour the batter into the prepared Bundt pan. Cover the pan with foil. 5. Pour 1 cup of water into the electric pressure cooker. Place the pan on the wire rack and lower it into the pressure cooker. 6. Close and lock the lid of the pressure cooker. Set the valve to sealing. 7. Cook on high pressure for 25 minutes. 8. When the cooking is complete, hit Cancel and quick release the pressure. 9. Once the pin drops, unlock and remove the lid. 10. Carefully transfer the pan to a cooling rack, uncover, and let it cool for 10 minutes. 11. Invert the cake onto the rack and let it cool for about an hour. 12. Slice and serve the cake.

Per Serving:
(1 slice): calories: 261 | fat: 11g | protein: 6g | carbs: 39g | sugars: 16g | fiber: 4g | sodium: 239mg

Southern Almond Pie

Prep time: 10 minutes | Cook time: 35 minutes | Serves 12

2 cups almond flour
1½ cups powdered erythritol
1 teaspoon baking powder
Pinch of salt
½ cup sour cream
4 tablespoons butter, melted
1 egg
1 teaspoon vanilla extract
Cooking spray
1½ teaspoons ground cinnamon
1½ teaspoons Swerve
1 cup water

1. In a large bowl, whisk together the almond flour, powdered erythritol, baking powder, and salt. 2. Add the sour cream, butter, egg, and vanilla and whisk until well combined. The batter will be very thick, almost like cookie dough. 3. Grease the baking dish with cooking spray. Line with parchment paper, if desired. 4. Transfer the batter to the dish and level with an offset spatula. 5. In a small bowl, combine the cinnamon and Swerve. Sprinkle over the top of the batter. 6. Cover the dish tightly with aluminum foil. Add the water to the pot. Set the dish on the trivet and carefully lower it into the pot. 7. Set the lid in place. Select the Manual mode and set the cooking time for 35 minutes on High Pressure. When the timer goes off, do a quick pressure release. Carefully open the lid. 8. Remove the trivet and pie from the pot. Remove the foil from the pan. The pie should be set but soft, and the top should be slightly cracked. 9. Cool completely before cutting.

Per Serving:
calories: 221 | fat: 19.0g | protein: 5.6g | carbs: 4.8g | net carbs: 2.4g | fiber: 2.4g

Daikon and Almond Cake

Prep time: 10 minutes | Cook time: 45 minutes | Serves 12

5 eggs, beaten
½ cup heavy cream
1 cup almond flour
1 daikon, diced
1 teaspoon ground cinnamon
2 tablespoon erythritol
1 tablespoon butter, melted
1 cup water

1. In the mixing bowl, mix up eggs, heavy cream, almond flour, ground cinnamon, and erythritol. 2. When the mixture is smooth, add daikon and stir it carefully with the help of the spatula. 3. Pour the mixture in the cake pan. 4. Then pour water and insert the trivet in the instant pot. 5. Place the cake in the instant pot. 6. Set the lid in place. Select the Manual mode and set the cooking time for 45 minutes on High Pressure. When the timer goes off, do a quick pressure release. Carefully open the lid. 7. Serve immediately.

Per Serving:
calories: 66 | fat: 5.7g | protein: 3.1g | carbs: 3.5g | net carbs: 3.0g | fiber: 0.5g

Deconstructed Tiramisu

Prep time: 5 minutes | Cook time: 9 minutes | Serves 4

1 cup heavy cream (or full-fat coconut milk for dairy-free)
2 large egg yolks
2 tablespoons brewed decaf espresso or strong brewed coffee
2 tablespoons Swerve, or more to taste
1 teaspoon rum extract
1 teaspoon unsweetened cocoa powder, or more to taste
Pinch of fine sea salt
1 cup cold water
4 teaspoons Swerve, for topping

1. Heat the cream in a pan over medium-high heat until hot, about 2 minutes. 2. Place the egg yolks, coffee, sweetener, rum extract, cocoa powder, and salt in a blender and blend until smooth. 3. While the blender is running, slowly pour in the hot cream. Taste and adjust the sweetness to your liking. Add more cocoa powder, if desired. 4. Scoop the mixture into four ramekins with a spatula. Cover the ramekins with aluminum foil. 5. Place a trivet in the bottom of the Instant Pot and pour in the water. Place the ramekins on the trivet. 6. Lock the lid. Select the Manual mode and set the cooking time for 7 minutes at High Pressure. 7. When the timer beeps, use a quick pressure release. Carefully remove the lid. 8. Keep the ramekins covered with the foil and place in the refrigerator for about 2 hours until completely chilled. 9. Sprinkle 1 teaspoon of Swerve on top of each tiramisu. Use the oven broiler to melt the sweetener. 10. Put in the fridge to chill the topping, about 20 minutes. 11. Serve.

Per Serving:
calories: 139 | fat: 13.4g | protein: 2.1g | carbs: 2.6g | net carbs: 2.5g | fiber: 0.1g

Lush Chocolate Cake

Prep time: 10 minutes | Cook time: 35 minutes | Serves 8

For Cake:
2 cups almond flour
⅓ cup unsweetened cocoa powder
1½ teaspoons baking powder
1 cup granulated erythritol
Pinch of salt
4 eggs
1 teaspoon vanilla extract
½ cup butter, melted and cooled
6 tablespoons strong coffee, cooled
½ cup water
For Frosting:
4 ounces (113 g) cream cheese, softened
½ cup butter, softened
¼ teaspoon vanilla extract
2½ tablespoons powdered erythritol
2 tablespoons unsweetened cocoa powder

1. To make the cake: In a large bowl, whisk together the almond flour, cocoa powder, baking powder, granulated erythritol, and salt. Whisk well to remove any lumps. 2. Add the eggs and vanilla and mix with a hand mixer until combined. 3. With the mixer still on low speed, slowly add the melted butter and mix until well combined. 4. Add the coffee and mix on low speed until the batter is thoroughly combined. Scrape the sides and bottom of the bowl to make sure everything is well mixed. 5. Spray the cake pan with cooking spray. Pour the batter into the pan. Cover tightly with aluminum foil. 6. Add the water to the pot. Place the cake pan on the trivet and carefully lower then pan into the pot. 7. Close the lid. Select Manual mode and set cooking time for 35 minutes on High Pressure. 8. When timer beeps, use a quick pressure release and open the lid. 9. Carefully remove the cake pan from the pot and place on a wire rack to cool. Flip the cake onto a plate once it is cool enough to touch. Cool completely before frosting. 10. To make the frosting: In a medium bowl, use the mixer to whip the cream cheese, butter, and vanilla until light and fluffy, 1 to 2 minutes. With the mixer running, slowly add the powdered erythritol and cocoa powder. Mix until everything is well combined. 11. Once the cake is completely cooled, spread the frosting on the top and down the sides.

Per Serving:
calories: 475 | fat: 44.2g | protein: 11.0g | carbs: 8.6g | net carbs: 4.2g | fiber: 4.4g

Hearty Crème Brûlée

Prep time: 5 minutes | Cook time: 30 minutes | Serves 4

5 egg yolks
5 tablespoons powdered erythritol
1½ cups heavy cream
2 teaspoons vanilla extract
2 cups water

1. In a small bowl, use a fork to break up the egg yolks. Stir in the erythritol. 2. Pour the cream into a small saucepan over medium-low heat and let it warm up for 3 to 4 minutes. Remove the saucepan from the heat. 3. Temper the egg yolks by slowly adding a small spoonful of the warm cream, keep whisking. Do this three times to make sure the egg yolks are fully tempered. 4. Slowly add the tempered eggs to the cream, whisking the whole time. Add the vanilla and whisk again. 5. Pour the cream mixture into the ramekins. Each ramekin should have ½ cup liquid. Cover each with aluminum foil. 6. Place the trivet inside the Instant Pot. Add the water. Carefully place the ramekins on top of the trivet. 7. Close the lid. Select Manual mode and set cooking time for 11 minutes on High Pressure. 8. When timer beeps, use a natural release for 15 minutes, then release any remaining pressure. Open the lid. 9. Carefully remove a ramekin from the pot. Remove the foil and check for doneness. The custard should be mostly set with a slightly jiggly center. 10. Place all the ramekins in the fridge for 2 hours to chill and set. Serve chilled.

Per Serving:
calories: 229 | fat: 22.2g | protein: 4.4g | carbs: 2.2g | net carbs: 2.2g | fiber: 0g

Coconut Squares

Prep time: 15 minutes | Cook time: 4 minutes | Serves 2

⅓ cup coconut flakes
1 tablespoon butter
1 egg, beaten
1 cup water, for cooking

1. Mix up together coconut flakes, butter, and egg. 2. Then put the mixture into the square shape mold and flatten well. 3. Pour water and insert the steamer rack in the instant pot. 4. Put the mold with dessert on the rack. Close and seal the lid. 5. Cook the meal on Manual mode (High Pressure) for 4 minutes. Make a quick pressure release. 6. Cool the cooked dessert little and cut into the squares.

Per Serving:
calories: 130 | fat: 12g | protein: 3g | carbs: 2g | net carbs: 1g | fiber: 1g

Glazed Pumpkin Bundt Cake

Prep time: 7 minutes | Cook time: 35 minutes | Serves 12

Cake:
3 cups blanched almond flour
1 teaspoon baking soda
½ teaspoon fine sea salt
2 teaspoons ground cinnamon
1 teaspoon ground nutmeg
1 teaspoon ginger powder
¼ teaspoon ground cloves
6 large eggs
2 cups pumpkin purée
1 cup Swerve
¼ cup (½ stick) unsalted butter (or coconut oil for dairy-free), softened
Glaze:
1 cup (2 sticks) unsalted butter (or coconut oil for dairy-free), melted
½ cup Swerve

1. In a large bowl, stir together the almond flour, baking soda, salt, and spices. In another large bowl, add the eggs, pumpkin, sweetener, and butter and stir until smooth. Pour the wet ingredients into the dry ingredients and stir well. 2. Grease a 6-cup Bundt pan. Pour the batter into the prepared pan and cover with a paper towel and then with aluminum foil. 3. Place a trivet in the bottom of the Instant Pot and pour in 2 cups of cold water. Place the Bundt pan on the trivet. 4. Lock the lid. Select the Manual mode and set the cooking time for 35 minutes at High Pressure. 5. When the timer beeps, use a natural pressure release for 10 minutes. Carefully remove the lid. 6. Let the cake cool in the pot for 10 minutes before removing. 7. While the cake is cooling, make the glaze: In a small bowl, mix the butter and sweetener together. Spoon the glaze over the warm cake. 8. Allow to cool for 5 minutes before slicing and serving.

Per Serving:
calories: 332 | fat: 21.9g | protein: 6.8g | carbs: 27.4g | net carbs: 26.2g | fiber: 1.2g

Lemon Vanilla Cheesecake

Prep time: 15 minutes | Cook time: 20 minutes | Serves 6

2 teaspoons freshly squeezed lemon juice
2 teaspoons vanilla extract or almond extract
½ cup sour cream, divided, at room temperature
½ cup plus 2 teaspoons Swerve
8 ounces (227 g) cream cheese, at room temperature
2 eggs, at room temperature

1. Pour 2 cups of water into the inner cooking pot of the Instant Pot, then place a trivet (preferably with handles) in the pot. Line the sides of a 6-inch springform pan with parchment paper. 2. In a food processor, put the lemon juice, vanilla, ¼ cup of sour cream, ½ cup of Swerve, and the cream cheese. 3. Gently but thoroughly blend all the ingredients, scraping down the sides of the bowl as needed. 4. Add the eggs and blend only as long as you need to in order to get them well incorporated, 20 to 30 seconds. Your mixture will be pourable by now. 5. Pour the mixture into the prepared pan. Cover the pan with aluminum foil and place on the trivet. (If your trivet doesn't have handles, you may wish to use a foil sling to make removing the pan easier.) 6. Lock the lid into place. Select Manual and adjust the pressure to High. Cook for 20 minutes. When the cooking is complete, let the pressure release naturally. Unlock the lid. 7. Meanwhile, in a small bowl, mix together the remaining ¼ cup of sour cream and 2 teaspoons of Swerve for the topping. 8. Take out the cheesecake and remove the foil. Spread the topping over the top. Doing this while the cheesecake is still hot helps melt the topping into the cheesecake. 9. Put the cheesecake in the refrigerator and leave it alone. Seriously. Leave it alone and let it chill for at least 6 to 8 hours. It won't taste right hot. 10. When you're ready to serve, open the sides of the pan and peel off the parchment paper. Slice and serve.

Per Serving:
calories: 207 | fat: 19g | protein: 5g | carbs: 4g | net carbs: 4g | fiber: 0g

Vanilla Cream Pie

Prep time: 20 minutes | Cook time: 35 minutes | Serves 12

1 cup heavy cream
3 eggs, beaten
1 teaspoon vanilla extract
¼ cup erythritol
1 cup coconut flour
1 tablespoon butter, melted
1 cup water, for cooking

1. In the mixing bowl, mix up coconut flour, erythritol, vanilla extract, eggs, and heavy cream. 2. Grease the baking pan with melted butter. 3. Pour the coconut mixture in the baking pan. 4. Pour water and insert the steamer rack in the instant pot. 5. Place the pie on the rack. Close and seal the lid. 6. Cook the pie on Manual mode (High Pressure) for 35 minutes. 7. Allow the natural pressure release for 10 minutes.

Per Serving:
calories: 100 | fat: 7g | protein: 3g | carbs: 12g | net carbs: 8g | fiber: 4g

Pumpkin Pie Pudding

Prep time: 10 minutes | Cook time: 20 minutes | Serves 6

Nonstick cooking spray
2 eggs
½ cup heavy (whipping) cream or almond milk (for dairy-free)
¾ cup Swerve
1 (15-ounce / 425-g) can pumpkin purée
1 teaspoon pumpkin pie spice
1 teaspoon vanilla extract
For Serving:
½ cup heavy (whipping) cream

1. Grease a 6-by-3-inch pan extremely well with the cooking spray, making sure it gets into all the nooks and crannies. 2. In a medium bowl, whisk the eggs. Add the cream, Swerve, pumpkin purée, pumpkin pie spice, and vanilla, and stir to mix thoroughly. 3. Pour the mixture into the prepared pan and cover it with a silicone lid or aluminum foil. 4. Pour 2 cups of water into the inner cooking pot of the Instant Pot, then place a trivet in the pot. Place the covered pan on the trivet. 5. Lock the lid into place. Select Manual and adjust the pressure to High. Cook for 20 minutes. When the cooking is complete, let the pressure release naturally for 10 minutes, then quick-release any remaining pressure. Unlock the lid. 6. Remove the pan and place it in the refrigerator. Chill for 6 to 8 hours. 8. When ready to serve, finish by making the whipped cream. Using a hand mixer, beat the heavy cream until it forms soft peaks. Do not overbeat and turn it to butter. Serve each pudding with a dollop of whipped cream.

Per Serving:
calories: 188 | fat: 17g | protein: 4g | carbs: 8g | net carbs:6 g | fiber: 2g

Chipotle Black Bean Brownies

Prep time: 15 minutes | Cook time: 30 minutes | Serves 8

Nonstick cooking spray
½ cup dark chocolate chips, divided
¾ cup cooked calypso beans or black beans
½ cup extra-virgin olive oil
2 large eggs
¼ cup unsweetened dark chocolate cocoa powder
⅓ cup honey
1 teaspoon vanilla extract
⅓ cup white wheat flour
½ teaspoon chipotle chili powder
½ teaspoon ground cinnamon
½ teaspoon baking powder
½ teaspoon kosher salt

1. Spray a 7-inch Bundt pan with nonstick cooking spray. 2. Place half of the chocolate chips in a small bowl and microwave them for 30 seconds. Stir and repeat, if necessary, until the chips have completely melted. 3. In a food processor, blend the beans and oil together. Add the melted chocolate chips, eggs, cocoa powder, honey, and vanilla. Blend until the mixture is smooth. 4. In a large bowl, whisk together the flour, chili powder, cinnamon, baking powder, and salt. Pour the bean mixture from the food processor into the bowl and stir with a wooden spoon until well combined. Stir in the remaining chocolate chips. 5. Pour the batter into the prepared Bundt pan. Cover loosely with foil. 6. Pour 1 cup of water into the electric pressure cooker. 7. Place the Bundt pan onto the wire rack and lower it into the pressure cooker. 8. Close and lock the lid of the pressure cooker. Set the valve to sealing. 9. Cook on high pressure for 30 minutes. 10. When the cooking is complete, hit Cancel and quick release the pressure. 11. Once the pin drops, unlock and remove the lid. 12. Carefully transfer the pan to a cooling rack for about 10 minutes, then invert the cake onto the rack and let it cool completely. 13. Cut into slices and serve.

Per Serving:
(1 slice): calories: 296 | fat: 20g | protein: 5g | carbs: 29g | sugars: 16g | fiber: 4g | sodium: 224mg

Ultimate Chocolate Cheesecake

Prep time: 10 minutes | Cook time: 50 minutes | Serves 12

2 cups pecans
2 tablespoons butter
16 ounces (454 g) cream cheese, softened
1 cup powdered erythritol
¼ cup sour cream
2 tablespoons cocoa powder
2 teaspoons vanilla extract
2 cups low-carb chocolate chips
1 tablespoon coconut oil
2 eggs
2 cups water

1. Preheat oven to 400°F (205°C). Place pecans and butter into food processor. Pulse until dough-like consistency. Press into bottom of 7-inch springform pan. Bake for 10 minutes then set aside to cool. 2. While crust bakes, mix cream cheese, erythritol, sour cream, cocoa powder, and vanilla together in large bowl using a rubber spatula. Set aside. 3. In medium bowl, combine chocolate chips and coconut oil. Microwave in 20-second increments until chocolate begins to melt and then stir until smooth. Gently fold chocolate mixture into cheesecake mixture. 4. Add eggs and gently fold in, careful not to overmix. Pour mixture over cooled pecan crust. Cover with foil. 5. Pour water into Instant Pot and place steam rack on bottom. Place cheesecake on steam rack and click lid closed. Press the Manual button and adjust time for 40 minutes. When timer beeps, allow a natural release. Carefully remove and let cool completely. Serve chilled.

Per Serving:
calories: 461 | fat: 40g | protein: 5g | carbs: 20g | net carbs: 15g | fiber: 5g

Chai Pear-Fig Compote

Prep time: 20 minutes | Cook time: 3 minutes | Serves 4

1 vanilla chai tea bag
1 (3-inch) cinnamon stick
1 strip lemon peel (about 2-by-½ inches)
1½ pounds pears, peeled and chopped (about 3 cups)
½ cup chopped dried figs
2 tablespoons raisins

1. Pour 1 cup of water into the electric pressure cooker and hit Sauté/More. When the water comes to a boil, add the tea bag and cinnamon stick. Hit Cancel. Let the tea steep for 5 minutes, then remove and discard the tea bag. 2. Add the lemon peel, pears, figs, and raisins to the pot. 3. Close and lock the lid of the pressure cooker. Set the valve to sealing. 4. Cook on high pressure for 3 minutes. 5. When the cooking is complete, hit Cancel and quick release the pressure. 6. Once the pin drops, unlock and remove the lid. 7. Remove the lemon peel and cinnamon stick. Serve warm or cool to room temperature and refrigerate.

Per Serving:
calories: 167 | fat: 1g | protein: 2g | carbs: 44g | sugars: 29g | fiber: 9g | sodium: 4mg

Vanilla Crème Brûlée

Prep time: 7 minutes | Cook time: 9 minutes | Serves 4

1 cup heavy cream (or full-fat coconut milk for dairy-free)
2 large egg yolks
2 tablespoons Swerve, or more to taste
Seeds scraped from ½ vanilla bean (about 8 inches long), or 1 teaspoon vanilla extract
1 cup cold water
4 teaspoons Swerve, for topping

1. Heat the cream in a pan over medium-high heat until hot, about 2 minutes. 2. Place the egg yolks, Swerve, and vanilla seeds in a blender and blend until smooth. 3. While the blender is running, slowly pour in the hot cream. Taste and adjust the sweetness to your liking. 4. Scoop the mixture into four ramekins with a spatula. Cover the ramekins with aluminum foil. 5. Add the water to the Instant Pot and insert a trivet. Place the ramekins on the trivet. 6. Lock the lid. Select the Manual mode and set the cooking time for 7 minutes at High Pressure. 7. When the timer beeps, perform a quick pressure release. Carefully remove the lid. 8. Keep the ramekins covered with the foil and place in the refrigerator for about 2 hours until completely chilled. 9. Sprinkle 1 teaspoon of Swerve on top of each crème brûlée. Use the oven broiler to melt the sweetener. 10. Allow the topping to cool in the fridge for 5 minutes before serving.

Per Serving:
calories: 138 | fat: 13.4g | protein: 2.0g | carbs: 2.3g | net carbs: 2.3g | fiber: 0g

Spiced Pear Applesauce

Prep time: 15 minutes | Cook time: 5 minutes | Makes: 3½ cups

1 pound pears, peeled, cored, and sliced
2 teaspoons apple pie spice or cinnamon
Pinch kosher salt
Juice of ½ small lemon

1. In the electric pressure cooker, combine the apples, pears, apple pie spice, salt, lemon juice, and ¼ cup of water. 2. Close and lock the lid of the pressure cooker. Set the valve to sealing. 3. Cook on high pressure for 5 minutes. 4. When the cooking is complete, hit Cancel and let the pressure release naturally. 5. Once the pin drops, unlock and remove the lid. 6. Mash the apples and pears with a potato masher to the consistency you like. 7. Serve warm, or cool to room temperature and refrigerate.

Per Serving:
(½ cup): calories: 108 | fat: 1g | protein: 1g | carbs: 29g | sugars: 20g | fiber: 6g | sodium: 15mg

Almond Butter Keto Fat Bombs

Prep time: 3 minutes | Cook time: 3 minutes | Serves 6

¼ cup coconut oil
¼ cup no-sugar-added almond butter
2 tablespoons cacao powder
¼ cup powdered erythritol

1. Press the Sauté button and add coconut oil to Instant Pot. Let coconut oil melt completely and press the Cancel button. Stir in remaining ingredients. Mixture will be liquid. 2. Pour into 6 silicone molds and place into freezer for 30 minutes until set. Store in fridge.

Per Serving:
calories: 142 | fat: 14g | protein: 3g | carbs: 9g | net carbs: 7g | fiber: 2g

Pumpkin Walnut Cheesecake

Prep time: 15 minutes | Cook time: 50 minutes | Serves 6

2 cups walnuts
3 tablespoons melted butter
1 teaspoon cinnamon
16 ounces (454 g) cream cheese, softened
1 cup powdered erythritol
⅓ cup heavy cream
⅔ cup pumpkin purée
2 teaspoons pumpkin spice
1 teaspoon vanilla extract
2 eggs
1 cup water

1. Preheat oven to 350°F (180°C). Add walnuts, butter, and cinnamon to food processor. Pulse until ball forms. Scrape down sides as necessary. Dough should hold together in ball. 2. Press into greased 7-inch springform pan. Bake for 10 minutes or until it begins to brown. Remove and set aside. While crust is baking, make cheesecake filling. 3. In large bowl, stir cream cheese until completely smooth. Using rubber spatula, mix in erythritol, heavy cream, pumpkin purée, pumpkin spice, and vanilla. 4. In small bowl, whisk eggs. Slowly add them into large bowl, folding gently until just combined. 5. Pour mixture into crust and cover with foil. Pour water into Instant Pot and place steam rack on bottom. Place pan onto steam rack and click lid closed. Press the Cake button and press the Adjust button to set heat to More. Set timer for 40 minutes. 6. When timer beeps, allow a full natural release. When pressure indicator drops, carefully remove pan and place on counter. Remove foil. Let cool for additional hour and then refrigerate. Serve chilled.

Per Serving:
calories: 578 | fat: 54g | protein: 12g | carbs: 11g | net carbs: 8g | fiber: 3g

Lemon and Ricotta Torte

Prep time: 15 minutes | Cook time: 35 minutes | Serves 12

Cooking spray
Torte:
1⅓ cups Swerve
½ cup (1 stick) unsalted butter, softened
2 teaspoons lemon or vanilla extract
5 large eggs, separated
2½ cups blanched almond flour
1¼ (10-ounce / 284-g) cups whole-milk ricotta cheese
¼ cup lemon juice
1 cup cold water
Lemon Glaze:
½ cup (1 stick) unsalted butter
¼ cup Swerve
2 tablespoons lemon juice
2 ounces (57 g) cream cheese (¼ cup)
Grated lemon zest and lemon slices, for garnish

1. Line a baking pan with parchment paper and spray with cooking spray. Set aside. 2. Make the torte: In the bowl of a stand mixer, place the Swerve, butter, and extract and blend for 8 to 10 minutes until well combined. Scrape down the sides of the bowl as needed. 3. Add the egg yolks and continue to blend until fully combined. Add the almond flour and mix until smooth, then stir in the ricotta and lemon juice. 4. Whisk the egg whites in a separate medium bowl until stiff peaks form. Add the whites to the batter and stir well. Pour the batter into the prepared pan and smooth the top. 5. Place a trivet in the bottom of your Instant Pot and pour in the water. Use a foil sling to lower the baking pan onto the trivet. Tuck in the sides of the sling. 6. Seal the lid, press Pressure Cook or Manual, and set the timer for 30 minutes. Once finished, let the pressure release naturally. 7. Lock the lid. Select the Manual mode and set the cooking time for 30 minutes at High Pressure. 8. When the timer beeps, perform a natural pressure release for 10 minutes. Carefully remove the lid. 9. Use the foil sling to lift the pan out of the Instant Pot. Place the torte in the fridge for 40 minutes to chill before glazing. 10. Meanwhile, make the glaze: Place the butter in a large pan over high heat and cook for about 5 minutes until brown, stirring occasionally. Remove from the heat. While stirring the browned butter, add the Swerve. 11. Carefully add the lemon juice and cream cheese to the butter mixture. Allow the glaze to cool for a few minutes, or until it starts to thicken. 12. Transfer the chilled torte to a serving plate. Pour the glaze over the torte and return it to the fridge to chill for an additional 30 minutes. 13. Scatter the lemon zest on top of the torte and arrange the lemon slices on the plate around the torte. 14. Serve.

Per Serving:
calories: 367 | fat: 32.8g | protein: 11.5g | carbs: 10.0g | net carbs: 7.0g | fiber: 3.0g

Strawberry Cheesecake

Prep time: 20 minutes | Cook time: 10 minutes | Serves 2

1 tablespoon gelatin
4 tablespoon water (for gelatin)
4 tablespoon cream cheese
1 strawberry, chopped
¼ cup coconut milk
1 tablespoon Swerve

1. Mix up gelatin and water and leave the mixture for 10 minutes. 2. Meanwhile, pour coconut milk in the instant pot. 3. Bring it to boil on Sauté mode, about 10 minutes. 4. Meanwhile, mash the strawberry and mix it up with cream cheese. 5. Add the mixture in the hot coconut milk and stir until smooth. 6. Cool the liquid for 10 minutes and add gelatin. Whisk it until gelatin is melted. 7. Then pour the cheesecake in the mold and freeze in the freezer for 3 hours.

Per Serving:
calories: 155 | fat: 14g | protein: 5g | carbs: 4g | net carbs: 3g | fiber: 1g

Cinnamon Roll Cheesecake

Prep time: 15 minutes | Cook time: 35 minutes | Serves 12

Crust:
3½ tablespoons unsalted butter or coconut oil
1½ ounces (43 g) unsweetened baking chocolate, chopped
1 large egg, beaten
⅓ cup Swerve
2 teaspoons ground cinnamon
1 teaspoon vanilla extract
¼ teaspoon fine sea salt
Filling:
4 (8-ounce / 227-g) packages cream cheese, softened
¾ cup Swerve
½ cup unsweetened almond milk (or hemp milk for nut-free)
1 teaspoon vanilla extract
¼ teaspoon almond extract (omit for nut-free)
¼ teaspoon fine sea salt
3 large eggs
Cinnamon Swirl:
6 tablespoons (¾ stick) unsalted butter (or butter flavored coconut oil for dairy-free)
½ cup Swerve
Seeds scraped from ½ vanilla bean (about 8 inches long), or 1 teaspoon vanilla extract
1 tablespoon ground cinnamon
¼ teaspoon fine sea salt
1 cup cold water

1. Line a baking pan with two layers of aluminum foil. 2. Make the crust: Melt the butter in a pan over medium-low heat. Slowly add the chocolate and stir until melted. Stir in the egg, sweetener, cinnamon, vanilla extract, and salt. 3. Transfer the crust mixture to the prepared baking pan, spreading it with your hands to cover the bottom completely. 4. Make the filling: In the bowl of a stand mixer, add the cream cheese, sweetener, milk, extracts, and salt and mix until well blended. Add the eggs, one at a time, mixing on low speed after each addition just until blended. Then blend until the filling is smooth. Pour half of the filling over the crust. 5. Make the cinnamon swirl: Heat the butter over high heat in a pan until the butter froths and brown flecks appear, stirring occasionally. Stir in the sweetener, vanilla seeds, cinnamon, and salt. Remove from the heat and allow to cool slightly. 6. Spoon half of the cinnamon swirl on top of the cheesecake filling in the baking pan. Use a knife to cut the cinnamon swirl through the filling several times for a marbled effect. Top with the rest of the cheesecake filling and cinnamon swirl. Cut the cinnamon swirl through the cheesecake filling again several times. 7. Place a trivet in the bottom of the Instant Pot and pour in the water. Use a foil sling to lower the baking pan onto the trivet. Cover the cheesecake with 3 large sheets of paper towel to ensure that condensation doesn't leak onto it. Tuck in the sides of the sling. 8. Lock the lid. Select the Manual mode and set the cooking time for 26 minutes at High Pressure. 9. When the timer beeps, use a natural pressure release for 10 minutes. Carefully remove the lid. 10. Use the foil sling to lift the pan out of the Instant Pot. 11. Let the cheesecake cool, then place in the refrigerator for 4 hours to chill and set completely before slicing and serving.

Per Serving:
calories: 363 | fat: 34.2g | protein: 7.0g | carbs: 7.6g | net carbs: 6.4g | fiber: 1.2g

Almond Pie with Coconut

Prep time: 5 minutes | Cook time: 41 minutes | Serves 8

1 cup almond flour
½ cup coconut milk
1 teaspoon vanilla extract
2 tablespoons butter, softened
1 tablespoon Truvia
¼ cup shredded coconut
1 cup water

1. In the mixing bowl, mix up almond flour, coconut milk, vanilla extract, butter, Truvia, and shredded coconut. 2. When the mixture is smooth, transfer it in the baking pan and flatten. 3. Pour water and insert the trivet in the instant pot. 4. Put the baking pan with cake on the trivet. 5. Lock the lid. Select the Manual mode and set the cooking time for 41 minutes on High Pressure. Once the timer goes off, perform a natural pressure release for 10 minutes, then release any remaining pressure. Carefully open the lid. 6. Serve immediately.

Per Serving:
calories: 89 | fat: 9.2g | protein: 1.3g | carbs: 2.5g | net carbs: 1.5g | fiber: 1.0g

Apple Crunch

Prep time: 13 minutes | Cook time: 2 minutes | Serves 4

3 apples, peeled, cored, and sliced (about 1½ pounds)
1 teaspoon pure maple syrup
1 teaspoon apple pie spice or ground cinnamon
¼ cup unsweetened apple juice, apple cider, or water
¼ cup low-sugar granola

1. In the electric pressure cooker, combine the apples, maple syrup, apple pie spice, and apple juice. 2. Close and lock the lid of the pressure cooker. Set the valve to sealing. 3. Cook on high pressure for 2 minutes. 4. When the cooking is complete, hit Cancel and quick release the pressure. 5. Once the pin drops, unlock and remove the lid. 6. Spoon the apples into 4 serving bowls and sprinkle each with 1 tablespoon of granola.

Per Serving:
calories: 103 | fat: 1g | protein: 1g | carbs: 26g | sugars: 18g | fiber: 4g | sodium: 13mg

Keto Brownies

Prep time: 15 minutes | Cook time: 15 minutes | Serves 8

1 cup coconut flour
1 tablespoon cocoa powder
1 tablespoon coconut oil
1 teaspoon vanilla extract
1 teaspoon baking powder
1 teaspoon apple cider vinegar
⅓ cup butter, melted
1 tablespoon erythritol
1 cup water, for cooking

1. In the mixing bowl, mix up erythritol, melted butter, apple cider vinegar, baking powder, vanilla extract, coconut oil, cocoa powder, and coconut flour. 2. Whisk the mixture until smooth and pour it in the baking pan. Flatten the surface of the batter. 3. Pour water and insert the steamer rack in the instant pot. 4. Put the pan with brownie batter on the rack. Close and seal the lid. 5. Cook the brownie on Manual mode (High Pressure) for 15 minutes. 6. Then allow the natural pressure release for 5 minutes. 7. Cut the cooked brownies into the bars.

Per Serving:
calories: 146 | fat: 11g | protein: 2g | carbs: 9g | net carbs: 5g | fiber: 4g

Lemon-Ricotta Cheesecake

Prep time: 10 minutes | Cook time: 30 minutes | Serves 6

Unsalted butter or vegetable oil, for greasing the pan
8 ounces (227 g) cream cheese, at room temperature
¼ cup plus 1 teaspoon Swerve, plus more as needed
⅓ cup full-fat or part-skim ricotta cheese, at room temperature
Zest of 1 lemon
Juice of 1 lemon
½ teaspoon lemon extract
2 eggs, at room temperature
2 tablespoons sour cream

1. Grease a 6-inch springform pan extremely well. I find this easiest to do with a silicone basting brush so I can get into all the nooks and crannies. Alternatively, line the sides of the pan with parchment paper. 2. In the bowl of a stand mixer, beat the cream cheese, ¼ cup of Swerve, the ricotta, lemon zest, lemon juice, and lemon extract on high speed until you get a smooth mixture with no lumps. 3. Taste to ensure the sweetness is to your liking and adjust if needed. 4. Add the eggs, reduce the speed to low and gently blend until the eggs are just incorporated. Overbeating at this stage will result in a cracked crust. 5. Pour the mixture into the prepared pan and cover with aluminum foil or a silicone lid. 6. Pour 2 cups of water into the inner cooking pot of the Instant Pot, then place a trivet in the pot. Place the covered pan on the trivet. 7. Lock the lid into place. Select Manual and adjust the pressure to High. Cook for 30 minutes. When the cooking is complete, let the pressure release naturally. Unlock the lid. 8. Carefully remove the pan from the pot, and remove the foil. 9. In a small bowl, mix together the sour cream and remaining 1 teaspoon of Swerve and spread this over the top of the warm cake. 10. Refrigerate the cheesecake for 6 to 8 hours. Do not be in a hurry! The cheesecake needs every bit of this time to be its best.

Per Serving:
calories: 217 | fat: 17g | protein: 6g | carbs: 10g | net carbs: 10g | fiber: 0g

Nutmeg Cupcakes

Prep time: 5 minutes | Cook time: 30 minutes | Serves 7

Cake:
2 cups blanched almond flour
2 tablespoons grass-fed butter, softened
2 eggs
½ cup unsweetened almond milk
½ cup Swerve, or more to taste
½ teaspoon ground nutmeg
½ teaspoon baking powder

Frosting:
4 ounces (113 g) full-fat cream cheese, softened
4 tablespoons grass-fed butter, softened
2 cups heavy whipping cream
1 teaspoon vanilla extract
½ cup Swerve, or more to taste
6 tablespoons sugar-free chocolate chips (optional)

1. Pour 1 cup of filtered water into the inner pot of the Instant Pot, then insert the trivet. In a large bowl, combine the flour, butter, eggs, almond milk, Swerve, nutmeg, and baking powder. Mix thoroughly. Working in batches if needed, transfer this mixture into a well-greased, Instant Pot-friendly muffin (or egg bites) mold. 2. Place the molds onto the trivet, and cover loosely with aluminum foil. Close the lid, set the pressure release to Sealing, and select Manual. Set the Instant Pot to 30 minutes on High Pressure, and let cook. 3. While you wait, in a large bowl, combine the cream cheese, butter, whipping cream, vanilla, Swerve, and chocolate chips. Use an electric hand mixer until you achieve a light and fluffy texture. Place frosting in refrigerator. 4. Once the cupcakes are cooked, let the pressure release naturally, for about 10 minutes. Then, switch the pressure release to Venting. Open the Instant Pot, and remove the food. Let cool, top each cupcake evenly with a scoop of frosting.

Per Serving:
calories: 219 | fat: 22g | protein: 3g | carbs: 3g | net carbs: 2g | fiber: 1g

Vanilla Poppy Seed Cake

Prep time: 10 minutes | Cook time: 25 minutes | Serves 6

1 cup almond flour
2 eggs
½ cup erythritol
2 teaspoons vanilla extract
1 teaspoon lemon extract
1 tablespoon poppy seeds
4 tablespoons melted butter
¼ cup heavy cream
⅛ cup sour cream
½ teaspoon baking powder
1 cup water
¼ cup powdered erythritol, for garnish

1. In large bowl, mix almond flour, eggs, erythritol, vanilla, lemon, and poppy seeds. 2. Add butter, heavy cream, sour cream, and baking powder. 3. Pour into 7-inch round cake pan. Cover with foil. 4. Pour water into Instant Pot and place steam rack in bottom. Place baking pan on steam rack and click lid closed. Press the Cake button and press the Adjust button to set heat to Less. Set time for 25 minutes. 5. When timer beeps, allow a 15-minute natural release, then quick-release the remaining pressure. Let cool completely. Sprinkle with powdered erythritol for serving.

Per Serving:
calories: 221 | fat: 21g | protein: 3g | carbs: 5g | net carbs: 3g | fiber: 2g

Coconut Lemon Squares

Prep time: 5 minutes | Cook time: 40 minutes | Serves 5 to 6

3 eggs
2 tablespoons grass-fed butter, softened
½ cup full-fat coconut milk
½ teaspoon baking powder
½ teaspoon vanilla extract
½ cup Swerve, or more to taste
¼ cup lemon juice
1 cup blanched almond flour

1. In a large bowl, mix together the eggs, butter, coconut milk, baking powder, vanilla, Swerve, lemon juice, and flour. Stir thoroughly, until a perfectly even mixture is obtained. 2. Next, pour 1 cup filtered water into the Instant Pot, and insert the trivet. Transfer the mixture from the bowl into a well-greased, Instant Pot-friendly pan (or dish). 3. Using a sling if desired, place the dish onto the trivet, and cover loosely with aluminum foil. Close the lid, set the pressure release to Sealing, and select Manual. Set the Instant Pot to 40 minutes on High Pressure, and let cook. 4. Once cooked, let the pressure naturally disperse from the Instant Pot for about 10 minutes, then carefully switch the pressure release to Venting. 5. Open the Instant Pot, and remove the dish. Let cool, cut into 6 squares, serve, and enjoy!

Per Serving:
calories: 166 | fat: 15g | protein: 6g | carbs: 3g | net carbs: 2g | fiber: 1g

Caramelized Pumpkin Cheesecake

Prep time: 15 minutes | Cook time: 45 minutes | Serves 8

Crust:
1½ cups almond flour
4 tablespoons butter, melted
1 tablespoon Swerve
1 tablespoon granulated erythritol
½ teaspoon ground cinnamon
Cooking spray
Filling:
16 ounces (454 g) cream cheese, softened
½ cup granulated erythritol
2 eggs
¼ cup pumpkin purée
3 tablespoons Swerve
1 teaspoon vanilla extract
¼ teaspoon pumpkin pie spice
1½ cups water

1. To make the crust: In a medium bowl, combine the almond flour, butter, Swerve, erythritol, and cinnamon. Use a fork to press it all together. 2. Spray the pan with cooking spray and line the bottom with parchment paper. 3. Press the crust evenly into the pan. Work the crust up the sides of the pan, about halfway from the top, and make sure there are no bare spots on the bottom. 4. Place the crust in the freezer for 20 minutes while you make the filling. 5. To make the filling: In a large bowl using a hand mixer on medium speed, combine the cream cheese and erythritol. Beat until the cream cheese is light and fluffy, 2 to 3 minutes. 6. Add the eggs, pumpkin purée, Swerve, vanilla, and pumpkin pie spice. Beat until well combined. 7. Remove the crust from the freezer and pour in the filling. Cover the pan with aluminum foil and place it on the trivet. 8. Add the water to the pot and carefully lower the trivet into the pot. 9. Set the lid in place. Select the Manual mode and set the cooking time for 45 minutes on High Pressure. When the timer goes off, do a quick pressure release. Carefully open the lid. 10. Remove the trivet and cheesecake from the pot. Remove the foil from the pan. The center of the cheesecake should still be slightly jiggly. 11. Let the cheesecake cool for 30 minutes on the counter before placing it in the refrigerator to set. Leave the cheesecake in the refrigerator for at least 6 hours before removing the sides and serving.

Per Serving:
calories: 407 | fat: 35.8g | protein: 10.3g | carbs: 6.8g | net carbs: 4.3g | fiber: 2.5g

Chocolate Cake with Walnuts

Prep time: 10 minutes | Cook time: 20 minutes | Serves 6

1 cup almond flour
⅔ cup Swerve
¼ cup unsweetened cocoa powder
¼ cup chopped walnuts
1 teaspoon baking powder
3 eggs
⅓ cup heavy (whipping) cream
¼ cup coconut oil
Nonstick cooking spray

1. Put the flour, Swerve, cocoa powder, walnuts, baking powder, eggs, cream, and coconut oil in a large bowl. Using a hand mixer on high speed, combine the ingredients until the mixture is well incorporated and looks fluffy. This will keep the cake from being too dense. 2. With the cooking spray, grease a heatproof pan, such as a 3-cup Bundt pan, that fits inside your Instant Pot. Pour the cake batter into the pan and cover with aluminum foil. 3. Pour 2 cups of water into the inner cooking pot of the Instant Pot, then place a trivet in the pot. Place the pan on the trivet. 4. Lock the lid into place. Select Manual and adjust the pressure to High. Cook for 20 minutes. When the cooking is complete, let the pressure release naturally for 10 minutes, then quick-release any remaining pressure. 5. Carefully take out the pan and let it cool for 15 to 20 minutes. Invert the cake onto a plate. It can be served hot or at room temperature. Serve with a dollop of whipped cream, if desired.

Per Serving:
calories: 240 | fat: 20g | protein: 5g | carbs: 10g | net carbs: 5g | fiber: 5g

Cardamom Rolls with Cream Cheese

Prep time: 20 minutes | Cook time: 18 minutes | Serves 5

½ cup coconut flour
1 tablespoon ground cardamom
2 tablespoon Swerve
1 egg, whisked
¼ cup almond milk
1 tablespoon butter, softened
1 tablespoon cream cheese
⅓ cup water

1. Combine together coconut flour, almond milk, and softened butter. 2. Knead the smooth dough. 3. Roll up the dough with the help of the rolling pin. 4. Then combine together Swerve and ground cardamom. 5. Sprinkle the surface of the dough with the ground cardamom mixture. 6. Roll the dough into one big roll and cut them into servings. 7. Place the rolls into the instant pot round mold. 8. Pour water in the instant pot (⅓ cup) and insert the mold inside. 9. Set Manual mode (High Pressure) for 18 minutes. 10. Then use the natural pressure release method for 15 minutes. 11. Chill the rolls to the room temperature and spread with cream cheese.

Per Serving:
calories: 128 | fat: 6g | protein: 5g | carbs: 12g | net carbs: 8g | fiber: 4g

Coconut Cupcakes

Prep time: 5 minutes | Cook time: 10 minutes | Serves 6

4 eggs, beaten
4 tablespoons coconut milk
4 tablespoons coconut flour
½ teaspoon vanilla extract
2 tablespoons erythritol
1 teaspoon baking powder
1 cup water

1. In the mixing bowl, mix up eggs, coconut milk, coconut flour, vanilla extract, erythritol, and baking powder. 2. Then pour the batter in the cupcake molds. 3. Pour the water and insert the trivet in the instant pot. 4. Place the cupcakes on the trivet. 5. Lock the lid. Select the Manual mode and set the cooking time for 10 minutes on High Pressure. Once the timer goes off, perform a natural pressure release for 5 minutes, then release any remaining pressure. Carefully open the lid. 6. Serve immediately.

Per Serving:

calories: 85 | fat: 5.7g | protein: 4.7g | carbs: 9.1g | net carbs: 6.8g | fiber: 2.3g

Vanilla Butter Curd

Prep time: 5 minutes | Cook time: 6 hours | Serves 3

4 egg yolks, whisked
2 tablespoon butter
1 tablespoon erythritol
½ cup organic almond milk
1 teaspoon vanilla extract

1. Set the instant pot to Sauté mode and when the "Hot" is displayed, add butter. 2. Melt the butter but not boil it and add whisked egg yolks, almond milk, and vanilla extract. 3. Add erythritol. Whisk the mixture. 4. Cook the meal on Low for 6 hours.

Per Serving:

calories: 154 | fat: 14g | protein: 4g | carbs: 7g | net carbs: 7g | fiber: 0g

Fudgy Walnut Brownies

Prep time: 10 minutes | Cook time: 1 hour | Serves 12

¾ cup walnut halves and pieces
½ cup unsalted butter, melted and cooled
4 large eggs
1½ teaspoons instant coffee crystals
1½ teaspoons vanilla extract
1 cup Lakanto Monkfruit Sweetener Golden
¼ teaspoon fine sea salt
¾ cup almond flour
¾ cup natural cocoa powder
¾ cup stevia-sweetened chocolate chips

1. In a dry small skillet over medium heat, toast the walnuts, stirring often, for about 5 minutes, until golden. Transfer the walnuts to a bowl to cool. 2. Pour 1 cup water into the Instant Pot. Line the base of a 7 by 3-inch round cake pan with a circle of parchment paper. Butter the sides of the pan and the parchment or coat with nonstick cooking spray. 3. Pour the butter into a medium bowl. One at a time, whisk in the eggs, then whisk in the coffee crystals, vanilla, sweetener, and salt. Finally, whisk in the flour and cocoa powder just until combined. Using a rubber spatula, fold in the chocolate chips and walnuts. 4. Transfer the batter to the prepared pan and, using the spatula, spread it in an even layer. Cover the pan tightly with aluminum foil. Place the pan on a long-handled silicone steam rack, then, holding the handles of the steam rack, lower it into the Instant Pot. 5. Secure the lid and set the Pressure Release to Sealing. Select the Cake, Pressure Cook, or Manual setting and set the cooking time for 45 minutes at high pressure. (The pot will take about 10 minutes to come up to pressure before the cooking program begins.) 6. When the cooking program ends, let the pressure release naturally for 10 minutes, then move the Pressure Release to Venting to release any remaining steam. Open the pot and, wearing heat-resistant mitts, grasp the handles of the steam rack and lift it out of the pot. Uncover the pan, taking care not to get burned by the steam or to drip condensation onto the brownies. Let the brownies cool in the pan on a cooling rack for about 2 hours, to room temperature. 7. Run a butter knife around the edge of the pan to make sure the brownies are not sticking to the pan sides. Invert the brownies onto the rack, lift off the pan, and peel off the parchment paper. Invert the brownies onto a serving plate and cut into twelve wedges. The brownies will keep, stored in an airtight container in the refrigerator for up to 5 days, or in the freezer for up to 4 months.

Per Serving:

calories: 199 | fat: 19g | protein: 5g | carbs: 26g | sugars: 10g | fiber: 20g | sodium: 56mg

Lime Muffins

Prep time: 10 minutes | Cook time: 15 minutes | Serves 6

1 teaspoon lime zest
1 tablespoon lemon juice
1 teaspoon baking powder
1 cup almond flour
2 eggs, beaten
1 tablespoon Swerve
¼ cup heavy cream
1 cup water, for cooking

1. In the mixing bowl, mix up lemon juice, baking powder, almond flour, eggs, Swerve, and heavy cream. 2. When the muffin batter is smooth, add lime zest and mix it up. 3. Fill the muffin molds with batter. 4. Then pour water and insert the rack in the instant pot. 5. Place the muffins on the rack. Close and seal the lid. 6. Cook the muffins on Manual (High Pressure) for 15 minutes. 7. Then allow the natural pressure release.

Per Serving:

calories: 153 | fat: 12g | protein: 6g | carbs: 5g | net carbs: 3g | fiber: 2g

Fast Chocolate Mousse

Prep time: 10 minutes | Cook time: 4 minutes | Serves 1

1 egg yolk
1 teaspoon erythritol
1 teaspoon cocoa powder
2 tablespoons coconut milk
1 tablespoon cream cheese
1 cup water, for cooking

1. Pour water and insert the steamer rack in the instant pot. 2. Then whisk the egg yolk with erythritol. 3. When the mixture turns into lemon color, add coconut milk, cream cheese, and cocoa powder. Whisk the mixture until smooth. 4. Then pour it in the glass jar and place it on the steamer rack. 5. Close and seal the lid. 6. Cook the dessert on Manual (High Pressure) for 4 minutes. Make a quick pressure release.

Per Serving:

calories: 162 | fat: 15g | protein: 4g | carbs: 3g | net carbs: 2g | fiber: 1g

Candied Mixed Nuts

Prep time: 5 minutes | Cook time: 15 minutes | Serves 8

1 cup pecan halves
1 cup chopped walnuts
⅓ cup Swerve, or more to taste
⅓ cup grass-fed butter
1 teaspoon ground cinnamon

1. Preheat your oven to 350ºF (180ºC), and line a baking sheet with aluminum foil. 2. While your oven is warming, pour ½ cup of filtered water into the inner pot of the Instant Pot, followed by the pecans, walnuts, Swerve, butter, and cinnamon. Stir nut mixture, close the lid, and then set the pressure valve to Sealing. Use the Manual mode to cook at High Pressure, for 5 minutes. 3. Once cooked, perform a quick release by carefully switching the pressure valve to Venting, and strain the nuts. Pour the nuts onto the baking sheet, spreading them out in an even layer. Place in the oven for 5 to 10 minutes (or until crisp, being careful not to overcook). Cool before serving. Store leftovers in the refrigerator or freezer.

Per Serving:

calories: 122 | fat: 12g | protein: 4g | carbs: 3g | net carbs: 1g | fiber: 2g

Pine Nut Mousse

Prep time: 5 minutes | Cook time: 35 minutes | Serves 8

1 tablespoon butter
1¼ cups pine nuts
1¼ cups full-fat heavy cream
2 large eggs
1 teaspoon vanilla extract
1 cup Swerve, reserve 1 tablespoon
1 c water
1 cup full-fat heavy whipping cream

1. Butter the bottom and the side of a pie pan and set aside. 2. In a food processor, blend the pine nuts and heavy cream. Add the eggs, vanilla extract and Swerve and pulse a few times to incorporate. 3. Pour the batter into the pan and loosely cover with aluminum foil. Pour the water in the Instant Pot and place the trivet inside. Place the pan on top of the trivet. 4. Close the lid. Select Manual mode and set the timer for 35 minutes on High pressure. 5. In a small mixing bowl, whisk the heavy whipping cream and 1 tablespoon of Swerve until a soft peak forms. 6. When timer beeps, use a natural pressure release for 15 minutes, then release any remaining pressure and open the lid. 7. Serve immediately with whipped cream on top.

Per Serving:

calories: 184 | fat: 18.8g | protein: 3.0g | carbs: 1.9g | net carbs: 1.8g | fiber: 0.1g

Traditional Kentucky Butter Cake

Prep time: 5 minutes | Cook time: 35 minutes | Serves 4

2 cups almond flour
¾ cup granulated erythritol
1½ teaspoons baking powder
4 eggs
1 tablespoon vanilla extract
½ cup butter, melted
Cooking spray
½ cup water

1. In a medium bowl, whisk together the almond flour, erythritol, and baking powder. Whisk well to remove any lumps. 2. Add the eggs and vanilla and whisk until combined. 3. Add the butter and whisk until the batter is mostly smooth and well combined. 4. Grease the pan with cooking spray and pour in the batter. Cover tightly with aluminum foil. 5. Add the water to the pot. Place the Bundt pan on the trivet and carefully lower it into the pot using. 6. Set the lid in place. Select the Manual mode and set the cooking time for 35 minutes on High Pressure. When the timer goes off, do a quick pressure release. Carefully open the lid. 7. Remove the pan from the pot. Let the cake cool in the pan before flipping out onto a plate.

Per Serving:

calories: 179 | fat: 15.9g | protein: 2.1g | carbs: 2.0g | net carbs: 2.0g | fiber: 0g

Crustless Creamy Berry Cheesecake

Prep time: 10 minutes | Cook time: 40 minutes | Serves 12

16 ounces (454 g) cream cheese, softened
1 cup powdered erythritol
¼ cup sour cream
2 teaspoons vanilla extract
2 eggs
2 cups water
¼ cup blackberries and strawberries, for topping

1. In large bowl, beat cream cheese and erythritol until smooth. Add sour cream, vanilla, and eggs and gently fold until combined. 2. Pour batter into 7-inch springform pan. Gently shake or tap pan on counter to remove air bubbles and level batter. Cover top of pan with tinfoil. Pour water into Instant Pot and place steam rack in pot. 3. Carefully lower pan into pot. Press the Cake button and press the Adjust button to set heat to More. Set time for 40 minutes. When timer beeps, allow a full natural release. Using sling, carefully lift pan from Instant Pot and allow to cool completely before refrigerating. 4. Place strawberries and blackberries on top of cheesecake and serve.

Per Serving:

calories: 153 | fat: 13g | protein: 3g | carbs: 14g | net carbs: 14g | fiber: 0g

Chocolate Fondue

Prep time: 5 minutes | Cook time: 2 minutes | Serves 4

2 ounces (57 g) unsweetened baking chocolate, finely chopped, divided
1 cup heavy cream, divided
⅓ cup Swerve, divided
Fine sea salt
1 cup cold water
Special Equipment:
Set of fondue forks or wooden skewers

1. Divide the chocolate, cream, and sweetener evenly among four ramekins. Add a pinch of salt to each one and stir well. Cover the ramekins with aluminum foil. 2. Place a trivet in the bottom of your Instant Pot and pour in the water. Place the ramekins on the trivet. 3. Lock the lid. Select the Manual mode and set the cooking time for 2 minutes at High Pressure. 4. When the timer beeps, perform a natural pressure release for 10 minutes. Carefully remove the lid. 5. Use tongs to remove the ramekins from the pot. Use a fork to stir the fondue until smooth. 6. Use immediately.

Per Serving:

calories: 200 | fat: 18.5g | protein: 2.7g | carbs: 6.3g | net carbs: 3.9g | fiber: 2.4g

Crustless Key Lime Cheesecake

Prep time: 15 minutes | Cook time: 35 minutes | Serves 8

Nonstick cooking spray
16 ounces light cream cheese (Neufchâtel), softened
⅔ cup granulated erythritol sweetener
¼ cup unsweetened Key lime juice (I like Nellie & Joe's Famous Key West Lime Juice)
½ teaspoon vanilla extract
¼ cup plain Greek yogurt
1 teaspoon grated lime zest
2 large eggs
Whipped cream, for garnish (optional)

1. Spray a 7-inch springform pan with nonstick cooking spray. Line the bottom and partway up the sides of the pan with foil. 2. Put the cream cheese in a large bowl. Use an electric mixer to whip the cream cheese until smooth, about 2 minutes. Add the erythritol, lime juice, vanilla, yogurt, and zest, and blend until smooth. Stop the mixer and scrape down the sides of the bowl with a rubber spatula. With the mixer on low speed, add the eggs, one at a time, blending until just mixed. (Don't overbeat the eggs.) 3. Pour the mixture into the prepared pan. Drape a paper towel over the top of the pan, not touching the cream cheese mixture, and tightly wrap the top of the pan in foil. (Your goal here is to keep out as much moisture as possible.) 4. Pour 1 cup of water into the electric pressure cooker. 5. Place the foil-covered pan onto the wire rack and carefully lower it into the pot. 6. Close and lock the lid of the pressure cooker. Set the valve to sealing. 7. Cook on high pressure for 35 minutes. 8. When the cooking is complete, hit Cancel. Allow the pressure to release naturally for 20 minutes, then quick release any remaining pressure. 9. Once the pin drops, unlock and remove the lid. 10. Using the handles of the wire rack, carefully transfer the pan to a cooling rack. Cool to room temperature, then refrigerate for at least 3 hours. 11. When ready to serve, run a thin rubber spatula around the rim of the cheesecake to loosen it, then remove the ring. 12. Slice into wedges and serve with whipped cream (if using).

Per Serving:
calories: 127 | fat: 2g | protein: 11g | carbs: 17g | sugars: 14g | fiber: 0g | sodium: 423mg

Chocolate Chip Brownies

Prep time: 10 minutes | Cook time: 33 minutes | Serves 8

1½ cups almond flour
⅓ cup unsweetened cocoa powder
¾ cup granulated erythritol
1 teaspoon baking powder
2 eggs
1 tablespoon vanilla extract
5 tablespoons butter, melted
¼ cup sugar-free chocolate chips
½ cup water

1. In a large bowl, add the almond flour, cocoa powder, erythritol, and baking powder. Use a hand mixer on low speed to combine and smooth out any lumps. 2. Add the eggs and vanilla and mix until well combined. 3. Add the butter and mix on low speed until well combined. Scrape the bottom and sides of the bowl and mix again if needed. Fold in the chocolate chips. 4. Grease a baking dish with cooking spray. Pour the batter into the dish and smooth with a spatula. Cover tightly with aluminum foil. 5. Pour the water into the pot. Place the trivet in the pot and carefully lower the baking dish onto the trivet. 6. Close the lid. Select Manual mode and set cooking time for 33 minutes on High Pressure. 7. When timer beeps, use a quick pressure release and open the lid. 8. Use the handles to carefully remove the trivet from the pot. Remove the foil from the dish. 9. Let the brownies cool for 10 minutes before turning out onto a plate.

Per Serving:
calories: 235 | fat: 20.2g | protein: 7.0g | carbs: 6.7g | net carbs: 2.7g | fiber: 4.0g

Chocolate Macadamia Bark

Prep time: 5 minutes | Cook time: 20 minutes | Serves 20

16 ounces (454 g) raw dark chocolate
3 tablespoons raw coconut butter
2 tablespoons coconut oil
2 cups chopped macadamia nuts
1 tablespoon almond butter
½ teaspoon salt
⅓ cup Swerve, or more to taste

1. In a large bowl, mix together the chocolate, coconut butter, coconut oil, macadamia nuts, almond butter, salt, and Swerve. Combine them very thoroughly, until a perfectly even mixture is obtained. 2. Pour 1 cup of filtered water into the Instant Pot, and insert the trivet. Transfer the mixture from the bowl into a well-greased, Instant Pot-friendly dish. 3. Place the dish onto the trivet, and cover loosely with aluminum foil. Close the lid, set the pressure release to Sealing, and select Manual. Set the Instant Pot to 20 minutes on High Pressure, and let cook. 4. Once cooked, let the pressure naturally disperse from the Instant Pot for about 10 minutes, then carefully switch the pressure release to Venting. 5. Open the Instant Pot and remove the dish. Cool in the refrigerator until set. Break into pieces, serve, and enjoy! Store remaining bark in the refrigerator or freezer.

Per Serving:
calories: 258 | fat: 22g | protein: 2g | carbs: 15g | net carbs: 12g | fiber: 3g

Almond Chocolate Fudge

Prep time: 5 minutes | Cook time: 5 minutes | Serves 30

2½ cups Swerve
1¾ cups unsweetened almond milk
1½ cups almond butter
8 ounces (227 g) unsweetened baking chocolate, finely chopped
1 teaspoon almond or vanilla extract
¼ teaspoon fine sea salt

1. Line a baking dish with greased parchment paper. 2. Place the sweetener, almond milk, almond butter, and chocolate in the Instant Pot. Stir well. Select the Sauté mode and cook for 2 minutes. 3. Set the Instant Pot to Keep Warm for 3 minutes, or until the fudge mixture is completely melted and well mixed. Fold in the extract and salt and stir well. 4. Pour the fudge mixture into the prepared baking dish, cover, and refrigerate until firm, about 4 hours. 5. Cut the fudge into 30 equal-sized pieces and serve.

Per Serving:
calories: 139 | fat: 11.1g | protein: 3.8g | carbs: 7.5g | net carbs: 4.9g | fiber: 2.6g

Blackberry Crisp

Prep time: 5 minutes | Cook time: 5 minutes | Serves 1

10 blackberries
½ teaspoon vanilla extract
2 tablespoons powdered erythritol
⅛ teaspoon xanthan gum
1 tablespoon butter
¼ cup chopped pecans
3 teaspoons almond flour
½ teaspoon cinnamon
2 teaspoons powdered erythritol
1 cup water

1. Place blackberries, vanilla, erythritol, and xanthan gum in 4-inch ramekin. Stir gently to coat blackberries. 2. In small bowl, mix remaining ingredients. Sprinkle over blackberries and cover with foil. Press the Manual button and set time for 4 minutes. When timer beeps, quick-release the pressure. Serve warm. Feel free to add scoop of whipped cream on top.

Per Serving:
calories: 346 | fat: 31g | protein: 3g | carbs: 13g | net carbs: 5g | fiber: 8g

Espresso Cream

Prep time: 10 minutes | Cook time: 9 minutes | Serves 4

1 cup heavy cream
½ teaspoon espresso powder
½ teaspoon vanilla extract
2 teaspoons unsweetened cocoa powder
¼ cup low-carb chocolate chips
½ cup powdered erythritol
3 egg yolks
1 cup water

1. Press the Sauté button and add heavy cream, espresso powder, vanilla, and cocoa powder. Bring mixture to boil and add chocolate chips. Press the Cancel button. Stir quickly until chocolate chips are completely melted. 2. In medium bowl, whisk erythritol and egg yolks. Fold mixture into Instant Pot chocolate mix. Ladle into four (4-inch) ramekins. 3. Rinse inner pot and replace. Pour in 1 cup of water and place steam rack on bottom of pot. Cover ramekins with foil and carefully place on top of steam rack. Click lid closed. 4. Press the Manual button and adjust time for 9 minutes. Allow a full natural release. When the pressure indicator drops, carefully remove ramekins and allow to completely cool, then refrigerate. Serve chilled with whipped topping.

Per Serving:
calories: 320 | fat: 29g | protein: 3g | carbs: 10g | net carbs: 8g | fiber: 2g

Tapioca Berry Parfaits

Prep time: 10 minutes | Cook time: 6 minutes | Serves 4

2 cups unsweetened almond milk
½ cup small pearl tapioca, rinsed and still wet
1 teaspoon almond extract
1 tablespoon pure maple syrup
2 cups berries
¼ cup slivered almonds

1. Pour the almond milk into the electric pressure cooker. Stir in the tapioca and almond extract. 2. Close and lock the lid of the pressure cooker. Set the valve to sealing. 3. Cook on High pressure for 6 minutes. 4. When the cooking is complete, hit Cancel. Allow the pressure to release naturally for 10 minutes, then quick release any remaining pressure. 5. Once the pin drops, unlock and remove the lid. Remove the pot to a cooling rack. 6. Stir in the maple syrup and let the mixture cool for about an hour. 7. In small glasses, create several layers of tapioca, berries, and almonds. Refrigerate for 1 hour. 8. Serve chilled.

Per Serving:
(½ cup): calories: 174 | fat: 5g | protein: 3g | carbs: 32g | sugars: 11g | fiber: 3g | sodium: 77mg

Coconut Almond Cream Cake

Prep time: 10 minutes | Cook time: 40 minutes | Serves 8

Nonstick cooking spray
1 cup almond flour
½ cup unsweetened shredded coconut
⅓ cup Swerve
1 teaspoon baking powder
1 teaspoon apple pie spice
2 eggs, lightly whisked
¼ cup unsalted butter, melted
½ cup heavy (whipping) cream

1. Grease a 6-inch round cake pan with the cooking spray. 2. In a medium bowl, mix together the almond flour, coconut, Swerve, baking powder, and apple pie spice. 3. Add the eggs, then the butter, then the cream, mixing well after each addition. 4. Pour the batter into the pan and cover with aluminum foil. 5. Pour 2 cups of water into the inner cooking pot of the Instant Pot, then place a trivet in the pot. Place the pan on the trivet. 6. Lock the lid into place. Select Manual and adjust the pressure to High. Cook for 40 minutes. When the cooking is complete, let the pressure release naturally for 10 minutes, then quick-release any remaining pressure. Unlock the lid. 7. Carefully take out the pan and let it cool for 15 to 20 minutes. Invert the cake onto a plate. Sprinkle with shredded coconut, almond slices, or powdered sweetener, if desired, and serve.

Per Serving:
calories: 231 | fat: 19g | protein: 3g | carbs: 12g | net carbs: 10g | fiber: 2g

Appendix 1: Measurement Conversion Chart

MEASUREMENT CONVERSION CHART

VOLUME EQUIVALENTS(DRY)

US STANDARD	METRIC (APPROXIMATE)
1/8 teaspoon	0.5 mL
1/4 teaspoon	1 mL
1/2 teaspoon	2 mL
3/4 teaspoon	4 mL
1 teaspoon	5 mL
1 tablespoon	15 mL
1/4 cup	59 mL
1/2 cup	118 mL
3/4 cup	177 mL
1 cup	235 mL
2 cups	475 mL
3 cups	700 mL
4 cups	1 L

WEIGHT EQUIVALENTS

US STANDARD	METRIC (APPROXIMATE)
1 ounce	28 g
2 ounces	57 g
5 ounces	142 g
10 ounces	284 g
15 ounces	425 g
16 ounces (1 pound)	455 g
1.5 pounds	680 g
2 pounds	907 g

VOLUME EQUIVALENTS(LIQUID)

US STANDARD	US STANDARD (OUNCES)	METRIC (APPROXIMATE)
2 tablespoons	1 fl.oz.	30 mL
1/4 cup	2 fl.oz.	60 mL
1/2 cup	4 fl.oz.	120 mL
1 cup	8 fl.oz.	240 mL
1 1/2 cup	12 fl.oz.	355 mL
2 cups or 1 pint	16 fl.oz.	475 mL
4 cups or 1 quart	32 fl.oz.	1 L
1 gallon	128 fl.oz.	4 L

TEMPERATURES EQUIVALENTS

FAHRENHEIT(F)	CELSIUS(C) (APPROXIMATE)
225 °F	107 °C
250 °F	120 °C
275 °F	135 °C
300 °F	150 °C
325 °F	160 °C
350 °F	180 °C
375 °F	190 °C
400 °F	205 °C
425 °F	220 °C
450 °F	235 °C
475 °F	245 °C
500 °F	260 °C

Appendix 2: Instant Pot Cooking Timetable 1

Instant Pot Cooking Timetable

Dried Beans, Legumes and Lentils

Dried Beans and Legume	Dry (Minutes)	Soaked (Minutes)
Soy beans	25 – 30	20 – 25
Scarlet runner	20 – 25	10 – 15
Pinto beans	25 – 30	20 – 25
Peas	15 – 20	10 – 15
Navy beans	25 – 30	20 – 25
Lima beans	20 – 25	10 – 15
Lentils, split, yellow (moong dal)	15 – 18	N/A
Lentils, split, red	15 – 18	N/A
Lentils, mini, green (brown)	15 – 20	N/A
Lentils, French green	15 – 20	N/A
Kidney white beans	35 – 40	20 – 25
Kidney red beans	25 – 30	20 – 25
Great Northern beans	25 – 30	20 – 25
Pigeon peas	20 – 25	15 – 20
Chickpeas (garbanzo bean chickpeas)	35 – 40	20 – 25
Cannellini beans	35 – 40	20 – 25
Black-eyed peas	20 – 25	10 – 15
Black beans	20 – 25	10 – 15

Fish and Seafood

Fish and Seafood	Fresh (minutes)	Frozen (minutes)
Shrimp or Prawn	1 to 2	2 to 3
Seafood soup or stock	6 to 7	7 to 9
Mussels	2 to 3	4 to 6
Lobster	3 to 4	4 to 6
Fish, whole (snapper, trout, etc.)	5 to 6	7 to 10
Fish steak	3 to 4	4 to 6
Fish fillet,	2 to 3	3 to 4
Crab	3 to 4	5 to 6

Fruits

Fruits	Fresh (in Minutes)	Dried (in Minutes)
Raisins	N/A	4 to 5
Prunes	2 to 3	4 to 5
Pears, whole	3 to 4	4 to 6
Pears, slices or halves	2 to 3	4 to 5
Peaches	2 to 3	4 to 5
Apricots, whole or halves	2 to 3	3 to 4
Apples, whole	3 to 4	4 to 6
Apples, in slices or pieces	2 to 3	3 to 4

Meat

Meat and Cuts	Cooking Time (minutes)	Meat and Cuts	Cooking Time (minutes)
Veal, roast	35 to 45	Duck, with bones, cut up	10 to 12
Veal, chops	5 to 8	Cornish Hen, whole	10 to 15
Turkey, drumsticks (leg)	15 to 20	Chicken, whole	20 to 25
Turkey, breast, whole, with bones	25 to 30	Chicken, legs, drumsticks, or thighs	10 to 15
Turkey, breast, boneless	15 to 20	Chicken, with bones, cut up	10 to 15
Quail, whole	8 to 10	Chicken, breasts	8 to 10
Pork, ribs	20 to 25	Beef, stew	15 to 20
Pork, loin roast	55 to 60	Beef, shanks	25 to 30
Pork, butt roast	45 to 50	Beef, ribs	25 to 30
Pheasant	20 to 25	Beef, steak, pot roast, round, rump, brisket or blade, small chunks, chuck,	25 to 30
Lamb, stew meat	10 to 15		
Lamb, leg	35 to 45	Beef, pot roast, steak, rump, round, chuck, blade or brisket, large	35 to 40
Lamb, cubes,	10 t0 15		
Ham slice	9 to 12	Beef, ox-tail	40 to 50
Ham picnic shoulder	25 to 30	Beef, meatball	10 to 15
Duck, whole	25 to 30	Beef, dressed	20 to 25

Made in the USA
Las Vegas, NV
31 August 2023